U

1987/1988 Edition

By the staff of Berlitz Guides
A Macmillan Company

How to use our guide

These 256 pages cover the highlights of the U.S.A., grouped under eight regional headings. Although far from exhaustive, our selection of sights will enable you to make the best of your trip.

✦ The **sights** to see are contained between pages 37 and 194. Those most highly recommended are pinpointed by the Berlitz traveller symbol.

The **Where to Go** section p. 35 will help you to plan your visit according to the time available.

For **general background** see the sections America and the Americans p. 8, Facts and Figures p. 15, and History p. 16.

Entertainment and **activities** (including eating out) are described between pages 195 and 215.

The **practical information,** hints and tips you will need before or during your trip begin on page 216.

The **map section** at the back of the book (pp. 240–251) will help you find your way round and locate the principal sights.

Finally, if there is anything that you cannot find, look in the **complete index** (pp. 252–256).

Text: Jack Altman
Layout: Doris Haldemann
🅵🅰️Cartography: Falk Verlag, Hamburg.

We wish to express our thanks to all the local tourist offices around the U.S.A. and the U.S. Rangers in the national parks. We are particularly grateful to Mrs. Darryl Kestler for her help.

3rd Printing
1987/1988 Edition

CONTENTS

CONTENTS

Although we make every effort to ensure the accuracy of all the information in this book, changes occur incessantly. We cannot therefore take responsibility for facts, prices, addresses and circumstances that are constantly subject to alteration. Our guides are updated on a regular basis as we reprint. We are always grateful to readers, however, who let us know of errors, changes or serious omissions.

Photos: pp. 169, 175, 178, 179, 182, 186/187, 191, 211, Claude Huber; pp. cover, 38, 39, 43, 53 Jean Mohr; pp. 8, 11, 13, 16, 33, 54, 56, 76, 77, 91, 96, 122, 132, 133, 138, 156, 193, 200, 204, 210, Georg Stärk; pp. 9, 22, 49, 64, 67, 70, 71, 80, 87, 90, 100, 129, 137, 147, 149, 157, 171 KEY-color/ZEFA; pp. 61, 153, 161, 166 KEY-color; pp. 17, 27, 34, 141, 201 Maximilien Bruggmann; p. 194 Kurt Ammann; pp. 107, 110, 115, 117 Jacques Bétant; p. 103 Philadelphia Convention & Visitors Bureau; p. 144 Denver & Colorado Convention & Visitors Bureau; p. 197 Keystone Photo, Colorado.

For those planning long stays in New York, Florida, California, Hawaii, Puerto Rico or the Virgin Islands, our handy regional guides provide information on those destinations in greater depth. Berlitz Travel Guides are available at most bookshops, newsstands and airport terminals.

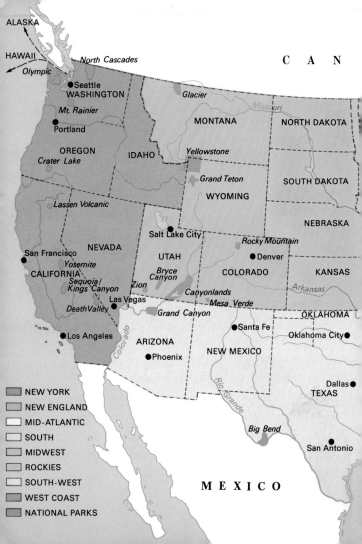

ALASKA

HAWAII

Olympic

North Cascades

C A N

Seattle
WASHINGTON

Glacier

Missouri

Mt. Rainier
Portland

MONTANA

NORTH DAKOTA

OREGON
Crater Lake

IDAHO

Yellowstone

SOUTH DAKOTA

Grand Teton

WYOMING

Lassen Volcanic

NEBRASKA

Salt Lake City

Rocky Mountain

San Francisco

NEVADA

UTAH

Denver

Yosemite

CALIFORNIA

Sequoia/
Kings Canyon

Zion

Bryce
Canyon

COLORADO

KANSAS

Arkansas

Canyonlands

Mesa Verde

Death Valley

Las Vegas

Grand Canyon

OKLAHOMA

Los Angeles

Colorado

ARIZONA

Phoenix

Santa Fe

NEW MEXICO

Oklahoma City

Dallas

Rio Grande

TEXAS

NEW YORK

NEW ENGLAND

MID-ATLANTIC

SOUTH

MIDWEST

ROCKIES

SOUTH-WEST

WEST COAST

NATIONAL PARKS

Big Bend

San Antonio

M E X I C O

A D A

Isle Royale
MINNESOTA
Minneapolis
WISCONSIN
IOWA
MICHIGAN
Detroit
Chicago
Cleveland
ILLINOIS
INDIANA
Indianapolis
OHIO
Montréal
Ottawa
Toronto
VERMONT
MAINE
Acadia
NEW HAMPSHIRE
NEW YORK
Boston
MASSACHUSETTS
RHODE ISLAND
CONNECTICUT
New York City
NEW JERSEY
PENNSYLVANIA
Pittsburgh
Philadelphia
MARYLAND
Baltimore
DELAWARE
Washington D.C.
WEST VIRGINIA
Shenandoah
St. Louis
MISSOURI
Mississippi
KENTUCKY
VIRGINIA
Tulsa
Nashville
NORTH CAROLINA
TENNESSEE
Great Smoky Mtns.
ARKANSAS
Memphis
SOUTH CAROLINA
Atlantic
Atlanta
Charleston
Ocean
MISSISSIPPI
GEORGIA
ALABAMA
LOUISIANA
Houston
New Orleans
FLORIDA
Orlando
Tampa
Miami
Gulf of Mexico
Everglades

AMERICA AND THE AMERICANS

It's significant that, despite the honourable competing claims of Canada, Mexico, Brazil or Argentina, when people talk of "America", they mean the United States. This cannot just be imputed to a political or economic dominance or a cultural or other form of "imperialism". It's simple tribute to the way the world's popular imagination has been captured by the fabulous adventure that has taken a pioneering people from the green fields of Massachusetts to the deserts, mountains and orchards of California—and up to the moon and back.

"America" is part of our global dream and the United States has embodied it with an infinitely varied continent that challenges the senses of the first-time visitor and remains a constant source of excitement for those who have lived there all their lives.

The old civilizations of Europe and Asia have always needed to come to the United States to recharge their batteries. For the U.S.A. is still a seemingly inexhaustible reservoir of energy, whether it be in its primary forms derived from oil in Texas and Alaska or uranium in Colorado and Utah, or the other, far more exciting energy of ideas, in the computer world of Silicon Valley, California, the movie industry down the coast in Hollywood, the business world of Wall Street,

American ways of life

the Washington "think tanks", or the cosmic explorations of Houston and Cape Canaveral.

But nobody knows better than the Americans that all work and no play would make Jack, Giovanni or Hans a dull boy, and so the United States is also blue jeans, tee shirts, fast food, surfboards and soft-wheeled roller skates. Other countries proudly display their glorious past in museums, palaces, temples and cathedrals. America joyfully displays its exuberant present — in the street and on the beach. Other countries talk of their culture, America talks of its way of life. Visitors to the United States are catching up with their own century.

And just when Europeans might hazard a patronizing observation on America's cultural life, they'll be made to eat their words by any one of half a dozen world-class symphony orchestras in Chicago, New York, Los Angeles, Philadelphia, Cleveland, Washington or Boston (an American half-dozen quite naturally has seven in it). Or by the endlessly innovative painting and sculpture of Manhattan, the great museums of New York, Washington and Chicago, and, nationwide, an architecture forever seeking surprising solutions — often superb, occasionally horrendous, but never timid — to the problems of housing in our overcrowded age.

Yet Americans, clearly the spoilt children of creation when it came to distributing the bounty of the earth, have at their disposal a huge diversity of landscapes to which they can run from that overcrowding. Luckily for them — and for foreign visitors — man's environmental reawakening came just in time to preserve much of the beauty of the continent's wide open spaces. For sailors and fishermen there are the wild Atlantic coast of Maine and its Pacific counterpart in northern California, Oregon and Washington. Or the calmer waters of Long Island Sound, Chesapeake Bay or the lazy beaches of Florida and southern California. In between, the Great Lakes of the Midwest might qualify as seas anywhere else in the world.

Stretching right across the country are the great national parks and nature reserves, luring people to paddle around the swamps of Florida's Everglades or hike and climb in the White Mountains of New Hampshire, the Great Smokies of North Carolina and Tennessee and the Rockies of Colorado. The vast parks of the West, with the geysers, waterfalls and evergreen forest of Wyoming's Yellowstone,

New York, New York!

the rainbow canyons of Utah's Zion, the massive granite and redwoods of California's Yosemite or Sequoia and of course Arizona's Grand Canyon, offer humbling sanctuaries in which to meditate on the natural beauty that is perhaps the soul of this industrial giant of America. Even the deserts—the Petrified Forest south-east of the Grand Canyon, or Death Valley in California's Mojave—grant you an enriching respite from civilization.

But civilization American-style is too much sheer fun to stay away from for too long. Each of the major cities offers its own adventure. The street life of New York is a carnival—endless movement, colour, noise and smell —sometimes hair-raising, always stimulating. Boston, Washington and Philadelphia are the metropolitan pillars of United States' history, proud and dignified but—this isn't Europe— never taking themselves too seriously. New Orleans offers an unashamedly theatrical view of a bygone elegance and pungent decadence, part Gallic, part Deep South, all tongue-in-cheek. Santa Fe is somehow its grand Spanish counterpart, quieter, more romantic. Nothing quiet or romantic about big, boisterous Chicago in America's heartland, but the town never fails to surprise visitors with the beauty of its lakefront architecture. Dallas and

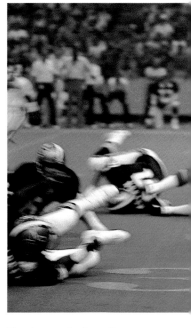

Houston are the bumptious concrete realizations of the Texan dream, ranchers gone urban. And crazy, amazing Los Angeles and lovely, non-conformist San Francisco are the last extravagant statements of America's push to the West. Big and small, America's cities—they may occasionally call themselves towns, but never villages—can be enjoyed both as playgrounds and as workshops displaying all the good and

12

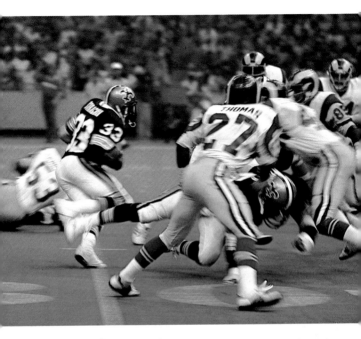

American football—war with a smile

bad aspects of our century's urban development.

And when you're tired of coping with the real world, you can sneak off to the fantasy realms of Disney World and Disneyland and Magic Mountain and Knott's Berry Farm and all the other "theme parks" that have mushroomed around the country. Here the thrills and excitement and joys and fears are carefully calculated not to create too much stress.

Good clean family fun. Children have a very important place in American life, and Americans have long understood that all of us, some of the time and more often than we care to admit, are children.

Americans love to play. Their

13

own versions of old European sports—baseball (which American encyclopaedias reluctantly admit is "doubtless derived" from English cricket and rounders) and what they call football, which looks to European eyes like something Roman gladiators would have played if they'd learned rugby—are marvellously exuberant spectacles. And in addition to the myriad spectator sports there's the endless flow of fads that spring up around the beaches of Florida, California or Hawaii—surfing, wind-surfing, skateboarding, roller-skating, hula-hooping—they come and go with the airy grace of a Frisbee. Where else in the world would the gruelling torture of marathon running be turned into a carnival for the whole family in towns like New York or Boston?

Americans, Americans—in a country as vast and varied as the United States, it's hazardous to claim that you know what you're talking about when you use the word "Americans". White Anglo-Saxon Protestants? Irish Catholics? Hispanics, Poles, Italians, Germans, Greeks, Scandinavians, Jews, Russians, Czechs, Africans, Chinese, Japanese or Sioux, Navajo, Cherokee and Cheyenne? Or, for that matter, New Yorkers and New Englanders, Southerners and Texans, Midwesterners and hill-billies, and again, to confound all generalizations, Californians? It's worth making out this long and far from exhaustive list just to be able to contemplate the incredible diversity of these people we call Americans.

And then you suddenly realize you have the answer. *There* is the valid definition of Americans. They are this people of boundless variety. Somehow people from every corner of the earth have landed up living together, by no means always peacefully, but this is the only place where that has happened on such a scale and, for all the revolution and civil war and riots, with such astounding success. Perhaps the greatest adventure of your whole American journey will be to encounter as many as you can of the different people making up these United States: the cool New Englanders, pushy New Yorkers, bluff and hearty Texans, earnest midwestern farmers—and their exact opposites, for no generalization stands up to more than five minutes' scrutiny in this place. But at least it can be said that they have not coalesced into one dull, homogeneous nation of look-alikes, talk-alikes and laugh-alikes. Martin Luther King, Jr., was right to contest the image of America as a melting pot. He said it was in fact a good bowl of vegetable soup in which you could taste the carrots, potatoes, leeks and peas, all separately, and together.

FACTS AND FIGURES

Geography: With an area of approximately 3,615,000 square miles (including Alaska and Hawaii), the U.S. is the fourth largest country in the world, or nearly 40 times bigger than the U.K. Mainland U.S.A. (excluding Alaska), called the 48 conterminous states, stretches for 3,000 miles from the Atlantic to the Pacific and for some 1,200 miles from the Canadian border to the Gulf of Mexico. Hawaii, the 50th state, is situated in the Pacific Ocean, some 2,500 miles to the south-west. The conterminous states consist, roughly, of the highland region of Appalachia in the east, the Rocky Mountains in the west and the Great Plains in the centre.
Highest point: Mount McKinley (Alaska), 20,320 feet. *Lowest point:* Death Valley (California), 282 feet below sea level.

Population: 230,510,000 of which 83% are Whites, 12% Blacks, 1% Indians and 4% of other races. The density is 64 people per square mile. 73% live in urban areas.

Capital: Washington, District of Columbia (pop. 638,000).

Major cities: New York (7,071,000), Chicago (3,005,000), Los Angeles-Long Beach (2,967,000), Philadelphia (1,688,000), Houston (1,594,000), Detroit (1,203,000), Dallas (904,000), San Diego (875,000).

Government: The U.S. is a federal republic (consisting of 50 states and 1 federal district), with a two-party system (Democrats and Republicans). The government is based on the Constitution of 1787. The president is elected for a period of 4 years, and can be re-elected once. The Congress is composed of the Senate (with 2 senators per state) and House of Representatives (435 members). Each state has its own semi-autonomous government (and local laws) headed by a popularly elected governor.

Religion: 55% Protestant, 37% Roman Catholic, 4% Jewish, 3% Orthodox (Eastern churches), 1% miscellaneous.

HISTORY

A European visiting an Indian village near the Grand Canyon was asked by one of the residents how long he'd been in America. "A month", he replied. "That's nice", said the Indian. "We've been here all the time".

If not all the time, for at least 25,000, maybe as much as 40,000, years. That's when scientists esti-

mate that mammoth and bison left Siberia in search of new pastures across a now submerged land bridge over the Bering Strait. Mongolian hunters, the Indians' ancestors, followed into what is now Alaska.

Over the centuries, some of them made their way down the Pacific coast and east across the continent. Between 500 B.C. and A.D. 500 the Hopi and Zuni had settled down in farming communities in the adobe-walled *pueblos* (villages) of New Mexico and Arizona. By 1500 the only truly nomadic Indians were the Plains Indians, roaming between the Rockies and the Mississippi River forests. Tribes living along the east coast were skilled farmers, growing beans, squash, maize and tobacco. But they had no wheel, either for wagon or pottery, nor metal tools. And no horses. Their only beasts of burden were dogs.

The Europeans Arrive
Although the claim that the 6th-century Irish monk, St. Brendan, got there first is considered a nice piece of blarney, historians do accept as fact that Norsemen living in Greenland made their way across to Newfoundland between 1001 and 1015. But they disappeared again without trace.

Not so the Spanish. It was 10 o'clock at night on October 11, 1492, when their Genoese captain,

Christopher Columbus, stood with his watchman looking at a pale light on the western horizon. It turned out to be on an island in the Bahamas, just 380 miles from Miami Beach. It wasn't *the* Indies Columbus had been looking for, but it would do.

Five years later, another Genoese-born sailor, John Cabot, set foot in Newfoundland, stopping just long enough to stake the fateful English claim to North America for his master, Henry VII. But it was the name of a third Italian explorer, Amerigo Vespucci, that was used by a German mapmaker and stuck to both northern and southern continents.

The first European contact with the future United States

Cliff Palace at Mesa Verde

mainland came in 1513 when Spanish explorer Juan Ponce de León was searching for the fabled Fountain of Youth. He stumbled, appropriately enough, on the coast of Florida, where elderly Americans still come from the chilly north and midwest to warm their tired bones. In 1565, the Spaniards built a fort in St. Augustine, the first permanent settlement in North America.

Other Spanish exploration touched on Texas, New Mexico, the Grand Canyon in Arizona and the Mississippi River. At their height, the Spanish brought to the New World an irresistible mixture of courage, brutality and civilization. If the Indians succumbed in the confrontation, it was due not only to their vulnerability to the strange European diseases and superior weaponry, but also—perhaps primarily—to their lack of unity. Each tribe had a name that was a variation of "We the People", considering all other tribes as potential enemies. Europeans were hailed as "Men from the Sky"—heaven-sent allies against their rivals. It took several generations for the Indians to unite in common cause and by then it was too late.

The British finally got into the colony business in 1607. After cursory examination of California (by Sir Francis Drake) and some unsuccessful efforts on the east coast (by Sir Walter Raleigh), they established their first settlement at Jamestown, Virginia.

Then on November 11, 1620, 102 Separatists landed on Cape Cod, Massachusetts, aboard the *Mayflower*. The seeds of American democracy were contained in a remarkable covenant drawn up by these "Pilgrims"—the Mayflower Compact which provided that laws accepted by the majority would be binding on all. They founded a community at Plymouth Bay, learning from friendly Indians how to fish the local waters and plant maize. Half the pilgrims died that first hard winter. The following October, after a good harvest, the survivors and 90 Wampanoag Indians held a three-day feast of wild turkey and waterfowl—their first Thanksgiving.

Between 1630 and 1646 many Puritans arrived in New England under the charter of the Massachusetts Bay Company, and groups from the "old country" stayed intact to form the new townships. Local affairs were decided and local officials elected at town meetings of the landowners. But all were not satisfied with the way things were run. Clashes between conservative elders and opponents of the religious oligarchy led to new community experiments a little further west—in Rhode Island and Connecticut. America was already on the move.

In 1626, the Manhattan Indians sold their island to the Dutch West India Company for the legendary sum of $24 and New Amsterdam sprang up as a classic seaman's town of taverns and seedy hang-outs for smugglers and illicit traders. The clergy of the Dutch Reformed Church and the few wealthy businessmen with houses there found it was none too safe to walk around Manhattan late at night. Apart from a few farms or *boweries,* the Dutch didn't invest much in their American property, concentrating their energies on the East Indies. Smart New Englanders moved down to Westchester and Long Island and the British began putting pressure on the Dutch to move out. In 1664, with the British fleet hovering in the harbour, the Dutch governor, Peter Stuyvesant, let New Amsterdam become New York without a shot being fired in protest. A few old Dutch families remained, including the Roosevelts.

Meanwhile the French, who had been up in Quebec since 1608 converting Indians into Christians and beavers into pelts, were extending their fur trade with expeditions down the Mississippi River. They founded Louisiana in 1682.

In the same year, William Penn set up a colony in Philadelphia. This energetic Quaker from London had inherited a useful fortune and established the proprietary province of Pennsylvania as a haven of free enterprise and religious tolerance. The Swedes, Finns and Dutch already settled there were now joined by farmers from Britain, France and Germany. The American adventure of ethnic coexistence was under way.

Things were slightly less peaceful back in Massachusetts. The Reverend Cotton Mather was stirring up hysteria arising from the horrendous Salem "witch hunts". Children told stories of broomstick-flights, witches' sabbaths, flying saucers and sexual relations with the devil. Trials led to the hanging of five men and 14 women by the summer of 1692. The fear of godlessness spreading through New England brought about a religious revival in the 1730s, known as the "Great Awakening", with hellfire-and-brimstone preachers roaring from their pulpits. Everything these Americans did, they did vigorously.

Towards Revolution

As the British Empire expanded in the middle of the 18th century, London demanded that the American colonies contribute more to its upkeep and defence. While accepting London's authority in foreign affairs, the colonists assumed they would enjoy the same freedoms and privileges as other Englishmen. But between

1764 and 1767 a series of special taxes (on newspapers and legal documents) and duties (on imported sugar, silk, linen, Madeira wine, paint, lead, paper and tea) made them realize they weren't just Englishmen abroad. They'd become something different. A South Carolina leader, Christopher Gadsden, drew the inevitable conclusion: "There ought to be no New England men, no New Yorkers known on the continent, but all of us Americans".

Groups known as "Sons of Liberty" formed in New York, Charleston and Boston and attacked the royal tax collectors' houses and burned their furniture. In Boston, the propagandist and agitator Samuel Adams led dances around the Liberty Tree, an elm from which unpopular officials were hanged in effigy. As unrest mounted, the British sent two regiments to Boston. In March 1770, a mob snowballed guards in front of the Boston Customs House. The attack grew fiercer and the British were ordered to fire, killing four Bostonians.

Most of the offending duties were repealed, and there followed three years of peace and prosperity. But the duty on tea remained. While Charleston, Philadelphia and New York staged boycotts, Sam Adams' Sons of Liberty (disguised as Mohawk Indians) boarded three British ships in Boston Harbour and dumped the cargo into the sea. The momentous Boston Tea Party of 1773 moved George III to say: "The colonies must either submit or triumph". The Americans agreed.

Britain stepped up its repressive measures and the American colonies called their First Continental Congress in Philadelphia in September 1774 to coordinate opposition. Once again, Massachusetts took the lead, declaring itself a "free state" and preparing to resist any British offensive with weapons and ammunition stored at Concord. The British moved 12,000 troops to Boston and, in April 1775, a contingent marched out to deal with the rebels. As any American schoolchild can recite, the patriots' messenger, Paul Revere, rode "through every Middlesex village and farm" to warn of the British advance on Concord. The first resistance took place at Lexington, but it was on the bridge at Concord that "embattled farmers" faced the British and "fired the shot heard round the world".

With a Virginian colonel, George Washington, as Commander-in-Chief of the newly constituted Continental Army, the Revolutionary War's first staged battle at Bunker Hill outside Boston resulted in a technical victory for the British with enormous casualties of 1,000 out of 2,200 troops.

But despite the Second Continental Congress's push for independence—led by Massachusetts' John Hancock, Virginia's Thomas Jefferson and Pennsylvania's Benjamin Franklin—many were still reluctant to sever the ties with Britain. In January 1776, the officers' mess at Washington's headquarters was still proposing a toast to George III. "Loyalists" were a considerable faction—big landowners in Virginia and Maryland and small farmers in New York and the Carolinas, even many merchants in Massachusetts.

Within a few months, though, the situation had changed. Success at Bunker Hill and the forced evacuation of Boston by the British, as well as a good deal of fervent propaganda in favour of independence—most notably Thomas Paine's *Common Sense* —brought the representatives around. They moved: "That these United Colonies are, and of right ought to be, Free and Independent States". Two days later, July 4, 1776, the Declaration of Independence was signed, proclaiming the aim of the United States of America's government to be the protection of "life, liberty and the pursuit of happiness".

But the war dragged on for seven more years, with a citizenry not at all keen on protracted warfare. The Americans liked the excitement of victory, vigorous skirmishes and then back to the farm, not this morale-sapping exhaustion of strategic attrition. After the Battle of Long Island in August 1776, the British took control of New York for the rest of the war. Philadelphia fell in September 1777, leaving Washington and his forces, depleted by large-scale desertions, to shiver out the winter in nearby Valley Forge.

Luckily the British became overconfident. Rather than press his advantage after taking Fort Ticonderoga on his way down from Canada, General "Gentleman Jack" Burgoyne preferred to wait for his silver plate, champagne and 30 wagons of personal baggage. The result was defeat for his German mercenaries at Bennington and his own humiliating surrender at Saratoga. Now the British were ready to negotiate a conciliatory peace, but the Americans chose to exploit their new military alliance with France for total victory.

At first, French help, under the inept leadership of Admiral d'Estaing, proved less than helpful. The British took control of the Atlantic coast with victories at Savannah and Charleston. American troops then forged north to Virginia, picking off British outposts along the way. There, French support paid off in a combined action with Washington in which 15,000 men won the deci-

The epic of the Far West re-enacted

sive Battle of Yorktown. On October 17, 1781, Lord Cornwallis's British soldiers surrendered with the band playing *The World Turned Upside Down*.

After two years of tedious negotiations led by Ben Franklin, the Peace of Paris ended the war on September 3, 1783.

The New Republic Expands Westwards

New York was the first capital of the new United States of America and it was on a balcony overlooking Wall Street on April 30, 1789, that George Washington was inaugurated as president. Endowed with great character, he made up for his lack of political talent by surrounding himself with men who possessed it in abundance, among them, Thomas Jefferson as secretary of state and Alexander Hamilton at the treasury. His vice president was John Adams —cousin of Sam, the troublemaker.

In the Republic's early years, Hamilton, a brilliant administrator, favoured a governing class of merchants, industrialists and bankers on the authoritarian European model, while Jefferson was eager to break with traditions that he felt had made Europeans "either hammer or anvil". As champion of a new democracy, Jefferson was disturbed by an obstacle to it on his own doorstep. The United States' first census of 1790 showed a population of nearly 4 million of whom 700,000 were black slaves. Himself a slave-owner on his Virginia farm, Jefferson expressed hopes for "a total emancipation", fearing otherwise the direst trouble for the Union of the states.

Jefferson was elected president in 1801, the first to be inaugurated in the new capital at Washington, on the Potomac River. Apart from the White House and the Capitol, there was little more than a collection of ramshackle boarding houses where many senators and congressmen had to bed down on the floor.

One of the major triumphs of the Jefferson presidency was the Louisiana Purchase of 1803. The French territory stretched from the Mississippi to the Rocky Mountains, 828,000 square miles that more than doubled the size of the country. Preoccupied with an insurrection in Haiti and his war with the British, Napoleon was happy to sell for $15 million. The next year, Captain Meriwether Lewis and Lieutenant William Clark set out from St. Louis to explore the uncharted West all the way to the Pacific Ocean.

The expedition was intended not only to lay American claim to the Oregon territory but also to size up the Indian situation in the north-west. Many suspected that the British were encouraging the Indians to resist American western expansion. This and disputes over free trade rights during Britain's naval blockade of Napoleon led, under President James Madison, to another war with the British, from 1812 to 1814. The U.S. invaded Canada, killing the great Indian leader Tecumseh and burning parliamentary houses in York (later Toronto) as well as surrounding villages. The British retaliated at Fort Niagara and Buffalo. Washington was attacked, the White House set on fire.

General Andrew Jackson made the reputation that was to win him the presidency 15 years later with ferocious assaults on the Indians in Tennessee and Florida, and on the British at New Orleans—a tragically absurd battle that left 2,000 British dead or wounded for the loss of only 13 Americans, although a peace treaty had been signed in Belgium two weeks before.

With Jackson turning his attention back to Florida, Spain hurriedly sold off its lands east of the Mississippi and its claim to the Oregon country for a flat $5 million. While participating enthusiastically in the great powers' expansionist spirit of the 19th century, President James Monroe proclaimed his famous doctrine warning Europeans to keep their hands off North and South America: "We should consider any attempt on their part to extend their system to any portion of this hemisphere as dangerous to our peace and security".

The Jacksonian era from 1829 to 1840 covered not only the presidency of crusty old Andrew Jackson but also that of his protégé Martin Van Buren. After years of gentlemanly rule by the Republic's founding fathers, this new generation of populist Democrats took power with no political programme beyond a general pride in their log-cabin origins and prowess in battle.

Jackson's was the spirit that pushed the American frontier to the west. Trappers and fur-hunters led the new pioneers from the Missouri River to the Rockies during the 1830s. Then, in canvas-covered wagons known as "prairie schooners", thousands of backwoodsmen who didn't like the treeless plains set out for the Oregon country in the 40s. America's drive to the Pacific was widely proclaimed to be the nation's "manifest destiny".

Other Americans moved beyond the U.S. frontiers to Mexican-owned Texas. By 1836 they were 20,000 strong, outnumbering the Mexicans there 4 to 1. They liked Mexican horsemanship, saddles and trappings, but rebelled against the authoritarian government. After fierce fighting in retaliation for the Mexican massacre of Americans at the Alamo (see p. 155), the Americans made Texas an independent "Lone Star Republic". In 1845 it was annexed to the U.S.

The tough, expansionist president, James Polk, blustered his way into war with Mexico for California and the south-west in 1848, ultimately winning California,

Nevada, Utah and parts of Arizona, New Mexico, Wyoming and Colorado. For all this, the U.S. paid $15 million, a bargain that turned into a bonanza with the discovery of gold in California.

Americans against Americans

Throughout the era of western expansion, the slavery issue festered. Slaves made up fully 40 per cent of the southern states' population. As long as cotton was "king", representing two-thirds of U.S. exports, the South felt it could justify working slaves on the plantations. But the cost of their upkeep was prohibitive and outweighed the cotton profits when settlement of the Great Plains opened up a new market for the north-east, making it less dependent on southern trade. But the economic factor proved secondary to the social status conferred in the South on slave owners. When rebellions broke out in South Carolina and Virginia, repression was ruthless and strict curfews were placed on all Blacks. Owners organized night patrols, and teaching slaves to read or write was forbidden.

In the North, the abolitionist movement grew to 200,000 by 1840. Since slave owners could legally reclaim fugitives in the northern states, an "Underground Railroad" was organized to help escaped slaves up into Canada. By the 1850s, any lingering moral considerations—the South had once regarded slavery as a "necessary evil", now they just regarded it as necessary—were blurred by the purely political issue of states' rights. The slave states insisted on the right to decide their own affairs without the interference of the federal government.

A new Republican Party was founded in 1854 on an anti-slavery platform and, by the 1860 presidential elections, was identified squarely with the North. The Democrats split on the issue of whether the new western territories should be obliged to permit slavery, and southern states fielded their own candidate in addition to the Democrats' official nominee. The Republicans chose a fellow of reassuringly simple personality who could get enough support in the new midwestern states to guarantee victory over the divided Democrats. The homespun Illinois attorney, honest Abraham Lincoln, did the trick.

When South Carolina immediately led Mississippi, Alabama, Florida, Georgia, Louisiana and Texas into secession from the Union, the stated reason was unambiguous: the North had "united in the election of a man whose opinions and purposes are hostile to slavery". In fact, Lincoln's aims were not that simple. As he wrote to a New York editor: "My paramount object in

this struggle is to save the Union and not either to save or destroy slavery". But he had said earlier: "I believe this government cannot endure permanently half *slave* and half *free*".

In February 1861, the Confederate States of America elected as their president Jefferson Davis, an aristocratic ex-soldier from Kentucky. Arkansas, Tennessee, Virginia and North Carolina joined the Confederacy, but Ken-

Washington, Jefferson, T. Roosevelt and Lincoln carved into Mt. Rushmore

tucky, after some hesitation, did not. Nor did Missouri, Maryland or Delaware. Virginia's great military leader, General Robert E. Lee, was more ambivalent than the politicians. "I can contemplate no greater calamity for the country", he wrote in January 1861, "than a dissolution of the Union. Still, a Union that can only be maintained by swords and bayonets and in which strife and civil war are to take the place of brotherly love or kindness, has no charm for me". This troubled, noble hero promptly emancipated his slaves but joined the Southern cause.

The Civil War began on April 12, 1861, when local South Carolina troops opened fire on the U.S. military base of Fort Sumter. The rest of the four-year war was a horror. Grand moments of heroism in the great pitched battles of Antietam (Maryland), Gettysburg (Pennsylvania), Fredericksburg (Virginia), Shiloh (Tennessee) and Vicksburg (Mississippi) were mere punctuation marks, however glorious, in the miserable, cold, wet, disease-ridden guerrilla warfare that characterized most of the campaign. In this war of Americans against Americans, dysentery, typhoid, malaria and consumption killed more than twice as many as did bullets and bayonets.

The South, with its proud military tradition, had superior officers and training, but the North, with an overwhelming supremacy in heavy industry, railways and arms manufacture, inexorably triumphed despite its frequently incompetent military leadership. While Lee brought a certain classical elegance and Thomas "Stonewall" Jackson a fatalistic sense of realism to Southern generalship, the North's heroes—Ulysses Grant and William Sherman—once they were able to assert themselves, demonstrated relentless willpower and sheer brute force.

After Grant occupied the Confederate capital of Richmond, Virginia, Lee submitted the South's surrender at Appomattox on April 9, 1865.

Just five days after victory, Lincoln was assassinated at Ford's Theater in Washington, by Confederate sympathizer John Wilkes Booth. This well-known actor leapt onto the stage after shooting the president, shouting *"Sic semper tyrannis!* The South is avenged!"

Reconstruction

But the revenge was not sweet for the South. Ravaged by the war, its major cities reduced to rubble, Georgia in utter ruin from Atlanta to Savannah, the South found its economy was shattered, its banks insolvent and the cotton crop of 1860 not matched again till 1879. As the planter-aristocracy moved out, either to towns in the North and West or abroad to England, Mexico or Brazil, the poor white farmers took over. The North had prospered, the war having profited a new class of millionaires—Armour in meatpacking, Rockefeller in oil, Remington in guns (later typewriters), Marshall Field in merchandising. Over 800,000 immigrants streamed into the North during the war and over 3 million more followed in the next ten years.

The Blacks, 4 million freed by the Union's victory, faced more hardships. After the first euphoria they woke to the embittered South's new "black codes" under which they could not vote, testify against Whites, bear arms or frequent public places reserved for Whites. In Washington, federal mismanagement could not make good on the "40 acres and a mule" which the government had promised each ex-slave who applied. The most positive achievement of the Freedmen's Bureau was to set up new hospitals and schools. Black activist Booker T. Washington wrote of the wholesale rush to the classrooms: "Few were too young and none too old to make the attempt to learn. The great ambition of the older people was to try to learn to read the Bible before they died". But many Blacks also faced greater violence than they'd ever known as slaves, and the Ku Klux Klan, founded in Tennessee in 1866, spread political terror throughout the South.

The federal government's Reconstruction Acts replaced recalcitrant southern state governments with northerners and Blacks, backed by federal troops, to guarantee "equal protection of the laws". While many northerners went south with the noble intention of protecting civil liberties, there were many more "carpetbaggers", aided by southern "scalawags", who exploited the situation for their private profit. Blacks participated in southern government but never had a controlling say, despite their overwhelming majorities in South Carolina, Mississippi and Louisiana.

The Reconstruction governments were often incompetent or corrupt but not more so than before or after. They did introduce tax reform, poor-relief and free public schooling, but white prejudice and hostility were unrelenting. By 1876 the nation was tired of the black civil rights issue, and a "soft" Republican, Rutherford Hayes, defeated tough, reform-minded Samuel Tilden in the presidential election. Enforcement Acts were nullified and for the next three generations southern Blacks were left in a limbo between slavery and freedom.

The World Stage

By 1914, America had established itself as the world's leading industrial power. Railways, steel, coal, oil and the vast agricultural resources of the Great Plains brought wealth such as the planet had never before witnessed.

From 1860 to 1920 the population more than tripled from 31 to 106 million. This was the period of massive immigration: 8 million British (half of them Irish), 6 million Germans, over 2 million Scandinavians, and Austrians, Hungarians, Czechs, Poles, Serbs, Italians and Russian Jews. Northern Europeans went west, to the farmlands; southern and eastern Europeans and the Irish stuck to the big eastern and midwestern cities. Jews went into the garment industry, Finns into the mines, Portuguese into textiles. The Chinese worked in the mines and on the railways—and suffered from anti-Oriental laws when white Americans became scared for their jobs.

The trade union movement —or organized labour as the Americans prefer to call it— proved less political than in Europe. Rather than question the virtues of the capitalist system, it preferred to demand its fair share of the profits. This proved hard enough, and the strikes, lock-outs and pitched battles between company militia and workers were as violent as anything in the most revolutionary "old country".

In keeping with the imperial spirit of the times, America bought Alaska from the Russians in 1867 and gradually absorbed Hawaii by negotiating trading and military privileges with these strategically vital Pacific islands. In the Caribbean, the U.S. proved itself adept at classical gunboat diplomacy. In the 1898 war against the Spanish, America ended up with Puerto Rico and Guam (in the Pacific), military occupation of the Philippines and the role of godfather to Cuba's independence.

As the old nations were butchering each other on the battlefields of Europe, America was clearly ready for the world stage. Woodrow Wilson, son of a southern Presbyterian minister and president of Princeton University, brought a decidedly moral and didactic flavour to the role. After helping the Allies to victory over Germany, the American President presented at the Versailles peace negotiations an elaborate plan for democracy, international peacekeeping through a League of Nations, and clemency towards the defeated. He ran into the anti-German jingoism of the British and the open cynicism of France's Georges Clemenceau: "Mr. Wilson bores me with his Fourteen Points; why, God Almighty has only ten!"

Boom and Crash

After the Russian Revolution, America fell victim to a Red Scare. Suspicious aliens were deported. The New York state legislature expelled five socialist members because their politics were felt to be "absolutely inimical to the best interest of the State of New York and of the United States". In 1927, Nicola Sacco and Bartolomeo Vanzetti, two Italian-born anarchists charged with murdering a shoe-factory paymaster in Massachusetts, were sent to the electric chair. Many believed the jury was swayed more by its fear of anarchic politics than its conviction of criminal responsibility.

But the '20s were also when the good times rolled: jazz, radio, silent movies, and cars—9 million in 1918, 26 million by the end of the decade. Materialism was respectable. As President Calvin Coolidge put it: "The business of America is business"—and it was enjoying a boom.

The growth of the big cities with their—to Anglo-Saxon Protestant eyes—exotic immigrant populations, brought a threat to the old American rural and small-town principles. Prohibition of alcohol in 1920 was justified with the argument that "Our nation can only be saved by turning the pure stream of country sentiment and township morals to flush out the cesspools of cities and thus save civilization from pollution". Far from upholding the old morality, Prohibition promoted gangland crime and even drove federal enforcement agents into league with Al Capone's bootleggers. The business of America is business.

In 1928, Herbert Hoover, very much the candidate of that American business, a great humanitarian in World War I with a mining engineer's efficiency, arrived in the White House with high hopes: "We shall soon with the help of God be in sight of the day when poverty will be banished from this nation". The next year came the Great Crash of the New York Stock Exchange and America slumped into the Depression. Between 1929 and 1932, 5,000 banks closed down.

By 1933, one third of the population were either unemployed or members of families in which the breadwinner was out of work. People went hungry while fruit, vegetables and grain were in abundance. Houses were unheated while coal piled up in mountains. America was stunned by the failure of its classic virtues of business leadership, organization and efficiency.

In 1933, Franklin D. Roosevelt embarked on a whirlwind "Hundred Days" of economic and social measures to conquer the catastrophe. With a canny sense of public relations, the president confided in the people with radio "fireside chats", and immediately cheered them up a little by legalizing wine and beer while Prohibition was dismantled federally and handed over to state legislation.

FDR's "New Deal" proliferated with new initials: NRA (National Industrial Recovery Act) to regenerate industry and improve working conditions; PWA (Public Works Administration) to create jobs with such projects as the Chicago subway, express highways in Virginia and new ships for the Navy; WPA (Works Progress Administration) to build parks and schools and encourage artists, writers, actors and musicians; and the TVA (Tennessee Valley Authority), a regional reconstruction experiment that attracted worldwide attention to its dams for flood control, electric power generation, resettlement of

31

small farmers and rural public health programmes. The New Deal did beat back the disaster of the Depression, but economic recession did not end till World War II. In 1939 there were still 10 million unemployed.

From World War II Onwards

After Woodrow Wilson's internationalist adventures, much of America preferred the small comforts of isolation, coupled with a pacifist reaction in general. Even FDR said in 1936: "We shun political commitments which might entangle us in foreign wars". But the neutralist policy was revoked after Hitler's 1940 *Blitzkrieg* against Belgium, France and the Netherlands. Congress appropriated $37 million for U.S. arms and aid to its allies—but still resisted military conscription. The Japanese raid on Pearl Harbor, on December 7, 1941, ended all hesitation.

The United States gave unstintingly in manpower and money to the Allied war effort against Germany and Japan. At the same time the war gave a huge boost to American industry. Meat, fuel and tyres were rationed, but the general standards of living remained high throughout the war.

Roosevelt was re-elected to an unprecedented fourth term in 1944. As a *Chicago Daily News* writer commented: "If he was good enough for my pappy and my grandpappy, he is good enough for me". After a long struggle against infantile paralysis that had been overcome by his iron will, FDR died in April 1945, before the final victory. It was left to Harry Truman to make the momentous decision to use the atom bomb that ended the war against Japan.

In some ways, events after World War II have followed the pattern of those after World War I—a Red Scare sparked by the Cold War and underlined by the McCarthyite witch-hunts; an era of happy materialism under Eisenhower; rock music in place of jazz; illegal marijuana in place of bootleg alcohol; boom prosperity alternating with recessions (stopping short, so far, of an all-out depression).

But two outstanding events set these years apart. In the 1960s, under Martin Luther King's inspired leadership, black Americans dealt with a piece of unfinished business in the U.S. Constitution, obtaining the emancipation promised them a century earlier, or at least as much of it as mere legislation can guarantee. At the end of that decade, Christopher Columbus's New World adventure achieved a new dimension when men took off from this continent to go to the moon. In the end, the business of America is *not* business, it's making dreams come true.

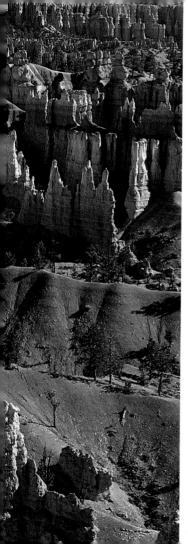

WHERE TO GO

Confronting your journey to the United States, you have to make some rather painful decisions. If this is likely to be a once-in-a-lifetime trip, you may want to get a feel for the whole country or at least a representative slice of it. Essential to this is a sense of the sheer size of America, in which case you may want to take in both the East and West coasts with some of the grand wide open spaces and natural wonders in between. This is an entirely feasible and financially reasonable proposition with the many special airline tickets that permit multiple destinations, often with almost unlimited mileage. But to "do" America this way, without exhausting yourself, you'll need at least a month.

If, however, this is to be just one of many trips to the U.S. or if you have only a couple of weeks at your disposal, it might be better to concentrate on one or two major regions. Don't forget, any one of these regions might embrace a whole European country, if not two or three.

First-time visitors with just two weeks available should, of course, begin with New York. Without it, they can't claim to have seen America. Manhattan itself will do for a start. In this car-dominated

Dramatic rock formations at Bryce Canyon

35

nation, you should realize—along with the wisest New Yorkers—that a car in Manhattan is worse than useless. Elsewhere, however, you'll find a car an important asset for excursions. In cities like Los Angeles or the big towns of Texas, you just can't do without a car. Those places were not built for pedestrians.

For cross-country trips two major national bus companies visit all important points on the continent. Trains are less practical, except along the East Coast. Obviously flying is the best choice for long distances, much cheaper and simpler than in Europe. On the "shuttles" between New York and Washington, Boston or Philadelphia or between Los Angeles and San Francisco, it's like taking a bus. But do try the bus or car if you can, just to get a taste of America's immensity.

From New York the most convenient regions to include in a two-week stay are the Mid-Atlantic (Washington D.C. and Philadelphia) for the historically minded, and/or New England (Boston and the resorts of Massachusetts and Rhode Island) for those who would like to mix history with relaxation. Or, the Florida part of the South for those who want nothing but fun.

Another possibility for the two-week holiday is to combine New York with an excursion further afield, either clear across the continent (4½ hours by plane) to California, or to one of the country's great natural wonders such as the Grand Canyon or Yellowstone. New York, especially in summer, is an exhilarating but also exhausting experience, so you'll need to pace yourself for the rest of the trip.

For the month-long stay, a typical itinerary might include New York–Boston–Washington, then directly to California, making your way back east via Yellowstone or Grand Canyon; then perhaps San Antonio or Santa Fe for a taste of Spanish America; a distinctive big city like New Orleans or Chicago, then rest up on a beach in Florida till your plane carries you home. If you want to see a lot of America in your four weeks, resist the temptation to start with California. You may be so seduced by it that you'll forget to look at the rest of the country.

The combinations are endless, but remember that Americans themselves like the good life to be both exciting and relaxed. If you want to survive your holiday, follow their example of enjoying both the big city and the parks and resorts that are always handy. Even a town like Chicago has sandy beaches on the lake; New Orleans has its restful bayou country; New York, its Long Island; Boston, its Cape Cod, and most of Los Angeles is beach anyway.

NEW YORK CITY

Perhaps more than any other place on earth, New York is a city people feel they know before they get there. Films and magazine photos have so stamped it into the popular consciousness that you believe you already possess its ferocious mystique of movement and noise, that you're already familiar with the gigantic chasms of skyscrapers, the flash of yellow taxis, the underworld steam puffing through the manhole-covers and the milling crowds of people.

Then, one day, you go. And it's more than you ever dreamed. Coming in from JFK airport, as you approach Manhattan, the city's skyscrapers loom higher, more impressively than in any film. In the flesh, the crowds on Madison, Fifth and Sixth avenues are a drama of motion and colour you could never conceive of in the abstract. Right in there among the city's Irish, Italians, Chinese, Jews, Germans, Puerto Ricans and Blacks, not to forget the poor put-upon white Anglo-Saxon Protestants, you'll plunge into one of the last travel adventures of our time. Every other place has been discovered, New York is new every time.

While you can't know America without first seeing New York, don't mistake New York for the rest of the U.S.A. Both New Yorkers and non-New Yorkers insist on that with equal vehemence. Facing east, it has always had a definite taste for the world of Europe. Founded by the Dutch as New Amsterdam in 1626 (see p. 19), the city numbered 1,500

> ### New York in Figures
> *The dimensions of New York are more than mere figures can express but here are a few to play with anyway:*
>
> *The five boroughs (Manhattan, Brooklyn, Queens, the Bronx and Staten Island) have a total population of 7 million. With the surrounding suburbs, this figure rises to 12 million, and if the outlying satellite cities are included, the total attains a phenomenal 16 million inhabitants.*
>
> *New York City covers an area of 300 square miles. It has 6,400 miles of streets and 18 miles of beaches. There are 1,100 parks, squares and playgrounds with a total area of 37,000 acres; 120 museums; 400 galleries; 30 department stores; 400 theatres; about 100 skyscrapers; 3,500 churches; 25,000 restaurants; 100,000 first-class hotel rooms and 12,000 taxis.*
>
> *About 4 million people ride the subway every day. Some 2½ million catch a bus. The number of shops is well up in the thousands. Roughly 17 million people visit New York each year, 2½ million of them from overseas.*

inhabitants speaking 18 different languages by 1644. From their earliest years, New Yorkers' loyalties have been divided between America and Europe. On the day George Washington left to take command of the Continental Army, half the town went to cheer him off. The other half was down at the harbour welcoming the British governor returning from London.

MANHATTAN

This island, 13 miles long and 2 miles wide, encompasses almost everything you will want to see or visit. The other four boroughs, mostly residential, have their own special flavours, but for locals and tourists alike New York *is* Manhattan.

As intimidating as it may seem at first glance, Manhattan is, in fact, a very easy place to get

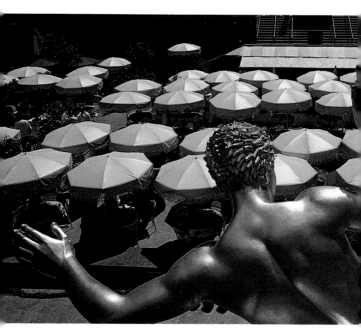

around. It divides up simply into three parts: Uptown, Midtown and Downtown (which, unlike in other cities, is the lower rather than the central part of town). Uptown is north of 59th Street, Midtown speaks for itself and Downtown is the area south of 34th Street.

The backbone of the island is Fifth Avenue; all areas to the west of it as far as the Hudson are

known as the West Side, while the East Side covers the area between Fifth Avenue and the East River. Fifth Avenue begins at Washington Square down in Greenwich Village. There and in the Wall Street area, streets still have the names and irregular lines of the colonial era. Otherwise, the roads intersect at right angles and the

Rockefeller Plaza in summer

streets have numbers rather than names. Avenues (First to Twelfth) run north-south, streets (1st to 220th) run east-west. Some avenues have names—York, Lexington, Madison and Park (attempts to rename Sixth the Avenue of the Americas seem doomed). Broadway, obeying no rules, runs more or less diagonally.

With the so-called grid system of rectangular blocks, you pinpoint a place not by street-number but by the nearest intersection of street and avenue; e.g. the Whitney Museum is at Madison and 75th, one block east and seven blocks south of the Metropolitan (Fifth and 82nd).

Midtown

Chances are your hotel will be located in Midtown so that you can cover the area on foot. At any rate, this is the centre, the place to begin.

Rockefeller Center

This soaring cluster of towers between Fifth and Sixth Avenue, from 48th to 51st Street, is the undisputed magnetic core of New York City. Without any one of them being an architectural masterpiece, this ensemble of Indiana limestone buildings achieves a power and harmony that attract thousands of shoppers, street-vendors, office workers and your better class of roustabout all day long.

The place breathes prosperity and that must please the ghost of John D. Rockefeller, Jr., who leased the site from Columbia University in 1928 to rescue it from the infamy of Prohibition speakeasy saloons. They quickly disappeared under the first skyscrapers of a booming business and communications centre, linked by an underground pedestrian concourse, which today includes over 200 shops and restaurants.

You immediately sense the cheerful genius of the place with the fountains and flower beds of the **Channel Gardens** that slope down from Fifth Avenue south of 50th Street to the sunken plaza. Akin to the English Channel, the gardens separate the Maison Française on the left and the British Empire Building on the right. At the end is the **Rockefeller Plaza,** parasoled garden café in summer and ice-skating rink in winter. Watched over by a gilded statue of Prometheus, the plaza is dominated by the Center's tallest tower, the **RCA Building,** home of NBC Television. Take its elevator to the 65th floor for a ticket to the **Observation Roof's** great view of Manhattan, five floors higher. Alternatively, try a drink or a meal at the elegant Rainbow Room (also on the 65th floor) and see Manhattan light up at night.

At one time, Rockefeller Center was supposed to be built around a new Metropolitan Opera House. Instead, we got **Radio City Music Hall,** one of the world's most marvellous cinemas-cum-variety-palaces—a brilliant 1930s pick-me-up for the Depression blues. Try to see a show there, with the gorgeous Rockettes, kicking their lovely legs to the Radio City's own symphony orchestra and wonderful Wurlitzer organ, naturally the world's biggest. (Or at least take one of the backstage tours organized seven days a week.) The shimmering chandeliers and mirrors of the lobby would have impressed King Louis XIV. The auditorium, seating a mere 6,200, is ornamented with fantastic semicircular bands of light. Can you imagine, they nearly tore it down in the 1970s but, as the *New York Times* said in support of the public outcry: "If Radio City Music Hall really closes, it will be a little like closing New York". Finally, they kept both open.

Fifth Avenue

Fifth Avenue—at least the stretch between 34th Street and Central Park—is synonymous with luxury, to sample or to look. If you can't afford to stay at the Plaza Hotel by the Park or to dance, like novelist Scott Fitzgerald's wife, Zelda, in its famous fountain, you can bask in the understated opulence of the diamond-studded windows of Tiffany's jewellery shop—or Cartier's or Van Cleef & Arpels'. Or stroll around the smarter department stores like Saks Fifth Avenue, Bergdorf Goodman or (just around the corner on 57th Street) Henri Bendel; or try the leather-shops of Mark Cross and Gucci and the high fashion of French and Italian boutiques cashing in on New York's affluent sophistication.

A stunning new addition to the Fifth Avenue scene is **Trump Tower** at 56th Street. Inside you will find the ultimate atrium, a cool, airy space, six storeys high, exquisitely finished in rich rose-coloured marble and gleaming brass. An appropriate collection of exclusive and expensive shops surrounds the courtyard.

Amid all this sometimes over-ripe elegance, turn off a moment at West 47th Street—**"Diamond Row"**—centre of the diamond trade, where bearded, black-coated Hassidic Jews from Eastern Europe hurry back and forth with a twinkle in their eyes and a glitter in their little paper bags, under the benign protection of uniformed and plain-clothes police.

The valiant effort of **St. Patrick's Cathedral** (between 50th and 51st) to imitate Cologne's Gothic cathedral is a little lost today among the skyscrapers of Rockefeller Center and the Olympic Tower next door. The 1879 building comes into its own for many New Yorkers on the occasion of the spirited Irish Catholic parade on St. Patrick's Day (March 17) when the Cardinal comes out to greet the marchers.

Times Square and Broadway

The august *New York Times* publishes, it says, "All the News that's Fit to Print" and the old Times Tower gave its name to that bizarre mixture of chic and sleaze —Times Square (on the north side of 42nd Street between Broadway and Seventh Avenue). Times Square in fact encompasses the area from 42nd to 47th Street, between Sixth and Eighth avenues. It's the heart of the theatre district with many first-run cinemas, and also headquarters for the city's nastiest strip joints and sex shops. Excellent restaurants rub shoulders with the seamiest bars. Sleek limousines deposit ladies in evening dress, just down the street from prostitutes, drunks and dope-dealers, serenaded by street-entertainers similarly varying between the sophisticated talents of an out-of-work jazz musician and the crummy twanging of someone who stole a guitar.

But New Yorkers make a neat distinction to cope with the incongruous intermingling. Though one and the same area, the pornography and drugs are "at Times Square" while the art and good food are "on Broadway". At all events, the area is generally too depressing by day—go at night when you can't see the garbage and when the neon lights earn Broadway the nickname "the Great White Way".

If the Times Square/Broadway atmosphere gets to be too much for you, take time out in the snug armchairs of the lobby or Blue Bar of one of the great monuments of Manhattan's 1920s, the Algonquin Hotel (44th, between 5th and 6th). Partake of the rarefied ambience of New York literati—or at least overhear people repeating the great lines of *New Yorker* magazine wits Dorothy Parker, Robert Benchley and Harold Ross.

42nd Street

Another haven of peace, *and an* architectural delight, is the **New York Public Library** (5th Avenue between 40th and 42nd). This truly is a masterpiece of Beaux-Arts, a 1911 American reinterpretation of the French design school's neo-classical style at its gentlest and restrained best. Set back at the end of a wide, gradually rising stairway, the noble façade's three arches with coupled Corinthian columns around the entrance invite you in off the

Manhattan—mineral and vegetables

street for an hour's tranquillity. In this most public of public libraries, relax with a book in the great reading room, admire the recently refurbished Periodical Room or laze outside on the steps, well protected by E.C. Potter's giant lions.

East on 42nd Street, at the end of Park Avenue, **Grand Central Station,** terminus of the Vanderbilt railway empire, is as much a legend as it is a building. Like the library, its Beaux-Arts pedigree is impeccable (although it took a U.S. Supreme Court decision to save it from destruction). Over the great clock of the façade, the sculpture of the eagle among various standing and reclining Roman deities apparently symbolizes America's special relationship with the gods. Completed in 1920, the station's 123 rail lines built on two levels, 66 above and 57 below, move half a million people in and out of the city every day, jaded commuters from the suburbs and wide-eyed newcomers from the great beyond. Watch them at rush hour in the vast barrel-vaulted **main concourse.** Fateful Zodiac formations painted in the blue heavens of the ceiling hover over these adventurers come to conquer New York.

The Pan Am Building over the station infuriated art critics, but the neighbourhood has some other impressive skyscrapers. A superb example of Art Deco can be seen in the stainless-steel swordfish pinnacle of the **Chrysler Building** (Lexington and 42nd). Its glazed enamel, white-brick silhouette is of course best viewed at a distance, but from the upper floors of nearby hotels you get a close-up of the weird gargoyles inspired by various radiator caps for Chrysler cars. **Citicorp Center** (Lexington between 53rd and 54th) brings an outstanding touch to the skyline with its dramatically sloping silver roof. At ground level, its urban consciousness is emphasized by a lively three-storey "market" of shops and restaurants around a skylit central courtyard and, by the same architect, Hugh Stubbins, the free-standing, polygonal **St. Peter's Lutheran Church.** By no means overwhelmed by its skyscraper environment, the church has a lovely chapel decorated by sculptor Louise Nevelson.

The best of the sleek office-blocks on Park Avenue is undoubtedly the **Seagram Building** (between 52nd and 53rd) by Mies van der Rohe and Philip Johnson. The pure lines of this bronze-tinted glass skyscraper, completed in 1958, are considered the ultimate refinement of Mies' International Style developed at the German Bauhaus. The lobby is decorated by Picasso's stage-backdrop for *Le Tricorne.*

The United Nations
(First Avenue, between 42nd and 48th)
John D. Rockefeller, Jr., donated the 17-acre site to persuade U.N. members to make their headquarters in New York. A disparate team of international architects, including the Swiss-French master, Le Corbusier, somehow managed to put up buildings in the early '50s with considerably more unity and harmony than are ever achieved inside by the diplomats. The Secretariat is housed in the tower (first smooth slab of its kind), the General Assembly in the lower block with the concave roof. The complex, including the Dag Hammarskjöld Library, memorial to the late secretary-general, and the Conference Building, is best seen as a whole from the East River on a boat ride around Manhattan.

At the information desk in the lobby (45th and First), you can get tickets for the General Assembly, when it's in session, and guided tours of the whole U.N. complex. Member states have made physical donations—the three Council Rooms, for instance, being the gifts of Norway, Denmark and Sweden, while Britain gave the Barbara Hepworth Sculpture in the Plaza pool (a donation from American schoolchildren).

For a pleasant view of the skyscrapers along U.N. Plaza, buy a sandwich to eat in the garden, or have your lunch (passholders only; reservations at the lobby information desk) in the Delegates' Dining Room overlooking the East River. You can get very reasonably priced craftwork from all over the world at the U.N. gift shop. The post office sells U.N. stamps only (not American) for letters and cards posted inside the complex.

Empire State Building
On the corner of Fifth Avenue and 34th Street, the Empire State Building is open to the public from 9.30 a.m. until midnight. Although Chicago's Sears Tower is currently the "world's tallest" title-holder, King Kong still prefers the Empire State. Follow him, but take the elevator—there are 1,860 stairs.

Everything about the Empire State Building is huge: 102 storeys; 60,000 tons of steel; 3,500 miles of telephone wires and cables; 60 miles of pipes; the building occupies 1½ million cubic yards and King Kong had to climb 1,472 feet. Built in 1931, most of its office space was empty in the early Depression years and it paid its taxes with income from the sightseers.

For your ticket to the **Observation Deck,** go down first to the basement—arrows point the way. Next to the ticket office is the Guinness World Records Exhibit. If you have a taste for a hair split 14 times, the longest earthworm in the world, the biggest guitar, smallest violin, thinnest waist and longest beard, you will find all these on display.

The elevator takes you to the 80th floor in under a minute, then you catch the "local" to the 86th. A heated shelter protects you in winter, otherwise the outside terrace offers a fantastic **view,** often of ships 40 miles out at sea. For those who want to go all the way, a third elevator goes to the observation deck on the 102nd floor, at the base of a 222-foot-high TV antenna.

Downstairs again on 34th Street, you're in a great popular shopping area, Macy's Department Store on 34th, rival Gimbels on 33rd. On 32nd Street and Seventh Avenue is the huge **Madison Square Garden,** Manhattan's most famous sports arena.

Downtown

Wall Street Area
Here at the southern end of Manhattan, the skyscrapers assert all their power, closing in on each other across narrow canyons to form ramparts for this almost awe-inspiring capital of capitalism known as Wall Street. Appropriately it was conceived in 1653 as a protection for America's first great financial bargain — a wooden stockade to keep the Indians from invading the island they had sold to the Dutch for $24 (60 guilders) 30 years earlier. Now the citadel is guarded from the towers of Chase Manhattan Bank, Citibank and Morgan Guaranty Trust, along with the offices of the world's other great banks and financial institutions at money's most prestigious address.

The beating heart of the Financial District is the **New York Stock Exchange,** reverentially designed as a Roman temple. During trading hours you can take a guided tour of the sanctuary through the 20 Broad Street entrance leading to the visitors' gallery. There you can watch the mad transactions on the trading floor that send the sacred Dow Jones Average up and down. A film and permanent exhibition relate the history and workings of the Stock Exchange, and lecturers teach you how to play the market. The famous ticker-tape is on display but these days it's been displaced by electronic screens. (The traditional ticker-tape parades for returning war heroes and astronauts have to be fed now with the "top secret" confetti of automatic shredding machines.)

From the temple of the money lenders take a look at the Episcopalian **Trinity Church** (1846) at the Broadway end of Wall Street. This first, and for many, most successful of America's Gothic Revival churches offers tired office workers—and sightseers—a moment's peace in the cemetery garden. Alexander Hamilton, first secretary of the treasury, is buried here.

During the brief period that New York was the United States' first capital, the **Federal Hall** (corner of Wall and Nassau streets, demolished in 1812 and rebuilt in 1842) was the home of Congress and the place where George Washington took the oath as president on April 30, 1789. His bronze statue stands outside. The other landmark from the birth of the Republic is **Fraunces Tavern,** corner of Pearl and Broad streets. Six years before his inauguration, Washington took leave of his officers here, at the end of the Revolutionary War. The black tavern-owner, Samuel Fraunces, became Washington's steward in the White House. The present building is an approximate reconstruction of the original, serving as a museum for the Revolutionary period.

North of Trinity Church, the twin towers of the **World Trade Center** (Church Street between Liberty and Vesey) are just so overpoweringly big that they sweep away all question of whether they're actually beautiful. The great surprise as your eye travels 1,350 feet from top to bottom is in those slim Venetian-

Gothic arches at the base. The buildings accumulate impressive figures: 43,600 windows, 198 elevators (46 express, 144 local and 8 freight). A gigantic bronze fountain globe highlights the central square. The whole Center covers an area of 16 acres. A railway station and various subway stations occupy the basement levels, and the concourse (street) level is the site of a vast shopping centre—a town in itself for tens of thousands of New Jersey commuters. The **observation deck** is up on the 107th floor of Two World Trade Center looking out over the metropolis, New Jersey and the ocean. You can have that fabulous view during a meal at the Windows on the World restaurant, also on the 107th floor, in One World Trade Center.

Statue of Liberty

(15-minute ferry ride from Battery Park.)

It is difficult to imagine a more eloquent symbol than the one this "Lady" of the Statue of Liberty offered those desperate refugees sailing to the New World at the end of the 19th century. Today few Americans or foreigners, however cynical about corny patriotism, can remain totally blasé about this monument, rising 305 feet from its pedestal base to the tip of the torch.

Start at the **American Museum of Immigration** in the base of the statue. This provides an excellent audio-visual introduction to the saga of all the ethnic groups flowing into America from colonial times, but also of those American Indians who were already there and of the Blacks who were scarcely willing passengers.

You can either pay to ride the elevator or climb the steps to the top of the pedestal. The ultimate feat is to continue up to the platform inside the Lady's crown. The **view** is worth it.

The statue's proper name is "Liberty Illuminating the World", a French idea linking the French and American Revolutions. The $250,000 it cost was jointly, and privately, funded, the French paying for the statue and the Americans for the pedestal. Sculptor Frédéric-Auguste Bartholdi took 10 years to complete it, with Gustave Eiffel taking time off from his tower to provide the inner steel casing for the copperplated figure. Once completed in Paris, it had to be taken apart and shipped over in 214 cases for its 1886 inauguration by President Grover Cleveland.

West of Liberty Island is **Ellis Island** where 12 million of those "huddled masses" passed through immigration checks between 1892 and 1924, where unpronounceable Polish names became Americanized, where the medically suspect were marked with chalk on their lapels—

H for heart, K for hernia, Sc for scalp, X for mental defects. Today, the "island of tears" has been declared a national monument, and is being restored for its centenary in 1992, when it will present a fascinating panorama of immigration to the U.S.

If you don't want to join the crowds on Liberty Island, but want a nice, cooling boat ride as well as a marvellous view of Manhattan, take the **Staten Island Ferry** (also from Battery Park)— take it anyway, it's the best bargain ride in town. For a superior view, stand forward on the second deck.

Lower East Side
(From Canal Street north to 7th Street)
This is where the immigrants headed first. Most stayed just long enough to learn English and then headed uptown or out west to the continent beyond the Hudson River. It says something about their special ethnic solidarity that substantial groups of Chinese, Jews and Italians chose to settle here a little longer in their own enclaves. The Chinese are still here in strength, but the colours, sounds and smells of the other communities also linger on vividly enough for you to capture, in an easy afternoon's stroll, the old flavour.

If you take the subway (underground) to **Chinatown,** you won't go wrong: the Canal Street Station has signs in both Roman and Chinese characters. The telephone booths have pagoda roofs, tiny shops sell ivory and jade jewellery, grocers display snow peas, Chinese cabbage and winter melon, and countless restaurants vie for attention with their Cantonese, Shanghai and Szechwan specialities.

Some 20,000 Chinese live in the nine-block area between Canal Street, the Bowery, Park Row, Pearl Street and Center Street.

Invitation to Hope
The famous inscription on the pedestal of the Statue of Liberty was written by Emma Lazarus, a New York poet, in response to the Russian pogroms of the 1880s which drove so many Jews to cross the Atlantic. Her lines have since taken on a universal significance for all the world's oppressed:

> "Give me your tired, your poor,
> Your huddled masses yearning to breathe free,
> The wretched refuse of your teeming shore,
> Send these, the homeless, tempest-tossed, to me:
> I lift my lamp beside the golden door."

The earliest arrivals came to this country during the California Gold Rush and railway construction of the 19th century; more recent immigrants here come directly from Hong Kong. Many of them barely understand English and continue to speak Chinese to their children; they have integrated very little in Manhattan life.

Join the Chinese from the rest of New York who come here on weekends to do their grocery shopping and to enjoy a meal out. The Canal Street supermarkets sell the finest China teas and cheap and pretty porcelain to drink it from. Take a look at the Chinese Museum (8 Mott Street) and the Buddhist Temple (64 Mott Street).

South of Mott Street, at 55 St. James Place, is New York's oldest "monument", the Shearith Israel cemetery, founded in 1683 by Portuguese Sephardic Jews from Brazil. But the **Jewish quarter,** settled mostly by Eastern European Ashkenazi Jews, is on the north-east side of Chinatown, around the old Hester Street market. Walk along Delancey and Orchard Street and you'll see only a shadow of its heyday at the turn of the century, but such a lively shadow that you sense how hectic it once was. Dormant on the Sabbath from Friday evening to Saturday night, the place springs to life on Sundays, when Orthodox Jews in black hats and long black frock coats pick their way among Puerto Rican dancers and Greek (non-kosher) shish-kebab vendors. Shuttered Yiddish theatres, publishing companies and second-hand bookshops — a couple of them still hanging on — attest to the cultural life that thrived amid the poverty of the old days. The delicatessen and kosher dairy restaurants ring with accents inherited from the *shtetl* (Jewish villages) of Polish Galicia and the Ukraine.

Little Italy, centred on Mulberry Street, is now principally a thriving tourist centre, polishing the rougher memories of Naples and Sicily with smart restaurants and high-quality caterers in place of the little old *trattorie* and mama-and-papa grocery stores. The mandolin music comes out of stereophonic amplifiers. Whenever they can, the merchants turn a saint's day into a street festival. But the salami smells good even if the pasta's not always *al dente*.

Greenwich Village and SoHo

The Village was once New York's artistic centre, home of distinguished writers like Henry James, Edith Wharton, John Dos Passos and O'Henry and painters like Edward Hopper, Ben Shahn and Franz Kline. In the '50s they went off to listen to the jazz of Charlie Parker and Miles Davis at the

51

Village Vanguard, in the '60s to
hear the first jokes of Woody
Allen at the Bitter End cabaret.

Today you can recapture something of the feeling in the crazy
second-hand clothing stores
around Bleecker and MacDougal
Street. At night the jazz cellars
are as aromatic as ever and a few
coffee houses still serve some very
good espresso over which you
read your weekly *Village Voice*.
The Jamesian gentility is to be
found in the attractive residential
area around Christopher Street,
the antique shops and, jarringly
less authentic, in the candlelit
bistros with checked tablecloths
and French-sounding food.

James himself lived for a few
months on **Washington Square,**
the title of one of his novels and
heart of the New York University
campus. His grandmother lived in
one of the Greek Revival houses
along the north side (no. 19),
among the most elegant dwellings
in New York. A gap in the middle
gives you a view up Fifth Avenue
from the **Washington Arch,** the
work of architect Stanford White,
commissioned in 1889 to mark the
centenary of Washington's inauguration as president. The park
has historically been a rendezvous
for criminals — the old oak which
was once a gallows for highway-
men today provides shelter for the
Village's many drug dealers.

The area south of West Houston Street, **SoHo** (short for South

of Houston), is following the pattern of Greenwich Village. Artists who couldn't afford the rents after the Village's commercialization moved south to the abandoned lofts and warehouse floors of the industrial district. The most successful artists were able to install kitchens, bathrooms and comfortable interiors. Others made do with bare walls and floors for the sake of the ample space and light. Through the curtainless windows you can admire either some affluent décors or some huge canvases and monumental sculpture in the making. With the success of the avantgarde galleries on West Broadway, especially number 420, where the old pillars of the Pop Art movement, Andy Warhol, Robert Rauschenberg and Roy Lichtenstein, exhibit, rents are soaring again. The interior decorators and gallery owners are taking over from the artists, many of whom have already moved on to the TriBeCa (*tri*angle *be*low *ca*nal) area.

Uptown

The Upper West Side—that is, west of Central Park—defies any label to its neighbourhoods other than "mixed". Intellectuals and artists live side by side with the shopkeepers and bus drivers of every ethnic and racial background. Street life manages to be both harmonious and lively.

Lincoln Center
(W. 62nd to W. 66th, between Columbus and Amsterdam)

With most of the prestigious fine arts museums situated on the affluent Upper East Side, the Lincoln Center for the Performing Arts provided a good balance and a perfect fillip for the revival of the neighbourhood in the 1960s. Since Daddy had to shelve his plan to put the Metropolitan Opera in the Rockefeller Center, John D. III led the drive to find it another home, along with the New York Philharmonic, the New York City Ballet and the Juilliard School of Music. The Center replaced a Puerto Rican neighbourhood of the kind immortalized by Leonard Bernstein's musical comedy *West Side Story* — Bernstein moved on, too, after a stint with the Philharmonic.

As you go up the steps to the plaza on Columbus Avenue — especially at night with the central fountain bathed in ethereal light — you may find the effect a shade too self-consciously "prestigious". New Yorkers do take their arts seriously. The undoubtedly important buildings around the plaza are overwhelmingly monumental, starting on the left with the severe modern classicism of Philip Johnson's **New York State Theater,** home of the New York City Ballet and New York City Opera. Men can't help adjusting their ties and women straightening their dresses when entering the opulent foyer with its gilded-chain drapery and gold-velvet ceiling.

At the back of the plaza, Wallace K. Harrison's grand design for the **Metropolitan Opera House,** with its tall glass façade arched in travertine marble, red-carpeted lobby with dazzling crystal chandeliers, makes it almost an impudence to call it the "Met". You can see the Chagall murals from the plaza.

Originally built in 1962, the Philharmonic or **Avery Fisher Hall,** on the right, had to be reconstructed several times over the next 14 years before achieving today's excellent acoustics and admired architectural simplicity. Beyond the Philharmonic, at the back of a handsome reflecting pool with sculpture by Henry

Moore, is the **Vivian Beaumont Theater,** originally intended as the base for a New York repertory company. Designed by Eero Saarinen, it houses both a large round auditorium with a versatile movable stage at plaza level and the small Mitzi Newhouse Theater below. Behind the Vivian Beaumont is the Library and Museum of the Performing Arts, the Lincoln Center's branch of the New York Public Library, housing thousands of records and books on the arts.

A bridge across 65th Street connects the Center to the **Juilliard School,** world-famous music conservatory. On the ground floor, in its Alice Tully Hall, you can hear fine chamber music ensembles, as well as free concerts by Juilliard School pupils. (One-hour guided tours of Lincoln Center start at the concourse level of the "Met".)

Central Park
The New Yorkers' daytime love affair with these 840 acres of greenery in the middle of Manhattan's concrete seems impervious to the stories of night-time muggings (simple to avoid — just don't go in there at night except for concerts and then stick with friends). Half a mile wide and two and a half miles long, Central Park remains the indispensable sports field, playground and picnic spot for tens of thousands

of city dwellers. A great place to contemplate the grandeur of Manhattan beyond the trees—or turn your back on it and forget it for a while.

The glades, copses, ponds, hillocks and rock outcroppings were landscaped in the 1860s by Frederick Law Olmsted, while Calvert Vaux designed the pavilions and delightful cast-iron bridges. The park has some 75,000 trees and what it lacks in variety of flowers it makes up for in sparrows, swans, ducks and squirrels.

Starting from the south-east corner in front of the Plaza Hotel, skirt the pond to the zoo. Then head up the tree-lined **Mall,** which looks much longer than it really is thanks to the perspective of the deliberately scaled-down, mock-medieval Belvedere Castle in the distance. Left of the Mall is Sheep Meadow where sheep really did graze until 1934 and where free concerts are given in spring and summer. West of the meadow, Tavern on the Green is an ornate greenhouse restaurant.

Scene of a lively oriental market on Sundays, **Bethesda Fountain** at the north end of the Mall is ornamented with some cherubs exhorting us, with typical New Yorker humour, to Purity, Health, Peace and Temperance. You can go rowing on the lake behind the fountain or, at the Conservatory Pond between the statues of Hans Christian Andersen and Alice in Wonderland, watch the model-sailboat enthusiasts egging on their vessels.

At the back of the Metropolitan Museum is **Cleopatra's Needle,** actually an obelisk from the reign of Thutmose III, some 1,500 years before the famous Queen of Egypt. West of the obelisk is the Great Lawn, filling in an old reservoir for the benefit of aficionados of baseball, touch-football and soccer. The **Delacorte Theater,** overlooking the lawn, hosts the summer "Shakespeare in the Park" festival (free, but queue up ahead of time for tickets).

Harlem

"Won't go to Harlem in ermine and pearls", says the old song, but that's no reason not to go at all, with the proper precautions. Of course, this place can be dangerous, a large part of it is a slum and slums everywhere are dangerous. But it's also part of New York's reality, which you may not want to avoid. This is one time when a guided tour is highly recommended as the best way to do it. So contact the Penny Sightseeing Company (telephone 246-4220) a day ahead and leave your valuables behind. The tour agency is run by Blacks who want to show their community to outsiders, concealing neither the best features nor the worst.

Harlem stretches from the top

end of Central Park, at 110th Street, to 162nd Street. A few years ago it was the home of a million Blacks from the southern states and the Caribbean. Today barely half a million remain. Optimists attribute this exodus to the new housing programmes and traditional "upward mobility". The pessimists say that dilapidation just drove people out to new ghettos such as the South Bronx, which has become another Harlem. Both are right.

Founded by Dutch settlers, Harlem remained a village separate from the rest of Manhattan until the end of the 19th century, when middle-class Americans moved north away from the new immigrants of the Lower East Side. You can still make out the genteel façades of some of their houses. Black people started moving in around 1920, the beginning of the Jazz Age. After the South, New York was the "Promised Land". Duke Ellington and Cab Calloway played the Cotton Club and the Apollo, drawing crowds of white people up to Harlem.

It's difficult to picture how it was in those days. The Apollo is still there and may come to life again one day as a resuscitated centre for jazz. But the rest looks like a bombed-out city, the result of a cataclysmic social civil war. Despairing tenants burned out their homes after unpaid land-lords cut off the services and made life unbearable.

The tragedy of what might have been can be seen in the few pleasant streets around Edgecombe Avenue, neighbourhood of the middle-class Blacks who proudly stay put. On the corner of Edgecombe and 160th is the **Morris-Jumel Mansion,** a stately house set in a garden, one of New York's last remnants of the colonial Georgian architecture. Built in 1765 and used by George Washington as his headquarters at the beginning of the Revolutionary War, it was bought in 1810 by a French wine-merchant, Stephen Jumel. Jumel's widow, Eliza, a remarkable woman who claimed to have slept with both George Washington and Napoleon, married her second husband, Aaron Burr (third Vice President of the U.S.), in the house. It's now a museum of American decorative arts from the 18th and 19th centuries.

The east side of Harlem is the domain of the Puerto Ricans— **Spanish Harlem.** Visit La Marqueta, the covered market under the railroad (Park Avenue from 111th to 116th Street). The mangoes, papayas, sugar cane, voodoo potions and aphrodisiacs take you out of Manhattan and drop you off in the Caribbean for a while. Best day is Saturday. A few words of Spanish will get you a better price.

Museums

With its 120 museums, New York performs a unique service to world civilization as a cultural bridge between the Old and New worlds. You could spend a lifetime in them.

Metropolitan Museum of Art (Fifth Avenue at 82nd Street). Indisputably one of the world's greatest museums, the Metropolitan consists of nearly 250 rooms with over 4,500 paintings and drawings, one million prints, 4,000 musical instruments and countless pieces of furniture and sculpture. Only a quarter of the collection is on display at any one time. Exhibits are ingeniously set out in their appropriate surroundings. Especially interesting are the American Wing, a glorious celebration of the architecture, decorative and fine arts of America; the Lehman collection of early Italian and French Impressionist painting; the primitive art in the Michael C. Rockefeller wing; the sections devoted to European painting from the 15th–20th century; and the Egyptian department.

Museum of Modern Art (W. 53rd Street between 5th and 6th avenues). MOMA to habitués, this private museum boosted by the Rockefeller family has more than 70,000 works of art from 1880 to the present, but only a portion of the collection is on view at any one time.

Guggenheim Museum (Fifth Avenue and 89th Street). Designed by Frank Lloyd Wright, the architecture is as important as the museum's contents. Late 19th- and 20th-century collection as well as works by Paul Klee, Kandinsky and Chagall. The annexe offers some fine Van Gogh, Gauguin and Modigliani and a superb group of Picassos.

Whitney Museum of American Art (Madison and 75th). Drawing on the great vigour of American 20th-century art, the museum has marvellously lit, imaginative and adventurous exhibitions.

Frick Collection (E. 70th Street and Fifth Avenue). Industrialist Henry Clay Frick's classical European paintings are presented in the opulent setting of his own home.

The Cloisters (Fort Tryon Park). Brings together medieval ruins from France, Spain and Italy in one combined fortified monastery.

American Museum of Natural History (Central Park West at 79th Street). Largest of the world's natural history museums, with a remarkable collection of minerals and gems and important anthropological exhibitions devoted to Asia and North American Indians.

Cooper-Hewitt Museum (Fifth Avenue and 91st Street). Houses America's largest collection of decorative art, an international history of design from the 15th to the 20th century.

Jewish Museum (Fifth Avenue at 92nd Street). Jewish ceremonial objects, archaeological remains from Israel, but also excellent avant-garde art shows.

Museum of the American Indian (Audubon Terrace, Broadway at 155th Street). World's largest collection of Indian art and artefacts of North, Central and South America.

Museum of the City of New York (Fifth Avenue and 104th Street). Important for the town's exciting history. Great old toys for kids.

Pierpont Morgan Library (Madison Avenue and 36th Street). Rare books, illuminated manuscripts, Old Master paintings, Florentine sculpture, etc., amassed by the American industrialist, J. Pierpont Morgan.

South Street Seaport Museum (Fulton and South streets). Restoration of 11-block historic seaport area, plus renovated sailing ships open for boarding (piers 15 and 16). Harbour tours aboard the schooner *Pioneer*.

And finally, a museum that isn't quite a museum: **The New York Experience,** in the McGraw-Hill Building (Avenue of the Americas and 49th Street). Shows featuring the history of New York on 16 screens, with 45 projectors and quadraphonic sound.

EXCURSIONS

Atlantic City *(New Jersey)*
(From New York, Lincoln Tunnel and south on New Jersey Turnpike and Garden State Parkway)

Atlantic City has made its way into most American homes on the board of the U.S. version of the famous parlour game Monopoly. Since the 1930s, when it was a fashionable seaside resort, the streets of Atlantic City served as the "properties" to be bought, bartered or mortgaged on your path to riches or ruin. With its rebirth as a casino town, the name of Atlantic City's game today is variously roulette, black-jack, craps or baccarat, and riches are paid out in real dollars. Big-time and small-time gamblers pour in from all over the East Coast with at least the hope of hitting one of the fantastic jack-pots pouring out of the one-armed-bandit slot machines.

Niagara Falls *(New York State)*
The true marvel of Niagara is how nature still manages to triumph over tawdry commercialism. No amount of pushy pedlars or tacky pink honeymoon motels (if you do stay overnight, take a look at one of the hilarious bridal suites)

can diminish the awesome spectacle of that mass of white water taking a plunge of nearly 200 feet on its way from Lake Erie down towards Lake Ontario.

It's worth looking at the Falls from more than one perspective. Make your first vantage-point Goat Island, a nice mini-tram ride from Prospect Point. The island divides the waters of the Niagara River into the eastern **American Falls**—182 feet high, 1,076 feet wide—and the western **Horseshoe (Canadian) Falls**—176 feet high and 2,100 feet wide—with a smaller cascade known as Bridal Veil off to the side. On Goat Island you can choose between a helicopter tour over the whole falls area or an elevator ride down to where the white water crashes into the lower river bed. There you can walk behind the wall of cascading water and experience the cataract's overpowering roar. Tour operators provide protective clothing, but nothing is totally waterproof against Niagara. Don't let that worry you—seeing Niagara and not getting wet would be silly.

Cable cars take you high above the rapids, three boats, all named *Maid of the Mist*, give you a safe view from the river. More adventurous, but not unsafe, is the raft trip through the rapids at the base of the falls. There are numerous observation towers and the best are on the Canadian side (no immigration or re-entry problems). The viewpoints of the Skylon and Panasonic Towers are respectively 770 feet and 665 feet above the falls.

At night the Horseshoe Falls gleam in multicoloured illuminations with 4,000 million units of candlepower generated by the falls themselves. The U.S. and Canada have collaborated to exploit Niagara's tremendous power resources—2,190,000 kilowatts on the American side and 1,775,000 kilowatts on the Canadian side.

Four miles north on Route 104, you can visit the interesting **Niagara Power Project** to see how this energy is harnessed. A geological museum in Prospect Park describes how rock erosion will completely flatten out the falls in the next 30,000 to 40,000 years.

While you're here, you might like to make a side-trip to **Buffalo,** a charming city—outside its ferocious winters—with a very lively cultural life. The Albright-Knox Art Gallery (1285 Elmwood Avenue) has some fine American and European art of the 18th, 19th and 20th centuries. The gallery is set in the lovely **Delaware Park,** landscaped by Frederick Law Olmsted and includes a zoo with some obligatory Buffalo buffalo. The Buffalo Philharmonic Orchestra is first class and gives concerts at the Kleinhans Music Hall.

NEW ENGLAND

From north to south, New England comprises six states—Maine, New Hampshire, Vermont, Massachusetts, Rhode Island and Connecticut, with Massachusetts' Boston as the undisputed capital. Their combined area would scarcely cover any one state in the west, but their historical significance in the Republic's exciting beginnings and their present role in American political and cultural life are impressive.

And beyond the historic prestige of New England, there's a terrific holiday to be had along the rugged coastline and little fishing ports from the Canadian border down to Boston. You may prefer the glorious sandy beaches of Cape Cod, or the rolling hills of the Berkshires in western Massachusetts and the White Mountains of New Hampshire, and everywhere among the woods, the splendid trees that cover four-fifths of the New England landscape. Even that grand past is a pleasure to behold in the spotless Massachusetts villages of white clapboard houses and red-brick mansions clustered around their church on its impeccably kept green.

Crisp spring and drowsy summer are delightful times in New England, but the trees claim a special short season to themselves in the place where the expression "Indian summer" came into its own. After the first cool spell in autumn, there's a sudden new burst of sunshine, when warm days and cool evenings combine to create a spectacular explosion of colour in the leaves. People travel from New York and from all over the north-east to see the gold of the poplars and birches, the scarlet of the oaks, dogwoods and maples and the magic copper-orange of the mountain ash and hickories. The green leaves of

---

Festivals
New England abounds in annual festivities—historic, social, sporting and cultural. Here are a representative few:

Patriot's Day *(Monday closest to April 19): pageants in Lexington and Concord, Mass., commemorating outbreak of Revolutionary War, 1775; and the Boston Marathon, massive international event.*

Berkshire Music Festival *at Tanglewood (Lenox, Mass.), July–August;* ***Newport Music Festival,*** *July;* ***Jacob's Pillow Dance Festival*** *(Berkshires), July–August.*

Pilgrim's Progress: *costumed Sabbath procession at Plymouth, Mass., every Friday in August.*

Thanksgiving Celebration *at Plimoth Plantation, Mass. (last Thursday in November).*

Autumn countryside in Vermont

Maine, New Hampshire and Vermont start turning in mid-September and a couple of weeks later in Massachusetts, Rhode Island and Connecticut. This natural spectacle has become so institutionalized that you can telephone state tourist offices to find out where and when to see the best displays, which usually peak around mid-October. This is also a great time for the country fairs, communal flea markets and individual garage-sales (see "Shopping" on p. 202) and pay-for-what-you-pick apples and pears in the orchards.

New England is packed with interesting and beautiful places to visit throughout its half-dozen states, and deserves, in many people's eyes, a whole vacation and a whole book to itself. But

64

BOSTON *(Massachusetts)*

This city encompasses the essence of America's origins and the blossoming of its 20th century. It's a bustling place of 600,000 inside the narrow city limits but nearly 4 million if you include all the townships of metropolitan Boston. Those small towns are how America began, and the big city, packing 70 colleges into the metropolitan area at the hub of the huge "brains industry", which is New England's greatest resource, is working on the country's future.

Apart from the transient thousands of students, Boston comprises first (though no longer foremost) the Anglo-Saxon descendants of the original settlers, the very proper "Brahmins" who favour the elegant neighbourhood of Beacon Hill in the city's north-west, down to the Charles River. They play a distinguished second fiddle now to the Irish who have spread through the town since fleeing their 1845 potato famine to become labourers, then "lace-curtain" bourgeois and finally to see first the Fitzgeralds moving into City Hall and then the Kennedys into Washington and the White House. The Italians make up an equally lively community, taking over from the Irish in the town's North End. The Black community, with a proud past in Boston as the first freed slaves, is largely centred on

a first-time visitor, who'll be taking in other parts of the U.S., can get a good feeling for the region by concentrating for a start on Boston and the surrounding Massachusetts countryside where America's Revolution began. Add a side-trip to the nearby seaside playground of Newport, Rhode Island, and you will have covered the historical, cultural and social heart of New England.

Roxbury and the South End of town.

Boston is a good town to walk in. The narrow streets of the most interesting sections make driving diabolically difficult. Bostonians claim to have found the knack and are dangerously oblivious of out-of-towners groping their way more slowly around. So park your car and start at the city's heart, the **Boston Common.** Between Tremont, Boylston and Beacon streets is the pleasant green nucleus of the 50 acres which the Massachusetts Bay Company bought from a beleaguered hermit, Reverend William Blackstone, in 1634. He was already there when the 900 Puritans arrived and sold out when he decided he couldn't take any more of their rather officious manners. As if to make his point for him, they subsequently set up on the green — apart from the usual grazing for livestock — a pillory and stocks, whipping post, sinners' cage and gallows. The first victim of the pillory was its carpenter, punished for charging too much for his labour. Today the Common is popular for baseball, touch-football and rock concerts. In the old Puritan days, it was the one public place where Bostonians were permitted to smoke tobacco.

Immediately west of the Common is the **Public Garden,** reclaimed in the 19th century from the marshes south of the Charles River. The neat little beds of tulips and pansies constituted the country's first botanical garden, and the artificial pond in the centre offers gentle rides on the whimsical, flat-bottomed swan boats.

The Visitors Information Center is on the Tremont Street side of the Common, a good place for maps and brochures and orientation for the 1½-mile **Freedom Trail** around the city's principal historical sights. The route is marked by a painted red line or by red bricks set in the pavement.

A good first stop is the tranquil-looking, white-steepled **Park Street Church,** built in 1809. But at one time this was called Brimstone Corner — the church served as a gunpowder storehouse during the war of 1812. Just as explosive were the first anti-slavery speeches delivered from its pulpit in 1829 by abolitionist William Lloyd Garrison.

In the church's **Old Granary Burial Ground** lie the victims of the Boston Massacre (see p. 20), as well as Paul Revere, Sam Adams and John Hancock. The last two signed the Declaration of Independence, but it was Hancock's name that was immortalized as synonymous with any more or less honourable signature in the phrase "put your 'John Hancock' here". Children may be

Boston's Hancock Tower

more interested in the tombstone of Mary Goose, said to be the original Mother Goose of the nursery rhymes.

King's Chapel (Tremont and School streets) was the colonies' first stone church (1754). Originally Anglican and then Unitarian, when the Church of England fell into disrepute after the Revolution, its dark granite walls and severe, columned portico make an austere exterior—it had to forgo a steeple when funds ran out. But the interior is more graceful, thanks to the canopied pulpit from an earlier church of 1719 and the red damask-lined box pews.

The **Old South Meeting House** (Washington and Milk streets), originally a Puritan church and now a museum of the Revolution, is best remembered as the assembly hall for Sam Adams' protests against the Massacre and the place where he planned the dastardly Tea Party. The British used it as a riding school during their occupation of Boston, burning the pews and pulpits for firewood, but the rest of the original woodwork is intact.

Further along Washington Street, the **Old State House** was the British Governor's Residence and it is still embellished by the lion and unicorn of the royal coat of arms (copies of the originals burnt on Independence Day 1776). It was on the Congress Street side of the building that the Massacre took place, a monument marking the spot where Crispus Attucks was shot, a black man and the first martyr of the Revolution.

Faneuil Hall (rhymes with "panel") has earned its name as the "cradle of liberty" with the speeches of two centuries of poli-

---

Indian Tea Time

On the night of December 16, 1773, Sam Adams led his Sons of Liberty in three companies of 50, all with coal dust on their faces disguised as Mohawk Indians, to board the Dartmouth, Eleanor and Beaver. *The ships were moored to unload their brew at Griffin's Wharf. Armed with hatchets for tomahawks, the Boston "Mohawks" split open the tea-chests to make sure the contents would steep properly when hurled overboard. The party was attended by a merry crowd cheering from the docks. Sam's cousin, (later president) John Adams, immediately recognized that this was not a childish act of irresponsibility, but an invaluable moment of grand historic theatre. He wrote in his diary the next day: "The Destruction of the Tea is so bold, so daring, so firm, intrepid and inflexible, and it must have so important Consequences, and so lasting, that I cannot but consider it as an Epoch in History." He wasn't wrong.*

ticians from Sam Adams to John Kennedy, not to mention Susan B. Anthony, who rocked the cradle. She spoke out here against the slavery both of Blacks and of women — she even had the gall to try to vote in national elections, 46 years before it was legal. If you like weapons, take a look at the collection of the Ancient and Honorable Artillery Company. If you like pewter, you can buy excellent handmade reproductions of old American pewter in the Heritage Shop. On the hall's dome is one of the city's most familiar landmarks, a grasshopper weathervane inspired by the one on London's Royal Exchange.

From Fan'l Hall, make your way via Union and Marshall streets under the unfortunate Fitzgerald Expressway to **North End,** now the colourful centre of the Italian community — aromatic grocery stores, fresh pasta shops and pizza parlours amid charming old houses coiffed by roof-gardens. Resume the Freedom Trail here on North Square at the wooden-frame **Paul Revere House,** the oldest house in Boston, built soon after the disastrous city fire of 1676. The Revolutionary hero moved here in 1770, five years before he set off on his historic ride. Take a look inside at the Revere family's own furnishings.

The intrepid horseman's statue can be seen north of his house on Paul Revere Mall, with the fine **Old North Church** (1723) rising behind him. It was in the church tower, designed in the style of Christopher Wren and restored after being toppled in a 1954 hurricane, that two lanterns were hung to signal to Revere that the British were marching out. The unusually tall pew-boxes were meant to keep out the winter draughts, the boxes built square to enable worshippers to sit around their communal footwarmer.

The Freedom Trail continues across Charlestown Bridge to the site of the Revolutionary War's first pitched battle at Bunker Hill, but you may feel that that's enough history for the time being, in which case, make your way back to Fan'l Hall. To the east of it is **Faneuil Hall Marketplace,** a cheerful haven tucked among the administrative buildings of Government Center and the new skyscraper office-blocks. This lively centre of boutiques, galleries, restaurants and cafés is one of the country's most successful pieces of urban restoration. Three run-down granite market buildings, which formed part of the seedy dockland back in 1825 before the land to the east was reclaimed from the sea, have been rehabilitated as light, airy halls around a pedestrian mall shaded by locust trees (the wholesale markets have moved to the suburbs). Glass-enclosed arcades open up in summer as café terraces, lit in the evening by attractive clusters of fish-bowl lamps posted among the parasol tables.

The central domed building is Quincy Market, specializing in gourmet foods. South Market offers jewellery, gift-stores and art galleries, while North Market has the fashion boutiques.

South of Fan'l Hall, at 60 State Street, you can see an excellent one-hour film, *Where's Boston*, on the city's rehabilitation since the 1960s under the direction of architect I.M. Pei, who provided a modern complement to its traditional historical image.

Part of that modern image is very much in evidence at the

Charles River; Quincy Market

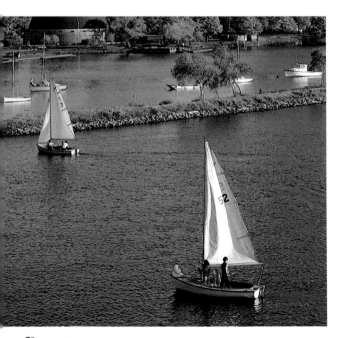

Government Center, dominated by the two towers of the John F. Kennedy Federal Building and the controversial inverted concrete pyramid of **City Hall.** The Plaza's aggressively 20th-century stance is offset by the traditional materials of red-brick paving.

Recapture the city's old serenity on **Beacon Hill,** the noble neighbourhood of Boston's best, sandwiched between Government Center and the Common. Here among the cedars and chestnuts and gas-lanterns of **Mount Vernon Street** and Louisburg Square, where, as the saying goes, "the Lowells talk only to the Cabots and the Cabots talk only to God", you can admire the restrained glories of Boston's finest residential architecture. It was here in the heady years of the 1790s that Boston-born Charles

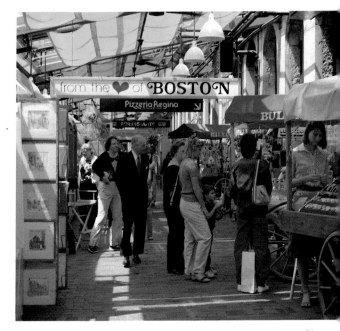

Bulfinch, one of the principal designers of the U.S. Capitol in Washington and America's first native-born professional architect, developed his Federal-style houses. Their simple red-brick façades, with a marble strip separating the storeys, plus a few classical details, are the very essence of Boston dignity. **Louisburg Square,** with its residents' fenced-off garden in the centre and the three-storey curved, bow-fronted houses, will remind many of Georgian London. Others, seeking something a touch more dashing in their houses — but still very dignified — went in for the Doric-columned porches of Greek Revival. This can be seen in its most monumental form in Bulfinch's gold-domed **State House** (1798), off Beacon Street, a building that got him his Washington commissions (it has been a little fussed up by later additions).

Back Bay, west of the Public Garden, was quite literally a bay at the rear of Boston's 19th-century city centre until landfill turned it into a residential neighbourhood with an essentially Victorian character for the city's newly rich merchants. It's now enlivened by some chic boutiques and art galleries and dominated by the Hancock and Prudential skyscrapers. Both offer excellent observation decks on their top floors, but the architecturally more satisfying of the two is

I. M. Pei's elegant **John Hancock Tower,** sheathed in reflective glass (now cured of an alarming early tendency to pop out). The slanted, rhomboid form escapes the standard rectangular block with an intriguing V-incision at either end. You get a grand view from the 60th floor (half a minute in the lift) over Cambridge and Charlestown all the way to the New Hampshire mountains in good weather.

Trinity Church, on Copley Square, is a solid, late-19th-century monument of American homage to the European Middle Ages. Its architect, Henry Hobson Richardson, makes no bones about it being a "free rendering of the French Romanesque" of the 11th century. Experts have spotted bits of Provençal Arles in the west porch and Spanish Salamanca in the central tower, but they find the whole combination unique enough to be dubbed "Richardsonian Romanesque". The interior is well worth a look for the rich polychrome décor of John La Farge — quite startling when the lights are turned on.

Museums

Museum of Fine Arts (465 Huntington Avenue) has one of the best collections in the country. American, European and Oriental works are well laid out according to departments. Don't miss I. M. Pei's West Wing.

Isabella Stewart Gardner Museum (280 The Fenway). Superb European collection in a building which recalls a Venetian *palazzo*.

Children's Museum (Museum Wharf). Among other things, children can work with intricate computers, anchor their own television newscasts, work on a factory assembly line or dress up in colonial-era clothes in "Grandma's Attic."

Museum of Transportation, housed in the same building as the Children's Museum, is a dazzling display of boats, buses and trolleys, scooters and skates, fire engines and sleighs, vintage cars, bicycles and aircraft.

Beaver II, Tea Party Ship (Congress Street Bridge on Fort Point Channel) is a full-scale replica of one of the three British ships raided by the Bostonians to protest the duties on tea.

CAMBRIDGE
(Massachusetts)

There's more to Cambridge (separated from Boston merely by the Charles River) than **Harvard,** but mostly it's Harvard and that's nothing to be ashamed of. Founded by the Massachusetts Bay Colony as America's first university in 1636, its name honours a young churchman, John Harvard, who bequeathed it £780, half his worldly wealth, and

his library of 320 books. Now it has an endowment of $2,500 million and about 100 libraries with over 10 million volumes. In 1965, Harvard merged with Radcliffe College for women (founded in 1894) and the combined institutions number over 36,000 students. They have the use of 17 university departments, nine faculties, more than 50 laboratories, two astronomical stations and nine museums. Other American universities rival Harvard in individual departments but overall the oldest has remained the country's best, both in the breadth of its undergraduate courses and in the seriousness of its dedication to research.

At the western end of Massachusetts Avenue, **Harvard Square** makes a bustling introduction to the town, with its cafés, restaurants, splendid bookshops and the "Coop" (short for "co-operative" but pronounced like a home for chickens) reputedly the country's biggest.

For orientation around the campus, start at the Information Center in the rather daunting modern block of Holyoke Center, just south of the square. The campus clusters mainly around **Harvard Yard.** Unlike much of the university architecture elsewhere in the country, Harvard's, with its earlier foundation, avoids the "Collegiate Gothic" of spired towers that too often unimaginatively recall Oxford and the other Cambridge. Harvard went red-brick, a more traditional New England style, to be seen in **Massachusetts Hall** (1720) and **Harvard Hall** (1766), along with the good old clapboard of **Wadsworth House** (1726), a residence formerly the home of college presidents. The one concession to Gothic Revival is Memorial Hall (1878), an imposing Victorian pile commemorating Harvard's fallen in the Civil War.

In front of **University Hall** (1815), a classical granite edifice by the indefatigable Charles Bulfinch, notice a statue described as "John Harvard founder 1638". A shameless falsehood. Not only was the college founded two years earlier, but John Harvard was a benefactor—not the founder—, and the fellow portrayed is an undergraduate who posed 150 years after Harvard's death.

There are some lovely 18th-century houses along Brattle Street, west of Harvard Square, known as Tory Row after their Loyalist owners. At 105 is the **Longfellow National Historical Site,** home of Henry Wadsworth Longfellow, sometimes unkindly called the best bad poet in the world. Built in 1759, it served as Washington's headquarters during the siege of Boston. Longfellow lived here from 1837 to 1882, wrote *Hiawatha* and taught modern languages at Harvard.

The most noteworthy of the campus's modern buildings is the **Carpenter Center of Visual Arts** (on Quincy Street), designed by Le Corbusier, his only American building (if you discount his collaborative effort on the United Nations Building in New York). With a characteristic touch, "Corb" moves the visitor up the outside of the building along an elevated ramp, from the studios and lecture hall to the art galleries at the top.

While the Carpenter is for students not taking an art degree, Harvard's fine arts department has its home in the **Fogg Art Museum** next door. It offers the public an impressive Oriental collection, including some fine Chinese jades and bronzes, and good representative European works, notably Italian paintings from the 14th century to the High Renaissance and the French Impressionists and Post-Impressionists.

Admirers of German art will find an astonishingly rich 20th-century collection at the **Busch-Reisinger Museum** (29 Kirkland Street).

On Divinity Avenue, the University Museum houses four distinct museums. The most prestigious is the **Peabody Museum of Archaeology and Ethnology.** This has been enriched over the years by the expeditions around the Americas and voyages of exploration to Africa and the Pacific sponsored by the university.

The **Geological and Mineralogical Museum** has a beautiful exhibition of minerals, gems and meteorites and a dramatic model of a Hawaiian volcano. At the **Zoology Museum,** look out for the world's oldest egg (225 million years old) and the 25,000-year-old Harvard Mastodon from New Jersey.

The **Botanical Museum** is also known popularly as the Glass Flower Museum because of its unique collection of 784 flowers modelled life-size in glass at the Dresden workshop of Leopold Blaschka and his son Rudolf over a period of 60 years. Botanists vouch for the models' scientific accuracy and the rest of us can just gasp at their beauty.

If you return to Boston via Harvard Bridge, stop off at **M.I.T.** With its research in the natural and social sciences, in engineering, architecture and urban planning, the Massachusetts Institute of Technology has created for itself the most prestigious academic initials in the world. Visitors enjoy the **Hart Nautical Museum,** displaying with models, prints and photos a thousand years of ship design. Two architectural oddities are the strangely warped-roofed **Kresge Auditorium** and moated cylindrical brick **M.I.T. Chapel** with its aluminium bell tower, both by Finnish designer Eero Saarinen.

OTHER NEW ENGLAND HIGHLIGHTS

Lexington *(Massachusetts)*
(From Boston, take Interstate 93 to the Woburn exit west.)
Almost engulfed by the ever-expanding web of metropolitan Boston, Lexington still has the classical elements of the small New England country town. There's an immaculate **village**

Revere for the Record
Thanks to Longfellow's exciting but frequently inaccurate poem, Paul Revere got all the glory for the ride to alert the fighting men of Lexington and Concord, but in fact he was, luckily, not alone. The British caught up with him soon after he reached Lexington and his co-riders William Dawes and Sam Prescott had to carry the news on to Concord without him. All the same, Revere's versatility and devotion to the American cause would have won him a prominent place in history. He rode with important Massachusetts legislative resolutions to the First Continental Congress in Philadelphia. As an accomplished engraver, he designed and printed the national currency during the war. An equally talented silversmith, he made the noble Liberty Bowl on show at Boston's Museum of Fine Arts. And, oh yes, he was also one of the "Mohawks" at the Boston Tea Party.

green, with on one side a tavern and on the other a church.

This was the town into which Paul Revere rode on the evening of April 18, 1775, to warn colonial leaders John Hancock and Sam Adams that the British were coming. Their target: American arms and ammunition in nearby Concord. The tavern is Buckman Tavern, rallying point for 77 Minutemen, rustic militia so-called because they had to be armed and ready at a minute's notice. At one end of the village green is a **statue** of the Minutemen's leader, Captain Parker. At the other end, inscribed on a boulder of the **Revolutionary Monument** are the Captain's heroic words: "Stand your ground; don't fire unless fired upon; but if they mean to have a war, let it begin here".

It did, at 5 a.m. on April 19, when the first of 700 British soldiers arrived. The British ordered the militia to disperse, but a shot rang out and the British opened fire. In the skirmish eight Minutemen died, and the wounded were taken to **Buckman Tavern,** which you can see today restored to its 18th-century state, ballroom, barroom and all. For those who spare a thought for the poor British — they did suffer 272 casualties before they got back to Boston from this fateful sortie — there are also guided tours of the 17th-century **Munroe Tavern,** which doubled as the British field hospital and headquarters.

Concord *(Massachusetts)*

Concord has successfully resisted the encroachments of the metropolis and would be worth a visit even without the Revolutionary associations. Its calm and serenity — still relatively unspoiled — made it a perfect haven for great thinkers like Ralph Waldo Emerson and Henry David Thoreau and for novelists Nathaniel

Hawthorne and Louisa May Alcott.

But let's go back first to the excitement of the Revolution. From a hill above the Concord River north of town, about 100 Minutemen watched the British searching for the military supplies. Seeing fires starting in town and fearing the hidden ammunition might blow the whole place up, the militia descended to the river and met up with the British on **Old North Bridge.** A replica of the bridge has been built west of Monument Street, with a Visitor Center organizing guided tours. The **Minuteman statue** of Daniel Chester French marks the spot, as Emerson wrote in his *Concord Hymn:* "Here once the embattled farmers stood / and fired the shot

Montpelier, Vermont

77

heard round the world." The farmers' stand was good enough to drive the British off.

But Concord, named after a peace treaty between early settlers and the Indians, regained its more natural, unbellicose role in the 19th century. In the **Ralph Waldo Emerson House** (28 Cambridge Turnpike), you'll find memorabilia of the philosopher-poet who lived in Concord, on and off, from his birth in 1803 to 1882. The meadows and woods around his house reinforced the mystical love of nature he developed in his transcendental philosophy.

Across Cambridge Turnpike at the **Museum of the Concord Antiquarian Society,** you can enjoy the genteel trappings of the good old Concord life — the Chippendale and Queen Anne furniture and the solid, more austere colonial style. The museum has a replica of Emerson's study and some of Henry David Thoreau's belongings from his **Walden Pond** cabin. (The 64-acre pond is still there, 1½ miles south of town off Walden Street.)

At **Orchard House** (399 Lexington Road), you'll see where Louisa May Alcott wrote her eternal best-seller, *Little Women* (1868), the story of her own New England childhood. Her royalties enabled her penniless philosopher-father, Bronson Alcott, Concord's school superintendent, to pursue his own esoteric brand of transcendentalism in his School of Philosophy, still operating today as a study centre on a hillside above the house.

At Sleepy Hollow Cemetery on "Author's Ridge" you can see the graves of Emerson, the Alcotts, and Nathaniel Hawthorne, who made his home for a time at the Old Manse (on Monument Street near the Old North Bridge).

Salem *(Massachusetts)*
(North on Route 1 and 1A from Boston)

Named in hope after the Hebrew word "Shalom" meaning peace, the town today revels both in the glory of its maritime past and the infamy of its witchcraft trials.

Down at **Derby Wharf,** you can stroll along the old waterfront, now consecrated as the Salem Maritime National Historic Site. For the story of the town's great seafaring days, visit the **Seaport Museum** on Pickering Wharf, a pleasant commercial center where you can sit outdoors and watch the boats in the harbour.

During the Revolutionary War, with Boston and New York both in British hands, Salem was the Americans' principal naval supplier. Salem ship-owners made a fortune out of the China trade, and **Custom House,** on Derby Street, today a museum, was a focus for the merchants' activities. Conveniently next door, Derby House (1761) was the home of Elias Hasket Derby, one of America's first millionaires.

Peabody Museum (East India Square) houses the riches and spoils (not all was obtained legitimately) of those voyages on the Eastern seas—artefacts from India, Burma, Indonesia, China, Japan and Korea.

Nathaniel Hawthorne, 19th-century novelist, was born in Salem. His famous **House of the Seven Gables** has been restored at 54 Turner Street, on the waterfront.

For the gory story of Salem's 1692 witch-hunt, follow the signs of old hags on broomsticks to the **Witch Museum** on Washington Square. Witch House in Essex Street was the home of hanging judge Jonathan Corwin, where he held preliminary examinations of suspected witches.

But Essex Street's serener glory is the splendid architecture of its houses under the protection of the **Essex Institute,** itself a first-rate museum of the town's decorative arts and historical furniture. At number 128, the **Gardner-Pingree House** (1805) by Salem architect Samuel McIntire is an outstanding example of the Federal style —both for the simple elegance of the rose-brick façade topped by a white wood balustrade and for the superb woodwork of the interior. Another grand residence by McIntire is the **Peirce-Nichols House** (1782) at 80 Federal Street.

Cape Cod *(Massachusetts)*
(Interstate 93 out of Boston, Route 3 to the Cape)

The beaches, sand dunes and marshlands of Cape Cod's east coast constitute a pleasure that is both invigorating and relaxing. It was a surprise to no one when President Kennedy in 1961 declared the coast a protected area—the **Cape Cod National Seashore.** It had, after all, been his family's holiday home for years.

He did the rest of us a favour, too, because the Rangers of the National Park Service have done a superb job of protecting the fauna, flora and fragile geological formations for the permanent benefit of cyclists, hikers and bathers. The 27,000 acres of parkland include more than 50 miles of beach between Chatham and Provincetown.

Start at the **Nauset Area's** Salt Pond Visitor Center, where Rangers will brief you on the area's history, the Indians, the local ecology and provide brochures about the various trails to the seashore and the regulations to observe for its continued protection. A bicycle trail takes you east to Coast Guard Beach or you can walk the Nauset Marsh Trail around the ponds and through a red maple swamp.

In the Marconi Area you can visit the few relics of the transatlantic radio station set up here in 1901 by the Italian inventor,

Guglielmo Marconi. Erosion of the shore has toppled most of the station into the ocean and your walk along the Atlantic White Cedar Swamp Trail will show you how brushwood and beach grass help resist the continued onslaught of the sea. The varied flora include midget scrub oaks and pitch pines, as well as the swampland cedars.

One of the best panoramic views of the dunes is from a hillock north-west of Pilgrim Lake in the **Pilgrim Heights** area. The Pilgrim Spring Trail takes you to a spot where in 1620 the good people of the *Mayflower* drank their first American fresh water, according to local legend.

At the north-west tip of the Cape, you can tour the dunes in

Rocky coastline in Maine

four-wheel-drive vehicles around **Race Point** and **Herring Cove,** two great swimming beaches. (A special permit may be obtained from the Rangers at the Province Lands Visitor Center.) The driving is not at all easy and you may prefer one of the guided tours organized from nearby Provincetown. The drivers are very knowledgeable and speak with great feeling for the natural environment, its erosion and enrichment. The best time to go, if you can't make it at dawn, is just before sunset when the play of light on the dunes and swaying beach grasses and brushwood is a pure joy.

The harbour of **Provincetown** or P-town was the *Mayflower* Pilgrim's first port of call after a voyage of extreme hardship, but soon they decided to continue on to Plymouth. P-town was subsequently settled by a more impudent breed—whalers, smugglers and bohemian artists—injecting that whiff of brimstone into the sober New England puritanism. Modelled like an Italian bell tower, the **Pilgrim Memorial Monument** pays due tribute to the *Mayflower* people and the view of Cape Cod from its observation deck is well worth the climb. The nearby **Provincetown Museum** admirably celebrates the town's seafaring past. Note the fine examples of scrimshaw carving.

MacMillan's Wharf is the centre of the fishing fleet's activities and the spot to hire a boat, take a harbour cruise or set off on a whale-watching expedition. (In season, boats leave daily in search of humpback and sperm whales. Reservations are strongly advised.)

Artists congregate around the Provincetown Art Association (corner of Bangs and Commercial streets), and the P-town Theater Company continues the town's traditions of avant-garde theatre. Eugene O'Neill got his start here and, if you don't spot his ghost or that of Tennessee Williams and other literary habitués of the past, you may at least see Norman Mailer swinging down the street with another Great American Novel on his mind.

At the southernmost tip of Cape Cod, Woods Hole ferries take you across to two island resorts very popular with discerning New Englanders and New Yorkers—Martha's Vineyard (45-minute crossing) and Nantucket (3 hours). There are no wild grapes growing on **Martha's Vineyard** any more, but the local artists and writers drink plenty of wine. You can get around the island by shuttle-bus or rent a bicycle or moped if you don't have a car. The beaches are excellent, Katama on the south shore being especially prized by surfers. There's a lovely view to be had west of Katama on the **Gay Head**

Cliffs, which consist of layers of coloured clay—red, white, orange, grey, blue and ochre. The local Indians turn it into pottery. Equally brightly coloured are the charming gingerbread cottages of **Oak Bluffs,** while the grander houses of **Edgartown** are of sparkling white clapboard.

Nantucket Island is just right for the family. Washed by the warm waters of the Gulf Stream, the beaches on the north side of the island—Jetties and Children's—offer easy swimming. Hardier swimmers go to Cisco and Surfside for the big breakers of the south shore. Nantucket town, beautifully preserved on the cobbled **Main Street,** has a proud whaling history (ending abruptly in the second half of the 19th century when Pennsylvania oil replaced whale blubber). The **Whaling Museum** (Broad Street) shows all the sailor's paraphernalia of the whaling industry. If you're taken by the impressive exhibition of scrimshaw, you may want to buy some of your own in the waterfront shops on **Straight Wharf,** at the end of Main Street, a delightful place to hang around the yachts.

Plymouth *(Massachusetts)*

On your way from Boston to Cape Cod or on your way back stop off on Route 3 to pay homage to the place where New England got its start. A boulder on the edge of the harbour is said to be the legendary **Plymouth Rock** onto which the first *Mayflower* Pilgrim stepped in 1620. Today, the sacred boulder is protected by monumental granite pillars. Few countries in the Western world celebrate the historic sites of their beginnings with more reverence. North of the Rock, at State Pier, is *Mayflower II*, an approximate replica which sailed from England in 1957. Just south of the town is **Plimoth Plantation,** reproducing the Pilgrims' first village of 1627—thatch-roofed, clapboard cottages with 16th- and 17th-century English furniture, barns and stables. Nearby is a 17th-century Wampanoag Indian Summer Encampment.

The Berkshires

(Massachusetts)
(Interstate 90 from Boston or Interstate 87 from New York)
These rolling foothills of the Taconic and Hoosac mountains offer wonderful opportunities in the summer to combine music, dance and theatre with hiking and fishing in the many lakes and streams of the region. The Berkshires are a prime place for watching the autumn foliage and there's skiing in winter. Dotted among the hills are the grand 19th-century estates that provided summer homes for wealthy New Yorkers and Bostonians and are now schools, resort-hotels and rest-homes.

Since 1934, the **Tanglewood** estate (just outside Lenox) has been the home of the summer Berkshire Music Festival, hosted now by the Boston Symphony Orchestra. Its Music Shed, designed by Finnish architect Eero Saarinen, seats 6,000. One of the nicest ways to enjoy the concerts in good weather is to come for a picnic a couple of hours early and listen to the music (much more cheaply) from the lawn. Saturday morning rehearsals are cheaper still. The Chamber Music Hall presents more intimate concerts.

The Berkshire Theater Festival is at the Playhouse in **Stockbridge** (south of Tanglewood on Route 7). The town itself is well worth a visit. It was established in 1734 with only four white families who had the explicit goal of converting the local Mohican Indians. Reverend John Sergeant's **Mission House** (1739), Route 102, austere and even gloomy by modern standards but considered plush in its day, is now a museum of that pious era.

The **Old Corner House,** quite properly on Main Street, was the home of painter Norman Rockwell, acute observer of American Main Street life for the magazine covers of the *Saturday Evening Post.* In the collection exhibited at Stockbridge, you can trace his evolution from the details of small-town Americana in the Depression years to the con-

temporary problems of racial integration and urban violence, along with portraits of his fellow Massachusetts men, the Kennedy brothers.

Further south, around Great Barrington, is some first-class fishing and hiking country along the Housatonic Valley.

Newport *(Rhode Island)*
(From Boston, Interstate 93 and Route 24 south; from Cape Cod, Route 6 and Interstate 195)
This playground of the legendary Astors and Vanderbilts, who accumulated fabulous fortunes from railroads and steamships in the 19th century, has remained a pleasant resort for those who like sailing, music—and gawking at the sumptuous relics of that playground. The summer music festival and yacht races have become world famous. It really is worthwhile to take time off for the 3-mile **Cliff Walk** south from Newport Beach to visit the incredible mansions inspired by—and plundered from—the châteaux and *palazzi* of Europe, called "cottages" by their owners.

Imagine at the turn of the century, dinners at which guests share caviar and champagne with their pet poodles before going off to Mrs. Astor's ballroom for the "400" (only room for 400 guests, but then, there *were* only 400 one could invite). Then look at the magnificent **Breakers,** Cornelius

83

Vanderbilt II's 70-room cottage, designed by Richard Morris Hunt. To call this crypto-Renaissance palace "an incredible display of tasteless vulgarity"—as did a member of the Society of Architectural Historians—is to miss the point. The marble, bronze, alabaster and gilt of the interior, especially the fantastic Grand Salon and two-storey dining room, are the ornaments of fantasy, not the realities of anything so mundane as good taste. If you're not convinced, go further down the coast to William Vanderbilt's **Marble House,** with almost as much gold as marble in it. Conscientious art-historians argue whether Hunt's model is the White House in Washington or the Petit Trianon in Versailles.

One of Newport's historically most important buildings is the beautifully preserved **Touro Synagogue,** east of Washington Square. Built in 1763, it was America's first synagogue, serving the Sephardic Jews from Lisbon and Amsterdam. Its austere beige façade contrasts with a richly handsome interior. The women's gallery is supported by 12 columns, Ionic below and Corinthian above, symbolizing the 12 tribes of Israel.

You can pick up a wealth of free material or rent a lively and informative 90-minute tape at the Chamber of Commerce Information Center.

MID-ATLANTIC REGION

Seven years after independence was declared in Philadelphia, the northern and southern states finally agreed on a site for the nation's permanent capital—right between the two regions, on land ceded by Maryland and Virginia. Your visit to Washington and a swing through the surrounding states will give you an opportunity to compare the businesslike North with the more leisurely South. Is Philadelphia as earnest as its reputation or Virginia as stately as its old plantation-days image? And Washington? In a moment of irritation, President John F. Kennedy once exclaimed that the capital had all the charm of a northern city and the efficiency of a southern town.

WASHINGTON D.C.

You couldn't mistake this city for anything but the capital of a great republic. Everything about it smacks of government. Monuments and ministries abound. But the architecture leans more to the temples of ancient Greece and Rome than the cathedrals of the European monarchies, and the government buildings are set in a green and pleasant landscape. The 69 square miles of the city (an area conterminous with the District of Columbia) include 33 parks, relics of the old Virginia and Maryland estates and plantations.

Over 3 million people live in Greater Metropolitan Washington and the suburbs in Virginia and Maryland, but the city itself numbers just 638,000 residents, more than half of them black, regularly electing a black mayor. The government centre of civil servants, congressmen, senators, diplomats and journalists leads a life largely separate from the concerns of the metropolis, which is beset like any other large American town with slums and crime. And so for foreign visitors, too, this underbelly remains mostly out of sight, as they stick to the downtown federal district and its residential neighbourhoods to the north-west.

When you see the attractive houses and diplomatic missions along and around Massachusetts Avenue and the university district of Georgetown, you may find it hard to believe that for a long time Washington was just a muddy mess, much of it marshland on the banks of the Potomac River. To lay out the new capital, George Washington called on the Paris-born engineer, Pierre Charles L'Enfant, the man who had remodelled Federal Hall in New York for the presidential inauguration. But the valiant Frenchman, a major with the U.S. Army during the Revolutionary War, produced a radial plan inspired by Rome and Versailles for the central federal district that proved too ambitious for the young Republic's treasury. After a quarrel with the bureaucracy, who called him "L'Enfant terrible", he was fired and died in misery.

Apart from the White House —only half-finished when John Adams moved in in 1800—the place looked much like a ramshackle frontier town for most of the 19th century, in part because it was sacked and burned by the British in 1814. The Capitol, for instance, took 70 years to complete and the streets weren't paved or properly lit till after the Civil War. Only in the 20th century did Washington finally assume the shape of L'Enfant's grand conception—perhaps it took that long to find the money —and the architect was reburied, with honours, at Arlington House.

Considering all there is to be seen, the area covering Washington's sights is mercifully compact. It's practically all in a rectangle extending from Union Station and the Library of Congress, on the east, to Watergate and the Lincoln Memorial near the Potomac River, on the west. Georgetown is just north-west of this rectangle and Arlington National Cemetery on the west bank of the Potomac. (Nearly all the monuments and museums are free of charge.)

Getting Around. When you no longer feel like walking—Washington can be very hot and sticky in high summer—there's a very agreeable system of open-sided Tourmobile shuttle trolleys. They follow a route past the main monuments, museums and government buildings, stopping at convenient points around the Capitol, the Mall and the White House. Guides provide cheerful commentaries as you ride. The great advantage is that you can get on and off as often as you like with one all-day ticket (bought on the trolley when you first board). The Tourmobile also makes excursions to Arlington and Mount Vernon (for information, call 554-7950).

Washington's public transport includes an efficient municipal bus and a growing underground Metrorail network. Taxis are plentiful, charging—not exorbitantly—by the zones into which they've divided the town (map in the cab) rather than by meter. Zone One covers most of the main sights. Keep your car for out-of-town excursions, as legal parking downtown is expensive and illegal parking disastrous because the police do not hesitate to tow vehicles away to one of 20 compounds without letting you know, even by telephone, to which one.

The White House
(1600 Pennsylvania Avenue, N.W.)
Unlike practically any other head of state, the American President lets you visit his home—often while he's working upstairs. Almost every day (Tuesday through Saturday) 6,000 people—9,000 in July and August—take him up on his hospitality. (During peak periods, you collect a free ticket from a booth at the south end of the Ellipse common, on Constitution Avenue. Otherwise just queue up at the East Gate on Executive Avenue, 10 a.m.-noon, later in summer.) Read this while you wait, as there is no guide inside.

Whatever detractors say, the place is magic. The house really is incredibly white, Virginia sandstone, not marble, repainted the moment the gleam even threatens to fade. And the stately interior positively glows with the pride of American history.

It was originally designed in 1792 by Irish-born architect James Hoban in the English Palladian style popular with the landed gentry. In the competition for a $500 gold medal, Hoban beat an anonymous entry submitted by Thomas Jefferson. Happy enough to reside there himself in 1801, Jefferson declared it "big enough for two emperors, one Pope and the grand Lama" and then promptly added a terrace

The Capitol building

86

pavilion on either side while Benjamin Latrobe was putting on the porticos. He was setting the pattern for nearly all his successors of remodelling or redecorating their temporary home — without the benefit of his architectural training.

The usual tourists' entrance is through the East Wing Lobby, decorated with portraits of past presidents and their first ladies. The cheerful **Garden Room** has the yellow-lacquered bamboo-style furniture of the early 19th-century English Regency period, when people liked things to look a little Chinese. Through the windows you can see the Jacqueline Kennedy Garden. Displayed in the East Foyer are gifts from foreign heads of state — since Watergate very carefully inventoried.

Toasting the White House
It wasn't always the president who redid the White House. In 1814, the dastardly British Admiral, George Cockburn, led an assault on Washington and the White House in retaliation for American pillage in Canada (see p. 24). While President James Madison had gone off to join the militia, wife Dolley stayed behind to take care of the valuables, getting out just before the British arrived and set fire to the place. A providential thunderstorm put out the fire but not before the White House turned decidedly black.

Upstairs on the first floor, the **East Room,** familiar for presidential press conferences, is used for concerts, balls and receptions —weddings for the president's children, funeral services for presidents who die in office, notably Lincoln, Franklin Roosevelt and Kennedy. The White House's first First Lady, Abigail Adams, used it as a drying room for her laundry. The famous 1796 Gilbert Stuart portrait of George Washington was saved from the 1814 fire by good old Dolley Madison.

First ladies often hold tea parties in the elegantly subdued **Green Room** under a superb 1790 cut-glass chandelier offered by the English to President Herbert Hoover. Jefferson liked to take his dinner here, showing off to baffled Americans the latest gourmet ideas he'd imported from Europe, such as macaroni, waffles and ice-cream.

The oval **Blue Room** (directly below the President's famous Oval Office, which one doesn't visit without a personal invitation) is decorated in grand French Empire style appropriate to the state dinners often held here. Outside the windows is "Truman's Balcony" where the man from Missouri used to take the air.

The **Red Room** with its red satin walls has some impressive gilded and marble tables. Its opulence contrasts with the restrained décor of the **State Dining Room** at the western end of this first floor (underneath the presidential living quarters). Dominated by a portrait of Abraham Lincoln, it's done in fine 18th-century English style, walnut Queen Anne chairs against oak panelling with Corinthian pilasters.

The Mall and Potomac Park

The Mall—an expanse of greenery and water from the Capitol to the Lincoln Memorial, crossing the axis between the White House and the Tidal Basin at the Washington Monument—is undoubtedly one of the world's great urban vistas. The place is alive with people strolling around, relaxing on the grass, flying kites and spinning Frisbies, surrounded by monuments and museums. It's certainly a posthumous triumph for planner Pierre Charles L'Enfant, whose dream it had been to achieve this interaction of town and nature.

If the Statue of Liberty represents America to the world, then the **Washington Monument** symbolizes the nation for Americans themselves. This 555-foot white marble obelisk seems to state, with the noble simplicity of George Washington himself, the people's loftiest aspirations. Construction of the monument began in 1848 but dragged on for 36 years because of lack of funds and the interruption of the Civil War. Inside, an elevator will take you

to the top for a great **view** of the Virginia and Maryland countryside. Take a map along to identify the landmarks.

West of the obelisk, wander along the tree-lined, 2,000-foot-long reflecting pool to the **Lincoln Memorial** (1922). This Greek-temple-like structure, a white rectangular box surrounded by 36 Doric columns, houses the 19-foot, seated statue of a pensive Abraham Lincoln by Daniel Chester French. If you care to make the vigil, there is a wonderful effect to be seen at daybreak when the majestic sculpture is first lit by the rising sun it faces, even more dramatic than its night-time illumination. On the left of the entrance is a plaque with Lincoln's speech after the Civil War Battle of Gettysburg, when he paid tribute to those who had died for a "nation conceived in liberty and dedicated to the proposition that all men are created equal".

You'll also want to pause for a while at the Vietnam Veterans Memorial, nearby. This simple black monument to the Vietnam war dead carries the names of 58,000 soldiers killed or missing in action.

From here you can make a detour across Potomac Park and around the Tidal Basin to the domed **Jefferson Memorial** (1943), a little unimaginatively inspired by the Pantheon in Rome. As you look at the bronze statue

Watch 'em Work

It's very easy to see American government at work. When the Senate or House of Representatives is in session, a flag flies over their respective wings. In the mornings, you can visit Congressional committee public hearings. This is where the real legislative work is done. (Advance details are published every day in the Washington Post's "In Congress" column.) You may be more interested in a floor debate, held after noon. Foreign visitors need only show their passports to get a pass to the Senate or House Visitors' Gallery, either from the Sergeant at Arms of the Senate or from the Doorkeeper of the House on the gallery floor. American citizens can get passes from their elected representatives. Senate debates tend to be more dignified, House debates more lively, because the latter's representatives are up for re-election every two years and must constantly impress visiting constituents. You'll rarely see all 100 Senators or more than half the 435 Representatives. Remember, Democrats sit to the Speaker's right, Republicans to his left, an arrangement that has no ideological significance.

Interior of the Library of Congress

of this philosopher, architect and most elegant of statesmen, think of the words of President Kennedy at a dinner for Nobel Prize winners: "I think this is the most extraordinary collection of talent, of human knowledge, that has ever been gathered together at the White House—with the possible exception of when Thomas Jefferson dined alone".

The Mall takes you past one of the world's most impressive concentrations of museums and galleries (see pp. 97-98). At the end, south of the characteristically casual statue of Civil War hero Ulysses S. Grant, stop off at the **Botanic Garden.** It's a joy to relax in spring among the azaleas. Year-round, orchid-lovers marvel at the 500 varieties.

Capitol Hill

The most powerful government in the Western world deserves a setting like the Capitol. This massive edifice imposes its will under a huge white dome that joins the Senate in the north wing to the House of Representatives in the south. The place exudes power.

William Thornton's original design in 1793 was a low-domed affair, but then, so was the United States. When Benjamin Latrobe expanded the design after the British burning of 1814, the homespun Congressmen complimented him only on the corncobs and tobacco leaves with which he whimsically decorated the Corinthian columns of their chamber. Charles Bulfinch came from Boston to put on a bigger and better dome, but by 1850 Congress, sensing America was going places, wanted it even bigger. So Thomas Walter, with nothing less than St. Peter's in Rome for his model, hoisted an iron monster up on a grandiose columned "drum" and that, with Thomas Crawford's statue of Freedom topping it off in 1863, is the way it stands today.

You enter the Capitol from the east side, starting at the **Rotunda** (there are 45-minute guided tours). The vast ceiling is decorated by a somewhat overblown fresco painted by Constantino Brumidi in 1865, *The Apotheosis of George Washington*, showing him glorified by the deities of Liberty, Victory and Fame and 13 ladies representing the 13 original states. Below is a 300-foot frieze devoted to American historical events from Columbus via Cornwallis's surrender at Yorktown to the flight of the Wright brothers' *Kitty Hawk* aircraft in 1903.

In **Statuary Hall** and the corridors leading off the Rotunda, you'll see what is widely regarded as one of the most delightfully horrendous sculpture collections in America. It's the result of an act of cultural democracy by which each of the 50 states was invited to exhibit two (now limited to one) of its most famous citizens, portrayed by the state's own sculptors.

Outside, the Capitol's grounds cover 131 acres of charming parkland designed by the 19th-century landscape architect, Frederick Law Olmsted, well known for his parks from Boston and New York via Chicago to California.

One of the great institutions of Capitol Hill is the **Library of Congress** (1st Street and Independence Avenue), packed with literally millions of books, maps, manuscripts, periodicals and photographs, recordings and rare instruments. For the visitor, the permanent exhibition of documents includes the 1455 Gutenberg Bible, one of only three in the world to have survived in perfect condition. See also the poignant Civil War photographs of Matthew Brady, first of the great American photo-journalists, in the Prints and Photographs section.

Behind the Library of Congress, the **Folger Library** (201 E. Capitol Street) offers in its Tudor interior the largest collection of Shakespeareana outside Britain, including a nicely reproduced Elizabethan theatre. Next door, the awe-inspiring **Supreme Court,** built in 1935, is the last of Washington's government buildings in the Graeco-Roman style (law enthusiasts can attend hearings from October to June).

North and South of the Mall

The scene of Abraham Lincoln's assassination, **Ford's Theater** (511 10th Street, between E and F streets) has been preserved as a National Monument, meticulously restored to how it looked on the night of April 14, 1865. Since 1968, it has been operating again as a theatre, complete with presidential box. The basement is now a museum of Lincoln's life. It preserves the clothes he wore to the play, the Derringer pistol that killed him, and the diary of assassin John Wilkes Booth, Shakespearean actor and embittered supporter of the lost Southern cause. Across the street, at number 516, is **Petersen House,** where the dying president was taken — the streets of Washington being too badly paved for a safe trip back to the White House. You'll see the bleak little bedroom where the 6-foot 4-inch Lincoln had to be laid diagonally across the bed.

Officially but not popularly named the J. Edgar Hoover Building (after the FBI's posthumously suspect director), the **Federal Bureau of Investigation** offers the most hair-raising tour in Washington (entrance E Street between 9th and 10th; reservations 324-3447). An introductory film explains the workings of the Bureau and documents its historic cases from the gang-busting days of the 1930s to the investigations of civil rights activities in the '60s and the threats to "national security" of the present day. Then you'll see the gangsters' guns and Hoover's Ten Most Wanted Men. The laboratory displays the FBI's latest gadgetry for uncovering criminals. For the tour's climax, you watch an agent shooting his .38 calibre revolver and a submachine-gun into a cardboard man-sized target—offered as a souvenir to perhaps your lucky kid.

More crime at the **National Archives** (Constitution Avenue between 7th and 9th streets) where you can listen to President Nixon and his associates plotting and cursing on the Watergate tapes (advance reservations necessary). More enlightening are the original documents of the Declaration of Independence, the Federal Constitution and the magnificent Bill of Rights, all of course handwritten on parchment. Some have faded badly but are now surrounded by light-filtering glass, with helium protection against decay.

South of the Mall, at 14th and C streets, is the fascinating **Bureau of Engraving and Printing,** where you can see the printing of U.S. paper money and postage stamps, anything from a one-cent stamp to a $500 million Treasury Note—no photographing allowed, no free samples. Follow the block-long gallery-tour of the gentle art of greenback-growing from blank white paper sheets through inking and cutting to the delicious stacking of nice crisp dollar bills at the other end. A one-dollar bill takes 15 days to produce and usually disintegrates after 18 months of normal use.

Arlington

Running north behind the Lincoln Parkway between the Rock Creek Parkway and the river is a delightful half-mile walk along the green river-bank. On weekends you can see polo, field hockey, even jousting on horseback, while less hectic types paddle by in canoes. On your way, you'll pass the **Kennedy Center for the Performing Arts,** less admired for its rather clumsy architecture than for its cultural activities in a capital that previously neglected the performing arts. The Center houses two theatres, an opera house, a concert hall and the American Film Institute's excellent "cinémathèque". A little further north is the appropriately convoluted mass of the notorious Watergate apartments where the 1972 dirty tricks were perpetrated, resulting in the downfall of Richard Nixon.

Beautifully situated on a hillside on the opposite bank of the Potomac is **Arlington House** (also known as the Custis-Lee Mansion). This very sober Greek Revival mansion fronted by eight Doric columns was built by George Washington's adopted grandson, George Washington P. Custis, in 1812. It later became the home of General Robert E. Lee until he left to lead the Confederate armies in 1861. Immediately in front of the house is the grave of architect Pierre Charles L'Enfant, quite properly commanding the best imaginable view across the river of the capital he had so lovingly planned. A granite slab is engraved with his original plan. It's a good vantage point from which to compare the result.

During the Civil War, Lee's house was confiscated by Union troops and part of its surrounding plantation used as a burial ground for the war dead. Out of this grew **Arlington National Cemetery,** where until recent years any American soldier who had seen active duty had the right to be buried. Pride of place goes to the **Tomb of the Unknowns** (soldiers of the two world wars and the Korean War), guarded by a solitary infantryman ceremoniously changed every half hour in summer, every hour in winter. In its own small park, the **John F. Kennedy Grave** is a square of simple paving set around an eternal flame. His brother Robert is buried nearby.

The Marine Corps War Memorial, better known as the **Iwo Jima Statue,** is outside the north entrance to the cemetery. The huge bronze group shows five marines and a sailor hoisting the American flag (a real one raised daily by the Washington-based marines) on Mount Suribachi during the battle for the Japanese Pacific island base of Iwo Jima on February 23, 1945. It took three more weeks to capture the island, with the loss of over 5,000 men — Japanese losses were four times higher.

Georgetown

Immediately north-west of the downtown federal district, Georgetown is the home of Washington's elite in government, the diplomatic corps, university establishment and better-paid journalists. It's also the liveliest part of town, with bright, pleasant shops, art galleries, cafés and restaurants, centred on M Street and Wisconsin Avenue. It's the only part of Washington with a cheerful street life after dark — the perfect antidote to any overdose of museums and officialdom.

Right from the beginning, Georgetown was the smart end of town. It was laid out in 1751 and was already established as a major tobacco market when Washington was still in the planning. Georgetown exported tobacco along the Potomac and imported luxury goods such as silks, wines, tinware, tea and powder for the

wigs of its high-stepping gentry. A couple of houses survive from that golden era but most of its better residential architecture is elegant Georgian and Federal-style from the first half of the 19th century, with a little Victorian "heavy pastry" from after the Civil War. Its narrow, tree-shaded streets provide a welcome change from the broad avenues of governmental Washington.

The oldest house in town is the **Old Stone House** (3051 M Street), built in rough stone in 1766 with an entrance up on the first floor and bedrooms gabled in the roof. Notable among the Georgian houses is **Dumbarton House** (2715 Q Street), remodelled by Benjamin Latrobe in 1805. It's now headquarters for the venerable National Society of Colonial Dames of America and houses some fine furniture, silver and china from the late 18th century. **Dumbarton Oaks** (3101 R Street), an imposing mansion built in 1801, gained its place in history as the site of a 1944 conference at which the U.S., Britain, the Soviet Union and China drew up the blueprint for the United Nations. The 16 acres of grounds are a delightful mixture of formal terraces and reflecting pools with more informal English-style landscaping on a lower level. The gardens include (at 1702 32nd Street entrance) the elegant, mushroom-domed Museum of

Pre-Columbian Art designed by Philip Johnson.

A charming surprise at the southern edge of Georgetown is the remnant of the **Chesapeake & Ohio Canal,** a joy for loafers, hikers, cyclists, canoeists and fishermen — and in winter, as in a Brueghel painting, skaters. Canal Square (1054 31st Street) is an old canalside warehouse converted into an attractive shopping centre.

Museums

National Gallery of Art (Constitution Avenue between 4th and 6th streets). The West Building, a classical, columned temple of art, is devoted to European and American painting and sculpture from the Middle Ages to the present day. Its great strength is in Italian art, but the French, Dutch, German, Flemish, Spanish, British and American schools are splendidly represented

Calder mobile, National Gallery of Art

New York. The museums have a combined inventory of 75 million artistic and scientific items, only one per cent of which is ever on display. To find your way around these vast riches, go first to the **Smithsonian Institution Building** (Jefferson Drive at 10th Street).

National Air and Space Museum (Jefferson Drive and 6th Street). The whole adventure of flying, whether it be across a meadow in North Carolina with the Wright brothers in 1903 or just 66 years later from Cape Canaveral to the moon, is packed into 23 galleries.

National Museum of Natural History (10th Street and Constitution Avenue). Everything from an 80-foot-long *diplodocus* to the creepy, crawly Insect Zoo. Building also houses the **Museum of Man,** with a fine display of Eskimo and American Indian artefacts.

National Museum of American History (Madison Drive, 12th to 14th streets). Americana are presented here with a delightful mixture of dignity and humour.

Corcoran Gallery (17th Street and New York Avenue). An outstanding array of American Art, plus European Masters. Every two years there's a fine all-American roundup.

Hirshhorn Museum (Independence Avenue between 7th and

as well. I.M. Pei's design of the East Building is a breathtaking combination of geometric forms —soaring triangles segmented into piercingly acute angles. The effect is even more exhilarating inside, where the museum's superb collection of contemporary art is on display.

The Smithsonian. Not one museum but a huge umbrella institution grouping 13 museums —12 in Washington and one in

9th streets). Distinguished collection of modern art, highlighted by the sculpture garden featuring Rodin's *Burghers of Calais* and important pieces by Moore, Picasso and David Smith. The painting collection does justice to Cubism, Social Realism, Op, Pop and Minimal.

The Phillips Collection (1600 21st Street). Duncan Phillips' lovely home has been turned into a showcase for a small but select collection of mostly modern European and American paintings.

Freer Gallery of Art (Jefferson at 12th). Oriental and American art.

Art and Industries (Jefferson at 9th) includes an important collection of Victorian Americana from the 1876 Philadelphia Centennial Exposition.

Museum of African Art (324 A Street). African arts and crafts at the home of 19th-century black abolitionist Frederick Douglass.

National Portrait Gallery (8th and F streets). All the presidents and great ladies including Pocahontas, Eleanor Roosevelt and Gertrude Stein.

Museum of American Art (8th and G streets). From colonial times via Winslow Homer, Cassatt and Whistler to O'Keefe and de Kooning.

Renwick Gallery (Pennsylvania Avenue and 17th Street). American design, crafts and decorative arts.

EXCURSIONS

Mount Vernon

(16 miles south on Mt. Vernon Memorial Parkway, also by tour-mobile in summer)

Not just a dutiful pilgrimage to the home of George Washington, Father of the Nation, Mount Vernon offers a delightful journey back to the life of an 18th-century Virginia plantation, beautifully restored, the lawns perhaps a shade more tailored than in the old days. Make the 35-minute drive early in the morning to avoid the spring and summer crowds and sit, as George and Martha did, on the graceful square-columned veranda overlooking the Potomac river valley and the Maryland hills beyond.

Great soldier and leader of men, George Washington was also an accomplished farmer. His lands, some 8,000 acres, were divided into 5 farms with 120 slaves to work them. At the border of the immaculate Bowling Green, you'll pass old trees planted by George himself. Inside the house, you can see Martha's account books, each item painstakingly recorded. The furniture is authentic 18th-century stuff, but only George's bedroom has the original pieces, including the bed he died in in 1799 and the portmanteau trunk that accompanied him during the Revolutionary campaign.

Colonial Virginia

(South from Washington on Interstate 95 via Richmond to State Highway 5)

Highway 5 takes you through some lovely James River plantation country to the Historic Triangle of Jamestown, where Virginia was founded, Williamsburg, its capital from 1699 to 1780, and Yorktown, where the Revolutionary War reached its triumphant climax in 1781. The towns are linked by the Colonial Parkway on which a Visitors Center dispenses tickets for Colonial Williamsburg.

Williamsburg is a complete "museum-town" where you can stroll around meticulously reconstructed 18th-century houses, shops and taverns—no cars, only horse-drawn carriages. Tourguides and the artisans working at the cobbler's, gunsmith's, apothecary and printer's workshop are all dressed in colonial costume. The restoration was carried out with funds from John D. Rockefeller, Jr., in 1927. Drawing on 18th-century engravings found across the Atlantic in the Bodleian Library, Oxford, architectural historians were able to restore the 1705 **Capitol** building and **Governor's Palace** in exact detail. For the latter, they were helped by a precise plan of the interior drawn by Thomas Jefferson, who lived here for six months as Governor of Virginia. The major

thoroughfare is **Duke of Gloucester Street** with some of the finest wooden weatherboard and red-brick Georgian houses. Revolutionary bigwigs met at Raleigh Tavern; you can eat authentic 18th-century food at the King's Arms, Chowning's and Christiana Campbell's taverns, all in fine restored state.

Jamestown, 6 miles south of Williamsburg, was the site settled by the first pioneers from London in May 1607 (13 years before the *Mayflower* reached Massachusetts). The only relic of colonial Jamestown is a crumbling church tower. The site was abandoned because of malarial mosquitoes (gone now). But **Jamestown Festival Park,** at the entrance to the causeway leading to Jamestown proper, has been built as a replica of the old three-sided fort, with a 17th-century pottery and an Indian ceremonial lodge. On the river are full-scale replicas of the tiny vessels—*Susan Constant, Godspeed* and *Discovery*—which brought John Smith and 103 settlers across the sea on their courageous voyage. You can go aboard the *Susan Constant* to inspect living conditions.

Yorktown, 18 miles to the east, is where Lord Cornwallis surrendered his British troops in October 1781, effectively sealing Britain's loss of its American colonies. Before visiting the battlefield, you may want to stop at the

Yorktown Victory Center, 2 miles outside town, to see a film restaging the decisive engagement. Actually, the most significant part of the fighting was played out in Chesapeake Bay in a naval engagement between the British and the Americans' French allies. In town, you can visit **Moore House,** where the British negotiated their capitulation with the Americans and French.

BIG CITIES NEARBY

Baltimore and Philadelphia provide interesting counterparts to the national capital. From the birthplace of American nationhood, Philadelphia has grown into an ebullient mixture of ethnic groups. Baltimore, a major seaport for Chesapeake Bay, is a great place for seafood, and the waterfront has become an exciting experiment in urban renewal.

Philadelphia *(Pennsylvania)*

It's one of the more charming aspects of America that a town which occupies such an important place in the history of the nation should also be a national joke. Philadelphia, after all, is the City of Brotherly Love that William Penn established as a model of religious freedom and colonial enterprise and where Benjamin Franklin and Thomas Jefferson championed the movement for independence. But it's a quiet, sedate town — to which comedian W. C. Fields preferred a graveyard, the town where the master of horror, Edgar Allan Poe, felt moved to write his famous poem "The Raven".

While the modern city has been enlivened by its thriving Italian and Jewish communities, it's the old Anglo-Saxon backbone that continues to set the dignified tone. According to Mark Twain, "In Boston, they ask 'How much does he know?' In New York, 'How much is he worth?' In Philadelphia, 'Who were his parents?'"

Today the town's past is still vitally important to its citizens. And they proudly proclaim **Independence National Historical Park** at the heart of old Philadelphia, containing all the great buildings of early America's government, as the "most historic square mile in America". At the grand red-brick Georgian **Independence Hall** (5th and Chestnut) you can see where America's founding fathers signed the Declaration of Independence and later the United States Constitution. Next door, the states' representatives met in **Congress Hall** and signed — without great enthusiasm — the Bill of Rights

Colonial houses in Williamsburg

101

that forced the government to protect rather than interfere with individual freedoms. On the pleasant tree-shaded green of Independence Mall (Market and 5th streets) you can touch (but not ring) the famous **Liberty Bell** in its new glass pavilion. This was the bell that came from England in 1751, cracked en route as if to symbolize the American fissure in Britain's empire, was repaired in time to ring out from the tower of Independence Hall on July 4, 1776, and cracked again in the 19th century. Now it's been laid to rest for visitors just to pat it with affection.

In case you still don't grasp the Philadelphians' view of their city's importance, take a look at the magnificently outrageous **City Hall** (Market and Broad streets). It took the Louvre in Paris as its architectural model and, locals like to point out, it's bigger than Washington's Capitol. On top stands William Penn.

The **Philadelphia Museum of Art** (26th and the Parkway) is a very good collection of American works, plus some fine Impressionist and Post-Impressionist paintings. Van Gogh's famous *Sunflowers* hangs here.

Edgar Allan Poe's House (530 N.7th Street) is now a museum of Poe memorabilia. He lived here with his young wife.

The **Rodin Museum** (22nd and Parkway) has the biggest collection of the French sculptor's work outside Paris.

And for the kids, the **Franklin Institute** (20th and Parkway) is a marvellous science museum where they make lightning—a permanent test for Ben's invention, the lightning rod.

Baltimore *(Maryland)*

Baltimore suffers even more than Philadelphia from what Baltimoreans consider unfair barbs. Edgar Allan Poe *died* here and was buried in Westminster Churchyard, but otherwise the town is somewhat lacking in historical monuments. However, it makes up for this with some of the boldest urban renewal in the country. **Charles Center** has turned the erstwhile blight of the downtown business district into a lively area of elegant architecture, cheerful plazas, shopping centers, theatres and cafés.

Equally successful and visually more attractive is the 95-acre **Inner Harbor** development using the once seedy waterfront of Baltimore Harbor for hotels, theatres, parks and promenades to bring the place back to life. Art shows, concerts and sports activities keep the place hopping all year round, a high point being the City Fair in mid-September, celebrating with ethnic festivities the city's multiracial community. The restaurants around the harbour serve some fine fresh seafood from the

Bountiful Italian Market, Philadelphia

bay—clams and oysters, soft-shell crab, crab cakes and the famous Baltimore speciality, hard-shell crabs.

At Constellation Dock you can tour the restored frigate *Constellation*, one of the U.S. Navy's earliest commissioned ships launched in 1797 and still in service in World War II. Another attraction appropriate to the waterfront is the **National Aquarium** (Pratt Street on Pier 3). Landlubbers who prefer old trains can see a superb collection at the **Baltimore & Ohio Railroad Museum** (Poppleton and Pratt streets).

Pride of the **Baltimore Museum of Art** (Charles and 31st streets) is the excellent Cone Collection of 19th- and 20th-century painting, well endowed with works by Matisse and Picasso.

THE SOUTH

For the holiday-maker, the South is above all the place where the sun is. For Americans, it's also an almost mythical place perceived through its history—an ante-bellum serenity and paternalism, the blood and fire of civil war, bitter resentments of reconstruction, and a 20th-century struggle for parity with the North and a new pride and prosperity. Parity, but not conformity. The South has held on to an exotic quality that spices courtly mellow decadence with a hint of contained violence below the surface. To sort out myth and reality would require a prolonged stay of months or years, criss-crossing the Carolinas, Georgia, Florida, Alabama, Mississippi, Louisiana and Arkansas. But for an introduction, start with Florida for the exquisite hedonism of its subtropical sun, then to Charleston for an echo of the golden past, to Atlanta for a look at the new South, and over to New Orleans, a grand old river city with a unique Creole flavour.

There is nothing ambiguous about a visitor's intentions in Florida: pleasure, sheer pleasure. Take in the sun, sea and sand along the coast from Miami up to Palm Beach, but allow some time off to visit the dreamlands of Walt Disney around Orlando and the outer space adventures launched from Cape Canaveral or perhaps to drift by the alligators in the Everglades swamps. In Florida's subtropical climate with air and sea-water temperatures ranging from an average low of 23°C (74°F) in January to an average high of 31°C (88°F) in August, fair-skinned northern Europeans should watch out. Sun-bathing here should begin with no more than 30 minutes the first day; the Florida sun can really scorch you.

MIAMI BEACH *(Florida)*

Connected to mainland Miami by causeways across Biscayne Bay, this is where the pleasure begins: 7 miles of gleaming sandy beaches in front of high-rise hotels and condominium apartment buildings. A few years ago these beaches nearly disappeared because of the erosion caused by undisciplined construction along the seafront. At the end of the 1970s, the U.S. Army Corps of Engineers came to the rescue by dumping 13½ million cubic yards of white sand along the reclaimed 100-yard-wide strip of seashore that is Miami Beach's *raison d'être*. It's a good place to get away from it all—just ask the ex-New Yorkers who are here all year round.

After a careful dose of sun your first day, you might like to check out the various beaches. If your hotel has commandeered its own piece of the shoreline—as is the case around 46th Street—you may be perfectly happy to stay there, but there are several good alternatives:

Haulover Beach, at the north end, is for the very active, with palm trees to shade their lazy companions. It's very good for surfing, Frisbee-spinning and fishing off the pier. There are barbecue grills to turn your catch into a picnic.

Bal Harbour is great for shell-collectors and jetsam-hunters with those strange battery-driven rods that may locate buried treasures—old Spanish coins or new Miami jewels, but most likely just beer cans. You can combine your beach stay with some shopping in the boutiques that quite happily proclaim themselves to be the most expensive in the world.

Surfside at 93rd Street and the **64th and 53rd Street beaches** are best for swimming, away from the crowds.

21st Street is a favourite of the young set, who turn the fast-food stands into swinging open-air clubs.

Away from the sands, Miami Beach offers architectural rewards for Art Deco buffs. In the area of **Washington Avenue,** on the blocks between 8th and 21st streets, you can stroll around hotels, apartment buildings, restaurants and shops that sprang up in the tourist boom of the '20s and '30s, with a flourish of chrome

and bakelite, gaily coloured ceramic tiles and mirrored glass, borrowing motifs from the Egyptians, Aztecs and other fellow sun-worshippers. After years of scorn by purists who found the buildings too "florid", it's now been declared by official art historians to be a "national preservation area".

Continuing the triumphant spirit from the '50s to the present day, **Collins Avenue** stretches for 100 blocks of more modern hotels, the flagship being the **Fontainebleau Hilton** (at 44th Street). Even if you're not staying there, plan to have a drink or meal (and a look around) in the unquestionable monument of American holiday-making. No expense has been spared at the serpentine pool, cabanas, waterfalls, grottoes, hidden bars, tennis courts, luxury shops and aquarium to make you feel, for a glorious change, anywhere but at home. After the extravagant décors of the '50s, it's gone beyond vulgarity—gilt and marble are "out"—to the higher realms of *de luxe* fantasy. Today everyone's a film star.

MIAMI *(Florida)*

The sun-sea-and-sand worshippers tend to avoid the city of Miami itself, but they're missing some major attractions. Like many Miami Beach residents, they've been frightened by the influx of immigrants from Cuba and Haiti and the stories of drugs, voodoo and violent crime. The stories are true—drugs are one of the four main sources of revenue in Florida, with tourism, citrus fruits and manufacturing—but with the reasonable care that you'd take in any large city these days, there's some fun to be had in this high-colour town.

Downtown is a conventionally bustling area of department stores, restaurants and nightclubs around Flagler Street and Biscayne Boulevard. But it's livelier south of downtown in the Cuban neighbourhood of **Little Havana,** centred on a 30-block section around "Calle Ocho" (8th Street) running east from 37th Avenue. More than a quarter of Miami's 2 million people are Cubans and here is where they hand-roll their cigars, roast their coffee and dance the *salsa.* The street life makes New York City seem sedate.

Try that strong Cuban coffee, served espresso-style on the street in paper cups, or cocoa for dipping your *churro* (a long thin doughnut). At Ocho and 14th Avenue is the open-air Domino Park where neighbourhood enthusiasts (male only, women can just watch) play with a concentration worthy of grand-master chess. A block further east is **La Ceiba,** the sacred kapok tree, where sorcery is very openly performed. (Miami cemetery guardians complain of having to clear up the dead chickens, goats' heads and voodoo dolls left by Haitian and Cuban voodoo-doctors.)

On Ocho and 12th Avenue, you can watch cigars being rolled, pressed, wrapped and cut with elegant dexterity.

The closest thing Miami has to a bohemian artists' quarter is **Coconut Grove** (South Bay Shore Drive), a pleasant self-contained community of boutiques, galleries and parks, with sailing boats bobbing in the harbour.

Across the Rickenbacker Causeway, **Key Biscayne** has some pleasant beaches at Bill Baggs Cape Florida State Recreation Area and an amusement park and nice little zoo at Crandon Park. But the star of Miami's many wildlife attractions is **Seaquarium,** just off the causeway on Virginia Key. There you will find whales, dolphins, sharks and turtles at work, play and in repose. The dolphins will leap any height for a few fish and the spectator's delight. On the other side of the causeway, **Planet Ocean** shows you the serious side of oceanography and marine ecology. And in **Parrot Jungle** (57th Avenue and 112th Street) the birds perform more tricks than the dolphins— ride bicycles, roller-skate, even do a bit of arithmetic. Some of them fly. The macaws and flamingoes are gorgeous.

Spanish Flavours
At any one of the myriad restaurants on Ocho and 12th Avenue, try the fish soup, sopa marinero (with rice, peas, pimentos and onions), arroz con pollo (yellow rice with chicken) or yuca con mojo (pork served in a sauce of sour orange juice, garlic and spices), and let yourself go with a tocino del cielo (tangy egg custard). The two most popular rum drinks are Cuba libre (Pepsi or Coca Cola, rum and lime juice) and daiquiri (rum, sugar, lime juice and ice, also made with crushed bananas or strawberries).

But man remains the most fascinating trickster. Look at what industrialist James Deering did with his **Vizcaya** home (3251 S. Miami Avenue). Now also the Dade County Museum, this 70-room Renaissance *palazzo* on Biscayne Bay contains in its opulent interior almost every artistic style known to Western man from the A.D. 200 altar to the 1915 gold plumbing fixtures. The formal gardens are properly bizarre and the huge barge in the little harbour is made of stone, a piece of sculpture by A. Stirling Calder, less mobile than the works done later by his son Alexander.

If that doesn't sufficiently impress you, how about the 12th-century Spanish cloisters intended for newspaper and copper tycoon William Randolph Hearst's home in California? In 1925, **St. Bernard's Monastery** (16711 W. Dixie Highway, off Biscayne Boulevard) was brought over from Segovia stone by numbered stone in 11,000 crates. Unfortunately, they were packed with hay that the U.S. Department of Agriculture deemed a health hazard to animals (there'd been foot-and-mouth in Segovia), so the dismantled monastery stayed on the East Coast until it was bought and reassembled by some entrepreneur. It is now under the auspices of the Episcopal Diocese of South Florida. The choral recitals here offer one of the most deliciously anachronistic experiences on the North American continent.

AROUND FLORIDA

The Everglades

(Toll road south to Homestead then take State Route 27, follow signs to the National Park)
This watery plain has given swamps a good name, replacing the image of a disease-ridden morass with that of a wonderland of natural beauty. A 50-mile band of brackish water from Lake Okeechobee flows lazily down through Florida and into the ocean. Called the "River of Grass", the slow-moving bog teems with wildlife. The **Everglades National Park** covering nearly 1½ million

acres is under the protection of U.S. Rangers, who are stationed at the various visitor centres throughout the park with advice about how best to enjoy—and not spoil—the wilderness.

From the park entrance southwest of Homestead (pick up a map at the Visitor Center), the road runs 38 miles to the coast. Several marked turnoffs along the way take you out to campsites and picnic grounds beside lakes or near "hammocks"—raised areas in the swamps. The first of these turnoffs leads you to **Royal Palm Visitor Center** on the edge of a fresh water slough (rhymes here with stew). Look down into the clear waters of the pond to see shoals of fish, among them the Florida garfish much appreciated by the alligator. You might like to see one of the brief slide-shows introducing the Everglades at the Visitor Center before taking the Anhinga and Gumbo Limbo foot-trails leading from this area.

The Anhinga Trail's raised boardwalk circles over sawgrass marsh where you can see alligators, egrets, herons and the anhinga snake-bird. The Gumbo Limbo Trail is a circular half-mile track through jungle vegetation. Keep your eyes open for racoons, opossums, tree-snails and lizards, very big hereabouts.

At the end of the main road is **Flamingo,** a fishing village on a shallow bay dotted with islands.

Alligators
The Everglades alligators are coming back. Recent legislation against hunting or trapping the reptiles has helped to reverse the population decline. Still, there are only about 10,000 alligators today (and some 500 crocodiles), where once they numbered in the millions. To provide the raw material for de luxe handbags, belts and shoes, they were almost hunted out of existence.

Alligators prefer fresh water; crocodiles like sandy beaches and salt water. And if you get close enough, you'll notice that alligators have shorter, blunter snouts.

Never, never underestimate an alligator—even if it appears to be dozing. Small or large, it will thrash towards anything that moves, snap with 2,000 pounds of pressure and drag its prey under water before devouring it at leisure.

In the old days, it produced illicit "moonshine" alcohol. Now, with all these rangers around, it's a tourist centre with a motel, housekeeping cabins and campsite. At the Flamingo Marina, you can rent tackle, boats and canoes to fish for trout, redfish, snapper and snook (tastes a little like pike). Find your own way up to Everglades City through a chain of lakes and rivers called "The Wilderness Waterway" or take a sightseeing boat from Flamingo.

The abundant wildlife on the coast and in the interior includes ibises, ospreys, white herons, snowy egrets, bald eagles, roseate spoonbills, otters, green turtles, manatees and rare Florida panthers.

Coat yourself with insect repellent, especially in summer. If you take the rangers' guidance about poisonous plants and snakes, you'll be fine.

The Gold Coast

The 70-mile-long Gold Coast offers half a dozen vacation resorts particularly favoured by Americans escaping the winter rigours of New York, New England and the Midwest. Hotels and condominiums gleam white across wide, palm-tree-lined boulevards that border on spotless beaches. Some of these resorts are just lazy, some crazy, some in another world.

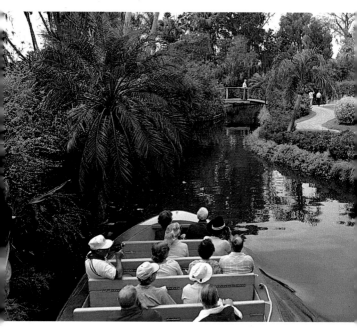

Fort Lauderdale is crazy. Its peak moment of madness is the month-long Easter vacation when a quarter-million sun-starved northern students descend on the town like the merry Mongol hordes of yore. They come not to pillage and rape but to boogie on the beach and try some gentle mating in the moonlight. Early evening, the kids cruise their cars bumper to bumper up and down the A1A "Strip" along the seafront, climbing from one convertible to another in search of an extra giggle. Summer and winter, the town settles down as private boats and yachts (estimated to number 30,000 on and off the canals) drift along the network of **inland waterways** past elegant marina homes. The best way to view them—if you're not thinking of chartering a yacht—is to take one of the paddle-boat cruises from the Bahia Mar marina.

Boca Raton is lazy. It's the winter home of a highly regarded polo club, but you can also enjoy the superb beaches tucked behind the dunes. Or rent a rod and pretend to fish off the rocks around the inlet. If you must be active, go bird-watching or hiking around Deerfield Island Park, once the home of Chicago's own Al Capone.

And **Palm Beach** is another world, the place that put the "gold" in the Gold Coast. (The "palms" in Palm Beach are said to have grown from coconuts spilled in a Spanish shipwreck.) The town was created after oil and railway magnate Henry Flagler was persuaded at the end of the 19th century that Florida's warm winters made the state a viable proposition for his railway expansion. While the railway

Cypress Gardens, Florida

was being built down the Gold Coast, the secluded location of Palm Beach struck Flagler as just the kind of place for his kind of person. Now one of America's wealthiest communities, it stretches its splendid *palazzi* along Ocean Boulevard, not too far from the proprietors' yachts in the harbour. You catch glimpses of these opulent residences as you wind through the impeccable landscaping. Flagler's own home is on Coconut Row, a white marble palace named Whitehall, now the **Henry Morrison Flagler Museum,** which traces the town's early history amid elegant old furnishings, with the master's private railway carriage on show in the grounds.

In this, Florida's ultimate consumer paradise, there is scarcely a luxury shop of the world that is not represented on its pride and joy: **Worth Avenue.** It's a street that ranks alongside Paris's Rue du Faubourg Saint-Honoré or London's Bond Street. Even if your holiday budget doesn't allow you to go wild and buy all the elegant goodies you want, you can still press your nose against the windows and see the super toys of the Florida élite.

You'll notice that the couturiers go a little crazy in the colours they choose here. It's the Florida sun that does it. You'll also see the most delightfully flamboyant golfing clothes ever offered to

Western man and woman. What's more, there are people actually wearing them on this hallowed avenue. And the Gucci store is worth the detour—nothing less than a Florentine *palazzo*, with fountains playing in the tree-shaded courtyard.

Kennedy Space Center

Situated a hundred-odd miles to the north on Merritt Island, this is the site of manned-craft launchings. Unmanned flights are launched from Cape Canaveral, across the Banana River. An ideal trip here would include watching a launching. You can get the schedule and information about reservations for the special viewing by calling 1-800-432-2153 (toll-free in Florida). Otherwise there's still plenty to see if you avoid the crowds by arriving very early at the Visitors Center on State Route 405 and catch one of the two-hour bus tours.

The Blue Tour takes you on a historical survey of space travel and includes visits to the Air Force Space Museum, former launching pads, and inside the old Mission Control building. The Red Tour concentrates on the facilities used in the current space-shuttle programme. The exhibits at the Visitors Center include films and simulated flights, the *Apollo-Soyuz* command module and a lunar roving vehicle.

Walt Disney World

(20 miles south-west of Orlando off Interstate 4 and State Highway 192)

With Walt Disney World, the grand old movie-maker's company has turned his fantasies into a mammoth holiday resort development, with its own hotels, campgrounds, golf courses, swimming and boating facilities, vacation villas and shops, surrounding the biggest theme park in the world. The area covers 27,400 acres—much of it reclaimed marshland.

The heart of the complex is the 100-acre theme park known as the Magic Kingdom. Just to the south of it is what might be called its brain, EPCOT Center, a multimedia projection of the world's past and future filtered through a Disney-inspired imagination.

The Magic Kingdom

On the drive from Highway 192, you'll pass lawns dotted with the weird shapes of topiary figures —first hint of the playful fantasy-land to come. At the enormous parking lots (note your car's parking area and row number), board one of the frequently passing "trams" for a free ride to the Transportation and Ticket Center.

Here you can choose between the *one-day ticket*, which is good for entry either to the Magic Kingdom or EPCOT Center and

---

Some Timely Tips

Plan your journey to Walt Disney World and EPCOT so that you'll be at the park entrance early in the morning—particularly important if you're not staying at one of the Disney hotels. By early afternoon in peak holiday season, there may just be no more room and they close the gates. Besides, it gets too hot to tour the attractions in the afternoon sun—that's the time to be inside one of the air-conditioned halls. (From September 1 to mid-December and January 3 to mid-February, things are easier.)

---

all rides and exhibits (but not the monorail, ferryboat, or bus), or the *World Passport* (3-, 4- and 6-day; one-year), which admits holders to the Magic Kingdom, EPCOT Center and all rides and exhibits (including unrestricted use of the Walt Disney World transport system). With a 6-day and one-year passport you also get free parking.

Once past the ticket booths, choose between the ultra-modern monorail or the more leisurely ferryboat across the lake to the Magic Kingdom's entrance. Now you're in fairyland, complete with Cinderella's castle, and surrounded by Mickey Mouse and a host of Disney movie characters. Take your choice of the Kingdom's six different sections.

Main Street, USA, is the very

113

symbol of the good old American Way of Life, from the entrance under the Railroad Station past gabled and turreted turn-of-the-century buildings to Town Square, where City Hall dispenses information about the rest of the Magic Kingdom and Walt Disney World in general. Roaring Twenties musicians, ice-cream parlours, candy stores, horse-drawn buses, stereoscope shows in the Penny Arcade—everything takes you comfortingly back to the sweeter things of the past.

Adventureland proposes exotic tropical flora and fauna. A gigantic (concrete) banyan tree supporting the Swiss Family Robinson Treehouse stands by the landing-stage for the Jungle Cruise, with trailing vines and all the horrors of hostile natives and pouncing (foam-rubber) wild animals. Pirates of the Caribbean take you to their treasure trove, or Tiki birds sing a Tropical Serenade.

Frontierland romanticizes the pioneer days—quick draw at the Shootin' Gallery, fast-food at Pecos Bill's Café or slow ride on the gaily coloured riverboat. The Tom Sawyer raft will carry you to his island. Ol' folks like the Diamond Horseshoe Revue.

Liberty Square doesn't quite save you from going to New England but makes a valiant effort to capture the atmosphere of the Republic's cradle at Liberty Tree

Tavern. The uncanny "Auto-Animatronic" robots in the Hall of Presidents reproduce the imagined voices of Washington and Lincoln.

Fantasyland takes you on a submarine voyage 20,000 Leagues Under the Sea or a dizzying whirl in the Mad Hatter's gigantic teacup. Every childhood hero seems to be here—Peter Pan, Snow White's Seven Dwarfs, Toad of Toad Hall, not forgetting Disney's own Mickey Mouse. But the favourite ride appears to be Cinderella's Golden Carousel, a classic merry-go-round with all the brass and glass fittings and hurdy-gurdy music. Visit the Cinderella Castle, too, with some nice mosaics of scenes from the film.

Tomorrowland is devoted to outer space and the accompanying technology. You can go on a Mission to Mars or pilot a Star-Jet. In the towering white-steel Space Mountain is a heart-stopping roller-coaster ride simulating a race through space. Much more reassuring is the WED-Way People Mover, cars floating oh-so-smoothly on a cushion of electro-magnetic force. You have free access to many of the technological attractions sponsored by their manufacturers—well worth the time.

You can take a last look at the whole Magic Kingdom with a 15-minute ride on the Walt Disney World Railroad.

EPCOT Center

Out of Walt Disney's last dream of an Experimental Prototype Community of Tomorrow has grown his company's most ambitious entertainment centre—partly built, constantly evolving—south of the Magic Kingdom. It attempts nothing less than to present in exciting visual terms the past and future of our planet, together with a showcase of some of the world's nations, all within a few hundred acres around an artificial lake.

In **Future World** a monorail takes you around polygonal, spherical, dome-shaped or pyramidal pavilions (each sponsored by a major American company) demonstrating the evolution of our civilization and the astounding new technologies that will be tomorrow's tools. The centrepiece is **Spaceship Earth,** a 180-foot-high, white geosphere. Inside, you will coast along in an egg-shaped vehicle on a rail past three-dimensional holograms of prehistoric man and frighteningly lifelike robots of his descendants, through the ancient civilizations of Greece and Rome via the Renaissance to the present day, at the top of the sphere.

World Showcase presents nations of the world through their monuments, landmarks and cuisines. You can enjoy French gastronomic delicacies in a bistro at the foot of a model Eiffel Tower. Wander through an Italian market of brilliantly faked onions, tomatoes and carrots before sitting down to a plate of real *fettucine* in a restaurant alongside a replica of Venice's Piazza San Marco.

If you intend doing both the Magic Kingdom and EPCOT, you'll need at least two days or a more leisurely three. For more information, including the wide range of Disney-run accommodation, contact Walt Disney World, Box 40, Lake Buena Vista, Florida 32830, U.S.A. For vacation packages: Walt Disney Travel Co., P.O. Box 22094, Lake Buena Vista, Florida 32830.

CHARLESTON
(South Carolina)

Standing somewhat aloof at the point where the Ashley and Cooper Rivers flow together into the Atlantic, this town evokes that elegant, courtly atmosphere that people still associate with the "Old South". After South Carolina had led the Southern states' secession from the Union, Charleston was the town that fired the first shots in the Civil War (see p. 27). Ever since, it has maintained, with winning self-consciousness, a sense of dignified separateness.

The **harbourside**—along the Battery curving north up to East Bay Street—is a delightful palmetto-shaded area to stroll around the 18th- and 19th-century houses with beautiful gardens of dogwood, wisteria and azalea. Most attractive of all are the pastel-washed façades—pink, blue, yellow—of Rainbow Row starting at 93 East Bay, formerly the townhouses of South Carolina planters and ship-owners.

Running west from East Bay Street, Market Street takes you to the colourful **Market Square.** Open-air cafés, restaurants, art galleries and boutiques have been installed in renovated warehouses in keeping with the nationwide movement for redeveloping derelict downtown neighbourhoods.

From the Municipal Marina at the junction of Calhoun Street and Lockwood Drive on the west, Ashley River side of the peninsula, you can take a boat out to historic **Fort Sumter.** This is the old military base that was wrested from the United States Army by South Carolina militia in April 1861, to the polite applause of the Charleston gentry assembled on the harbour. It was recaptured, after a two-year siege, in February 1865. The two-hour cruise includes a visit to the Civil War museum and a tour of the fort's remains.

Two excursions out of town will complete your glimpse of the old days of the cotton plantations. **Boone Hall,** 7 miles north on Highway 17, was used as the Tara plantation for the filming of *Gone with the Wind*—Georgia, apparently, had nothing as appropriate. Stroll through an avenue of splendid 250-year-old oaks and a grove of 140 acres of pecan trees around the well-restored mansion. But the most spectacular grounds are the **Magnolia Gardens,** 14 miles north of Charleston on Highway 61. This lovely 400-acre nature reserve that was once a huge plantation combines exotic displays of flowers and shrubs—camelia, azalea and, yes, magnolia—with fine opportunities for bird-watching, hiking, biking and canoeing. The plantation house stages "Magnolia by Moonlight" dinners, with a lamplit tour of the gardens. (Enquire at the Visitor Center in Charleston about reservations—essential.)

ATLANTA *(Georgia)*

This historic capital of Georgia is also the bouncing capital of the new South. Its symbol, which you can see in two fine sculptures —one on Broad Street by the First National Bank, the other on Martin Luther King Drive beside Rich's Department Store—is the phoenix, the mythical bird that rose from the ashes. The town's modern prosperity has been motivated by its total destruction in the Civil War in 1864. Two years later it was the federal headquarters for the South's Reconstruction (see p. 28) and the dynamism has not abated. Today its exhilarating contemporary architecture, elegant shops, smart restaurants and shiny discos are the backdrop for a people cannily combining yankee sophistication with the savvy of redneck good ol' boys who sometimes sound as if they just hit town, but hit it hard.

To get the ideal overview, start your tour with a trip to the 70th-floor revolving restaurant on top of the **Peachtree Plaza Hotel** —the elevators whiz up through glass tubes on the outside of the building. The **view** is spectacular, all the way to the Blue Ridge Mountains.

(No need to rent a car if you're on a brief visit, the buses of Atlanta's highly efficient MARTA public transport system give you a comprehensive tour of the major sights, stopping off at the main hotels.)

Linked to the plaza, **Peachtree Center** is the unmistakeable heart of downtown, an airy shopping and business centre with attractive landscaping among the skyscrapers, drooping vines and tropical plants, reflecting pools and splashing fountains. Even if you're not staying there, be sure to visit the Hyatt Regency Hotel, a pioneer in the updated atrium architecture: the skyscraper is built around a skylit courtyard with its own indoor-outdoor café-

---

Sing with Care

A mistake that foreign visitors sometimes make in Atlanta is to whistle the jolly tune of "Marching through Georgia". Atlantans don't dwell unduly on the past, but this ditty is still not appreciated here. It recalls the march of Northern troops who left Atlanta in September 1864, having carried out the orders of General William Tecumseh Sherman to burn it to the ground. Though he ruthlessly carried out the tactics of scorched earth throughout Georgia, Sherman was a soldier of much more compassion than Southerners understandably credit him with. Whether or not he actually made the remark often attributed to him: "War is hell", he did say to the protesting mayor of Atlanta: "War is cruel and you cannot refine it".

---

terrace inside the hotel, a boon on hot humid summer days.

South of Peachtree Center, Central City Park, like London's Hyde Park, attracts some strange soap-box orators along with the picnicking office workers and visiting out-of-towners in this pleasant green space.

The **Martin Luther King Memorial** (407 Auburn Avenue, NE) marks the tomb of the great civil rights leader assassinated in Memphis in 1968. Atlanta was his home, and the tomb, bearing the inscription 'Free at last" stands beside the Ebenezer Baptist Church where he and his father preached the message of non-violence (his mother was murdered there in 1974). A research institute next door provides an information centre on King's life and works.

One of the newer testimonies to Atlanta's entrepreneurial energy is the **Omni International Complex** (100 Techwood Drive), a dazzling 34-acre megastructure, as Atlantans like to call it, containing a sports coliseum for basketball, ice-hockey, circuses and concerts and a convention centre with cinemas, shops, discothèques, a skating-rink and restaurants. Multicoloured laser beams light up the huge interior at night while hundreds of "sun sculpture" prisms set in the skylight create a kaleidoscopic effect by day.

The **High Museum of Art**

(Peachtree and 16th streets) will take your breath away. The stunning white structure contains a superb collection, including American decorative art, 19th- and 20th-century photography, African art and modern paintings.

Atlanta is also the home-base of Coca-cola, and the company's museum (310 North Avenue) gives a fascinating glimpse of the history and advertising of this bubbly symbol of Americana.

NEW ORLEANS
(Louisiana)

Whatever is exotic, lurid, even sinful in the popular image of the South stems in large part from this port town at the mouth of the Mississippi River. In New Orleans, the jazz that grew up in its brothels and seamy saloons is still hot and the Creole cooking brought from the West Indies by the old French and Spanish settlers is as spicy as ever. You'll find them both in the French Quarter. And if the elegant decadence of the ante-bellum aristocracy is at best a whispered legend handed down to a few strutting diehards, take a look at their granddaddies' splendid Greek Revival townhouses in the Garden District and you'll see what a proud world they lost when they had to give up their slaves. Mississippi gamblers no longer fleece wealthy widows on riverboats coming down from Natchez, but the sternwheeler steamboats are back in service again for lazy cruises along Ol' Man River.

The closest they get to being exotic, lurid and sinful these days is at the great Mardi Gras carnival, so successful that the city fathers are now turning every imaginable occasion—St. Patrick's Day, Bastille Day, the arrival of spring, summer or the fishing fleet—into another festival, however hot and steamy it may get. New Orleans loves parades, but if they haven't found an excuse for one when you're visiting, you'll still find a public party going on somewhere, with all the trumpets and trombones blowing full blast.

French Quarter

Known locally as the Vieux Carré (Old Square), this is the historic heart of town, bounded by Canal Street and Rampart Street (originally a fortification), Esplanade Avenue and the Mississippi River. Great fires in 1788 and 1794 destroyed over 1,000 houses in the quarter, but the 19th-century reconstruction has maintained the old two- and three-storey houses with filigreed wrought-iron galleries providing the roof for shaded colonnades at street level. This, despite the encroachment of new hotels and garish saloons, remains the French Quarter's dominant architecture.

Start at **Jackson Square.** Around the prancing equestrian statue of General Andrew Jackson, this place bustles all day with clowns, magicians, balloon-vendors and assorted eccentrics sporting strange costumes even when there's no carnival for months. Flanking the cathedral are the two relics of the colonial era—the **Cabildo**, built as a police station and later used as the City Hall, and the **Presbytère,** a priests' residence, that became a courthouse. They are now parts of the Louisiana State Museum. The Cabildo's exhibits tell the colourful history of trade on the Mississippi River, while the Presbytère shows old Mardi Gras costumes and carnival paraphernalia and an exhibition of the history of Louisiana's Blacks from slavery to the present day. St. Louis Cathedral is an 1851 restoration of the 18th-century church of the French Catholic diocese, more famous for the duels in its rear garden than for its architecture. Framing the square are two rows of **Pontalba Buildings,** prime examples of the elegant ironwork (though, in this case, cast- rather than wrought-iron) on the upper-storey galleries.

Take Dumaine Street past Madame John's Legacy, a nicely preserved French colonial cottage, to Royal Street, one of the most gracious in the quarter with some high-class antique shops.

Mardi Gras

Shrove Tuesday, the British call it, but people here like to translate the French—"Fat Tuesday" is the last fling before an effort at Lenten austerity leading up to Easter. It's New Orleans' great moment of madness bringing hundreds of thousands of revellers— book your hotel room months in advance—to see the parade of papier-mâché floats down St. Charles Avenue, as well as many others throughout the city. King or Rex of the main parade is often a television or movie star. While the round of private masked balls starts on Twelfth Night (January 6), the pageants only begin 11 days before Mardi Gras. In costumes, anything goes—fat old men in baby's romper-suits, thin young ladies in fat old men's suits. The kinky may well wear a fabulous black leather cowboy suit on the front and absolutely nothing behind. Although Mardi Gras takes place in February or early March, the weather is delightfully balmy.

Carnival derives from the Latin meaning "Goodbye, meat", which scarcely cramps the style of New Orleans. The people here prefer seafood anyway.

Turning right past Ursulines Street (at 1132 Royal Street) is the **Gallier House,** named after its architect James Gallier, one of the few authentic old New Orleans

Jazz Town

Cotton is no longer king, but jazz has returned to its throne in New Orleans. The once disreputable music is now celebrated officially in the 14-acre Louis Armstrong Park on the edge of the French Quarter, complete with a 12-foot statue of "Satchmo", trumpet in one hand, handkerchief in the other. The local Tulane University's sociology department has special archives of recordings, photos and other documents devoted to the history of jazz.

It all began at the end of the 19th century when black marching bands wailed to the funerals and swung all the way home. At night, they played the bawdy-houses on Basin Street, and when the red-light district was closed in 1917, the action moved to Bourbon Street. The nightclubs and saloons there today are bouncing and shaking more loudly than ever — ragtime, blues, easy-going Dixieland or the heavier driving "Chicago" style, swing and boogie woogie, but none of the bop, cool and acid-electronic stuff that has come along since World War II.

The jazz joints dispensing beer and stronger stuff come and go, change their name and location from season to season, but one solid institution remains in place — Preservation Hall. Just old-time traditional jazz played straight by old black musicians.

houses open to the public. It has been beautifully restored to its original 1857 condition and when you walk out on the wrought-iron balcony you get a lovely view of the neighbourhood's old tranquillity before attacking the hurly-burly of **Bourbon Street's** saloons and nightclubs.

If you want to save Bourbon Street till night, cut down Governor Nicholls Street towards the waterfront. On the corner of Decatur is the old *Streetcar Named Desire* made famous by Tennessee Williams' play. (Desire is in fact a street a dozen or so blocks east of here—this streetcar doesn't run

Mississippi paddle steamer

any more but you can still take the St. Charles Avenue one through the Garden District starting from Carondelet at Canal.) Close to the waterfront is the ever-expanding **French Market,** pleasant boutiques and ice-cream parlours at this east end along with the traditional French (and Italian) fruit, vegetables and fish, and the lively 24-hour **Café du Monde** back near Jackson Square. It makes a good claim to the best coffee and *beignets* (doughnuts) in town, on a very Gallic terrace.

Garden District

South-west of the French Quarter, between Magazine Street and Louisiana, St. Charles and Jackson avenues, is the Garden District where the new American cotton and sugar aristocracy built their townhouses after the Louisiana Purchase, while the Creoles stayed on in the Vieux Carré. Surrounded by gardens of magnolias, oaks and palm trees, the spacious mansions—Victorian, Louisiana "raised cottage" or Greek Revival style with columned porticos—rival outlying plantation homes. There are some fine examples along **Prytania Street:** one of them (no. 2343) is now the Louise S. McGehee School.

The district's golden era ended with the double blow of the Civil War and the elimination of the Mississippi steamboat trade by the railways. Now the steamboats have been restored to service for **river tours** starting from Toulouse Street Wharf or the Canal Street docks. Most of the cruises take you past Chalmette National Historical Park (also an easy 10-mile drive south-east on Route 46). Andrew Jackson's crushing victory here over the British in the Battle of New Orleans came after a peace treaty had been signed (see p. 24), but it was enough to give him the national renown that won him the White House 14 years later. For those who make the drive out here, the pretty **Beauregard Plantation House** serves as an information centre for the battlefield and cemetery.

THE MIDWEST

Americans who work hard bring a lot of energy and imagination to their leisure, too. Foreign visitors are often surprised at how attractive life can be in America's busiest cities and few are busier than those of the Midwest. The area, popularly known as the Heartland, is the industrial and agricultural core of the U.S. It covers Ohio, Indiana, Illinois, Michigan, Wisconsin, Minnesota, Iowa, Missouri, Kansas and Nebraska. From the Great Lakes across the prairies to the Great Plains, the Midwest is dominant in dairy and pig farming, corn and wheat, but it is also a flourishing industrial center specializing in steel and rubber and car manufacture.

Chicago, business headquarters for many of the big steel companies, is the transportation hub of the continent, main junction for the national railway system and today blessed—occasionally cursed—with the world's busiest airport. In the neighbouring state of Michigan, it's still an economic truth that if car-capital Detroit sneezes, America catches cold. These two cities have achieved their industrial and commercial pre-eminence with a rich and fascinating "ethnic" mix that makes them increasingly vibrant centres of cultural activity, too—well worth a visit.

CHICAGO (Illinois)

Vigorous, tough, even brutal—these are the adjectives that many people associate with Chicago. But beautiful? Yes, there is a beauty to this vigorous, tough and sometimes brutal town that startles newcomers flying in over Lake Michigan or driving up from the south past the ugly steel towns of Gary and Hammond, Indiana. The skyline is simply one of the most spectacular in the world and something, for once, that does not make Chicago play second fiddle to New York.

For this is the city that taught the rest of the world how to build skyscrapers. It was a technique learned from necessity. In 1871, a fire swept through the largely wood-built city—scarcely 30 years old—leaving 100,000 homeless. Chicago had to rebuild in a hurry, new fireproof structures making maximum use of available ground space. The men who worked out how to construct a building around a metal skeleton so that it could "go as high as you like", but with elegance and style, became collectively known as the Chicago School. They included Louis Sullivan, Daniel Burnham and later Mies van der Rohe. Frank Lloyd Wright also worked in Chicago, but mostly on residential architecture. Their works and those of their pupils have made of Chicago a veritable lived-in and worked-in museum of

modern architecture. In quality of design, architectural critics insist, the more famous Manhattan skyline is in no way superior to the urban panoramas along Chicago's lakefront and around the downtown area.

The other visual surprise in this resolutely commercial city is the 15-mile stretch of sandy beaches and green parkland along the lakefront. Unlike many other big cities on the Great Lakes, Chicago did not build factories or railways all along its lakeshore, but reserved most of the land for parks and residential neighbourhoods. As a result, it's possible to sunbathe, swim or go fishing just a couple of blocks from the major centres of town.

The population of Chicago is 3 million, big by any standards, but still a long way behind New York, giving them a "Second City" complex that sometimes makes them defensive, but also acts as a spur to achievement. It was inevitable that the town's proud architectural tradition would prompt it one day to build something higher than New York's Empire State Building or World Trade Center and, sure enough, the Sears Tower is now the world's tallest. The Chicago Symphony is one of the world's great orchestras and the Art Institute is a museum of international renown. But the people themselves, rather than aspire to the sophistication of Manhattanites, have a distinctively warm, robust and cheerfully sardonic attitude to life that makes them much more approachable in public places. That old image of gangland machine-gunnings is hard to live down, but you'll not find any monuments to Al Capone, and the Mafia is no more powerful here than in any other wealthy American city. There's an Anglo-Saxon business establishment, but the public tone is set much more by the Irish, Polish, German, Italian and Jewish segments of the population, and in 1983 the town elected its first black mayor.

Getting Around. The Chicago Transit Authority (CTA) runs a very efficient bus system, taxis are not too expensive, but for once we recommend renting a car to move around the city, except in the congested downtown area, if you're staying more than a day. Orientation is not too difficult: the city centre is known as the Loop, after the elevated railway track that loops around the downtown business district immediately south of the Chicago River. The other neighbourhoods are defined in geographical relation to the Loop—North Side, South Side, West Side.

Michigan Avenue

Rather than start in the bustle of downtown, we suggest you first take stock of the city from its

most elegant street, certainly busy, but more measured in its pace. With a well-developed knack for boosterism, Chicagoans call the tree-lined stretch from Oak Street to the river the **Magnificent Mile.** It contains the town's smartest high-fashion boutiques, jewellery shops, department stores, art galleries and bookstores. Its image is such that when McDonald's fast-food chain (corporate HQ: Chicago) wanted to open a branch here, neighbouring merchants insisted that the décor be appropriate to the location. The result is a very dignified hamburger stand indeed.

But the dominant landmark is the gigantic black-steel 100-storey

---

Stable Stable

It has been established that the Great Fire began in the stable of Patrick and Catherine O'Leary over on the West Side on the evening of October 8, 1871. Then Chicago bar legend takes over to insist — and it's not wise to question stories told in a Chicago bar — that it was all the fault of Mrs. O'Leary's cow kicking over a paraffin lamp. At any rate, history does record that the fire raged for 27 hours, wiping out over 17,000 buildings, and when a rainstorm put it out, not only was the Water Tower still standing, but — fact, no legend — so was Mrs. O'Leary's stable.

127

John Hancock Center with its dramatic exterior, a diagonally strutted skeleton. This is a vertical street unto itself, soaring 1,107 feet in the air. The first five floors are for shops, then half a dozen floors for parking, and above that the building has offices and apartments, with a supermarket and swimming pool for the residents. From the 94th floor observatory there are marvellous views across to the Michigan shores of the lake, down over the Loop to the steel mills of Indiana, up the lakefront towards Wisconsin and out across the flat residential neighbourhoods of the West Side. Above or below, the effect of the Hancock is like Chicago itself, vigorous, tough, even brutal, but beautiful, too.

Down the street at Chicago Avenue is a strange, almost comical white-limestone turret that is in fact the city's most cherished historic monument, the **Water Tower.** Built in 1869 to house a pumping-station for water from the lake, it was the only public building to survive the Great Chicago Fire. Today it houses a very helpful Visitor Information Center. Its little park makes a pleasant place for a mid-town picnic.

One block west on Chicago Avenue, **Rush Street** is a lively entertainment area with outdoor cafés, nightclubs, restaurants and taverns that come alive after dark.

Back on Magnificent Mile,

Water Tower Place (845 N. Michigan) is—inside at least—a very attractive shopping centre with waterfalls playing alongside the escalators taking you up seven floors of shops and restaurants. Four blocks south, **Ontario Street** is "gallery row" for a thriving contemporary art scene.

Just before you reach the river, you should notice one of the city's more bizarre skyscrapers, the cathedral-like **Tribune Tower** with its Gothic pinnacles and porch and 30 storeys in between. Built in 1925 for the *Chicago Tribune* newspaper, it was the winning entry in America's most famous architectural competition. Many of the world's leading architects—233 entries from 23 countries—submitted designs, with Bauhaus master, Walter Gropius, and the great Finnish designer, Eero Saarinen, among the losers. Having persuaded the world by default that modern buildings should henceforth have modern designs, the tower settled down as a unique and even lovable eccentricity.

From **Michigan Avenue Bridge,** you have an excellent ensemble view of the varied skyscrapers immediately around the Chicago River. The white terra-cotta, clock-towered building just north of the bridge is the **Wrigley** of chewing-gum fame, particularly

Panoramic view of lakeside Chicago

attractive when floodlit at night (a revolutionary thing to do back in 1921). West along the river are the striking twin towers of **Marina City,** resembling two huge corncobs. The circular concrete towers, with apartments shaped like slices of pie on the upper floors, go right down to the river and have docking space for 500 boats for residents or for businessmen commuting to work by motorboat from the lake's northshore suburbs. In stark contrast behind is the pure black-steel-and-glass slab of Mies van der Rohe's **IBM Building.**

The Loop

With the "El" (elevated railway) rattling around its periphery of Wabash Avenue, Lake, Wells and Van Buren streets, the Loop unmistakably means business. LaSalle Street is the heart of the financial and banking district and has the same canyon-like quality as New York's Wall Street. The major downtown department stores are on State Street and Wabash Avenue. One of them, **Carson, Pirie & Scott,** is a mecca for architectural scholars attracted, like the earliest shoppers in 1899, by Louis Sullivan's incredibly intricate ironwork ornament over the Madison Street entrance, as well as by the then revolutionary, horizontally elongated windows.

But the most successful feature of Chicago's business district is the space devoted on its many open plazas to monumental modern sculpture and mosaics rather than statues of famous men. This **plaza art,** as it has become known, began with Picasso's great *Sculpture* (1967) in front of the Richard J. Daley Center (Washington and Dearborn streets), a complex of courthouse and local government buildings named after the late mayor. Like the elegant skyscraper courthouse, the 50-foot sculpture is made of CorTen steel that weathers to the colour of rust, but without the corrosion. To people who want to know whether the sculpture is to be understood as a woman or a horse, Picasso himself said they might just as well "try to understand the song of a bird". At any rate it draws to the plaza a constant flow of admirers and locals who just like to eat their sandwiches around it.

Other notable pieces of plaza art are Chagall's *Four Seasons,* a 70-foot mosaic on the First National Plaza (Monroe and Dearborn streets); a 53-foot, bright red *Flamingo* stabile by Calder (Adams and Dearborn streets)—this graces what is regarded as the most elegant set of U.S. Government buildings in the country, the **Federal Center,** designed by Mies van der Rohe; and, perhaps the most provocative, pop-artist Claes Oldenburg's

Beethoven on the Lawn
Among the Windy City's many monuments, few are more respected than the world-famous Chicago Symphony Orchestra, where Hungarian George Solti is the latest of a long series of distinguished European resident conductors. Tickets for their autumn and winter concerts at Orchestra Hall (220 S. Michigan) are difficult to get, but if you know well in advance when you'll be in Chicago, you can write directly to Orchestra Hall for programme details and reservations. In summer, it's slightly easier to get tickets, when the orchestra plays at Ravinia Park in the northern suburb of Highland Park. There you can listen to their music and that of other major performers at this summer festival on the lawn with a traditional "Ravinia picnic" of chicken, strawberries and wine.

States, because that's the limit set by the Federal Aviation Administration. Actually the building consists of nine towers packed together, as its designers Skidmore, Owings & Merrill suggest, like squared cigarettes. They pop out of their packet at different heights. The structure's steel frame is sheathed in black aluminium with 16,000 bronze-tinted windows—that works out to one window for each of the workers employed there. Built for the Sears, Roebuck merchandising company as the ultimate status symbol, it has been criticized for packing all those people into a confined location without providing quick transport facilities for getting them out. Morning and evening rush hours are indeed a bewildering sight. The impact of the building at ground level —some people lie on their backs on the plaza to take it all in— is enormous. Then, of course, there's the top, or at least the 103rd-floor **Skydeck** observatory. If you went up the Hancock in the daytime, try the Sears at night, you get a great view, among other things, of the Hancock.

filigreed *Batcolumn*, a 100-foot high baseball-bat made of 1,608 pieces of welded steel (just outside the Loop at the Social Security Administration Building, 600 W. Madison Street).

On the edge of the Loop, but you really can't miss it, is, yes, the world's tallest building, the **Sears Tower** (Wacker Drive and Adams Street). Its 110 floors rise 1,454 feet and it's not likely that it will soon be topped, at least in the United

Lake Shore Drive
A trip along the Outer Lake Shore Drive expressway is a delightful way to see the lakefront skyline unfold behind the parks. On the South Side you drive from

Jackson Park past the sailboats moored in Chicago Harbor at Grant Park up around Oak Street Beach to Lincoln Park on the North Side and the boats of Belmont Harbor.

(You can also make a boat tour of the lakefront on one of the cruises starting from Michigan Avenue Bridge on the Chicago River.)

Lincoln Park is worth a separate visit for the delight of the **zoo.** It has a terrific ape house, but better than all the usual tropical exotica (of which there's a good sample) is the charming idea of presenting farm animals—that's it, pigs, cows, goats, ducks and chickens—for city kids who never saw a chicken that wasn't

Fun and fantasy around Chicago

fried or barbecued and know little else besides cats, dogs and pigeons. Similarly, the **Lincoln Park Conservatory** not only has a beautiful orchid collection and amazing African and South American trees, but also the simple enchantment of hollyhocks and hyacinths and snapdragons and daisies in Grandmother's Garden.

Museums

The **Museum of Science and Industry** (South Lake Shore Drive and 57th Street) is the city's most popular museum because you don't just stand there and look, you get *into* the exhibits and do things. Go down a coal mine, walk through a 16-foot high model of the human heart, creep around a captured World War II German submarine, and press buttons and pull all kinds of levers with scarcely a "Don't Touch" in sight.

Museum Point (1300 S. Lake Shore Drive) combines three fascinating exhibitions. The **Shedd Aquarium,** largest in the world, has 7,500 species of fish, including a gorgeous Coral Reef collection of 350 Caribbean creatures. If you're lucky, you'll be there when scuba divers go down to feed the big fish. The **Field Museum of Natural History** also encourages visitors to "play" with some of the exhibits, though you may be intimidated at first by the giant rogue elephants fighting in the

main hall. The **Adler Planetarium** offers attractive multi-media sky shows. Apart from the well-presented but by now quite usual exhibits about space exploration, a highlight is the display of old astronomical instruments dating back to when people still had to be persuaded that the earth was not flat.

The **Museum of Surgical Sciences** (1524 N. Lake Shore Drive)

133

is the place for those with a sense of the macabre. Inspect the 18th-century amputation devices, antique artificial limbs, but also a reassuring apothecary shop nicely reconstituted from 1873.

The **Art Institute of Chicago** (Michigan Avenue and Adams Street), at first an art school, now ranks as one of the great American museums. In less than a century it has acquired a collection highlighted by a magnificent range of French Impressionist, Post-Impressionist and the major 20th-century movements.

Practically all of Chicago's ethnic groups have their own museum, often set in the neighbourhoods where they still live. Among them are the Polish (984 N. Milwaukee Avenue), Swedish (5248 S. Michigan Avenue), Ukrainian (2247 W. Chicago Avenue), Jewish (618 S. Michigan Avenue), Lithuanian (4012 S. Archer Avenue) and Chinese (2238 S. Wentworth).

If you want to learn more about the riches of Chicago's architecture, the **ArchiCenter** (330 S. Dearborn) has a collection of historic models and photographs and organizes walking and bus tours of the city's landmarks. In Oak Park there are several tours of the many houses that the great Frank Lloyd Wright built, including his own home, in this western suburb, declared a National Historic District.

DETROIT *(Michigan)*

Much older than Chicago, Detroit was established in 1701 by a French aristocrat, Antoine de la Mothe Cadillac, whose name is now attached to the aristocrat of General Motors' cars. To protect the burgeoning Canadian fur-trade, Cadillac set up Fort Ponchartrain d'Etroit—the fort on the straits, between Lake St. Clair and Lake Erie. Subsequently, as an important shipping centre on the Canadian border, its shipbuilding industry was accompanied in the 19th century by carriage-building. From that it was a natural step for Detroit to become the American capital of car manufacturing after Henry Ford built his first motor-driven vehicle in 1892 and revolutionized the American way of life in 1908 with his "Model T" which made cars available to everyman.

The car industry made the city the gauge of the country's economic health, but it was not always good for the town itself. Over-industrialization turned the city centre into a slum of derelict docks, warehouses and railway yards. In the 1950s and '60s, the middle classes fled to the suburbs. But dissatisfaction with the homogenized life out there has prompted civic leaders and most especially the Henry Ford family and fellow car-manufacturers to revive the downtown business district. The result is an exciting new interest in civic and cultural buildings around the core, quite rightly named Renaissance Center (RenCen to locals). It attracts thousands of people back to the new downtown shops, cafés and restaurants, and now apartment dwellings are going up along the waterfront to carry on the renewal.

The centrepiece of the **Renaissance Center** (Jefferson and Brush streets), in the dramatic group of five shining black-steel and tinted-glass towers, is the 73-storey, cylindrical **Detroit Plaza Hotel.** The vast lobby has an indoor "lake" surrounded by trees and lounges reached by ramps and spiral staircases. There are a couple of bars and a revolving restaurant on the 73rd floor for you to view the city—and Canada. The interconnecting office buildings and hotel stand on a four-level podium that comprises 70 shops and four cinemas. The place is constantly abuzz with people.

Civic Center continues the new downtown bustle outdoors around **Hart Plaza** with its striking Noguchi fountain. Jefferson Street takes you past the Ford Auditorium (corner of Woodward) where the fine Detroit Symphony Orchestra gives its winter concerts, along an esplanade enlivened in summer by street musicians, mimes and acrobats. You can take an old, reconditioned trolley car that rattles from the exhibition centre of Cobo Hall, past the outdoor cafés and boutiques on Washington Boulevard to **Grand Circus Park.** The theatre there, Grand Circus Exchange (47 E. Adams), stages both avant-garde and traditional drama.

The **Cultural Center** (around Woodward and Kirby avenues) brings the city's museums together. The **Detroit Institute of Arts** has some fine Old Masters, including Pieter Brueghel's *Wedding Dance,* but the most intriguing works are the frankly provocative frescoes of Mexican Marxist painter Diego Rivera on work in Detroit automobile plants, as an epitome of industrial America.

The **International Institute** (111 E. Kirby) assembles under one roof the cultural artefacts, folklore, costumes and dolls of 50 different countries, many of them represented in the work force of the automobile plants.

To escape the city for a while, just take MacArthur Bridge at the end of E. Grand Boulevard over to **Belle Isle,** a lovely island park in the Detroit River. You can play tennis or golf there and attend free open-air concerts by the Detroit Concert Band at the Remick Music Shell. For the children, there's a zoo reserved for baby animals and the **Dossin Great Lakes Museum** has a fine exhibition of model ships.

THE ROCKIES

The Rockies are a series of mountain ranges extending all the way from Mexico to the Canadian Arctic, running along the great Continental Divide that forms the backbone of America. In Montana, Wyoming, Utah and Colorado, they bring the holiday-maker face to face with the inspiring natural beauties of America's back-country, its vast forests and torrents, delightful Alpine meadows in summer and superb ski-slopes in winter.

Formidable barrier to the 19th-century pioneers' westward trek beyond the Great Plains, the Rockies also proved to be sources of mineral wealth—gold, silver, copper, and today, uranium.

It was appropriate that the first natural region to receive the federally protected status of National Park (in 1872) should be Yellowstone, the fabulous mountain plateau 8,000 feet up in the Rockies. To the south, Denver has established itself as the major city to have grown out of the Rockies' old mining towns and today provides the ideal starting point for exploring Colorado's mountain beauty. On the west of the Continental Divide the Mormons established their Salt Lake City, originally with the hope that the barrier of the Rockies would protect them from the intolerance of non-believers.

YELLOWSTONE NATIONAL PARK
(Wyoming)

Yellowstone is more than a vast landscape of mountains, valleys, rivers and forests—both living and petrified—it's a perpetual spectacle of exuberant geysers (including star performer Old Faithful) shooting hundreds of feet into the air, volcanic mudpots exploding, hot springs bubbling out of the earth, waterfalls cascading from heights that make Niagara look like an overflowing bathtub. And all against a backdrop of colours that only begin with the yellow of the canyon rock that gives the park its name.

Headquarters for the park are at **Mammoth Hot Springs** on the north side of Yellowstone, so we recommend that first-timers come, if possible, through the north entrance at Gardiner (Montana Highway 89) or make their way first up to Mammoth from the West Yellowstone entrance. The information centre provides important tips about camping sites as well as park regulations, trail maps and a museum of the region's flora, fauna and geological phenomena.

Old coal-mining town, Silverton

One of the great geological phenomena of the park is right there at Mammoth, the lovely silver travertine shelves of a **terrace mountain** being created daily before your eyes. Volcanically heated springs are thrusting up mineral-laden water from underground limestone beds and laying their deposits in terraced pools that form at least a couple of tons of new travertine each day.

Drive 21 miles south of Mammoth to the Norris junction on the 142-mile **Grand Loop** road that will take you around the major landmarks. A visitors centre at the junction organizes hikes (on boardwalks) across the steaming **Norris Geyser Basin.** You'll get good explanations of the workings of geysers and hot springs. With exceptional luck, you may even witness here the world's biggest active geyser, the Steamboat. But unlike steady, reliable Old Faithful further down the road, its performance is almost as erratic as a volcano, varying in appearances from every few days to just once a year. When it does blow, it shoots water, steam, rocks and mud 300 to 400 feet into the air.

Further south, at Madison Junction, the Loop meets the road from the West Yellowstone entrance and curves down along

Mammoth Hot Springs, Yellowstone

the **Firehole River.** This well-named river is fed by hot springs and in places feels like a pleasantly warm bath, compared with the plateau streams' chilly 39° F.

Old Faithful, the most famous sight in the park, is 16 miles south of Madison Junction. This is the geyser that you can rely on to blow an average of every 65 minutes or so. Some geysers in the park are larger, and others are more regular in their habits. But none are as dependable as Old Faithful, which erupts the most frequently of them all. Another Visitors Center nearby has some excellent audio-visual exhibits to explain the phenomenon. This is also the area of three of the park's most active geyser basins, named simply Upper, Midway and Lower. Be on the lookout, too, for some intriguing, smelly mudpots. These vats of hot, soupy clay are activated by a steam vent or fumarole.

To escape the crowds that gather at Old Faithful, take the Loop east over to West Thumb (junction with the southern park-entrance road, the John D. Rockefeller Memorial Highway) on the shore of the beautiful **Yellowstone Lake.** Within strict limitations, you are allowed to fish for cut-throat trout, averaging 16 to 18 inches. Boats and tackle can be rented either at Grant Village on the lake's south-west tip or at Fishing Bridge on the north shore. Remember, you're competing with otters, osprey hawks and grizzly bears, as well as coyotes hanging around for what others drop.

From the lake's north shore, the Loop follows the Yellowstone

Leaving Well Alone
Human beings are only guests in the park and park guides will warn you not to interfere with the residents—the moose (elk) antelope, bighorn sheep, bear, bison and myriad fish and birds. Under no circumstances should you feed the bears. There ferocious grizzlies number about 350 in Yellowstone, black bears about 500. They are doing much better since they have learned not to rely any more on handouts. After being reduced in the 19th century by wanton slaughter from millions to just a few hundred on the whole continent, the bison are back up to 2,000 in this park. Yellowstone now has an ecological policy of strict non-interference with nature. That means, for instance, that no attempt is made to save the moose herds from starvation in the bitter winters. To do so would deprive their predators— grizzlies, coyotes and eagles—of an important food source. Many moose survive the winter by standing in water warmed by hot springs, others fall into very hot springs and provide grizzlies with a boiled supper.

River down to the **Grand Canyon** of the Yellowstone. Approaching from the south, you catch a first sight of the cascading waters of the 109-foot Upper Falls. Park a little further on near the short trail that will take you to **Inspiration Point** where you can survey the even more dramatic 308-foot **Lower Falls** and a panorama of

the winding 24-mile-long canyon. It drops 1,200 to 4,000 feet to the banks of the Yellowstone River. The canyon walls are impregnated with arsenic sulfides that produce every shade and variation of yellow—lemon, saffron, gold, ochre, burnt sienna, orange —wonderfully enhanced by the brilliant greens of the surrounding lodgepole-pine forests.

At the northern end of the

Bighorn sheep

141

canyon is **Tower Fall** (near the junction with the north-east park-entrance road from Cooke City). On a sunny day at noon you are almost certain to see a bewitching double rainbow across the 132-foot-high falls. And if you think that the huge boulder perched on the rim is about to tumble down, don't hold your breath. "Discoverers" of the Tower Fall on August 27, 1870, placed bets that it would be gone by August 28.

East of Tower Junction, off the Lamar Valley Road, lies a **petrified forest.** These trees, still upright after millions of years, include sycamores, magnolias, maples, oaks, redwoods, walnuts and willows, suggesting Yellowstone was once a lot warmer than today. Botanists have also identified 76 flowering plants. The forest was covered by volcanic ash rich in silica with which groundwater impregnated the trees and plants, turning them to stone.

Yellowstone Logistics

Most of its 3,472 square-mile expanse is in Wyoming, but Yellowstone also spills over into Montana to the north and Idaho to the west. Only one of the park's entrances, Gardiner, remains open year-round; the others close between November and May. Both Salt Lake City and Denver have local airline services to Yellowstone's airport, where you can rent a car. Though all of the major sights can be reached by car, do plan on some good walking too.

Hotels, mostly comfortable but simple cabins, must be reserved well in advance. For reservations: write to TWA Services, Yellowstone National Park, WY 82190, or call 307-344-7311 (for information: Superintendent, Yellowstone National Park, WY 82190, tel. 307-344-7381). Camping can be a scramble for the choice spots in high season, but well worth the trouble of getting up earlier than the others. Obviously, it's best if you can visit Yellowstone outside the peak months of July and August, but even then the park is vast enough for you always to be able to move off the beaten track.

DENVER *(Colorado)*

If you don't believe Denver was once the mining capital of Colorado, look at the 24-carat gold leaf dome on its Capitol Building, or at the local branch of the U.S. Mint that handles one quarter of the nation's gold supplies. The Wild West days have long gone, but locals still like to sport a stetson hat and checked shirt, for old times' sake. This is the mile-high town, but the air here is unfortunately as polluted as in many other major American cities and the architecture is relentlessly modern, apart from one colourfully preserved street from the old mining days. But what counts for the holiday-maker is what you see almost on the city's doorstep—the marvellous backdrop of the Rocky Mountains, Denver's backyard.

Take a look around town, get used to the altitude and then hit the road out to Colorado's mountains. There's no better place to start than the Visitors Bureau at 225 W. Colfax, well prepared to provide you with local and travel information.

Across the street, the **U.S. Mint** gives free weekday tours of its money-making plant. You can see gold bullion, but most people seem to like the counting-room, full of the finished product, stacked in millions.

Also on Colfax is the august **Capitol Building** (E. 14th and E. Colfax streets). Make sure to take the west staircase and stand on the 13th step—that's exactly one mile above sea level.

The best of the modern city is the dazzling **Denver Art Museum** (W. 14th Avenue and Bannock Street). When you see its seven-storey walls covered with one million glass tiles over a surface broken up higgledy-piggledy with slotted windows, you know what its Italian architect, Gio Ponti, meant when he said: "Architecture must create spectacles." The museum, by the way, contains a first-class collection of American Indian art—totem poles, costumes and rugs.

Old Denver is over on **Larimer Street,** which has conserved its Victorian buildings as art galleries, shops, leathersmiths', silversmiths' and cafés—some good Mexican restaurants, too. Larimer Square is quaintly done up with courtyards and arcades lit by gas lanterns. But the most authentic piece of old Denver is to be found in the grand lobby of the 1892 **Brown Palace Hotel** (17th and Tremont Place), genteel forerunner of the skylit atrium style of today's glass tower hotels.

From September to May, the Denver Symphony Orchestra plays at **Boettcher Concert Hall** (14th and Curtis streets), an acoustically sophisticated auditorium-in-the-round with the audience encircling the performers. A unique opportunity to see the conductor's facial expressions. Classical and popular music concerts are held 16 miles south-west of town in the fantastic open-air arena of **Red Rocks,** set amidst towering red sandstone outcroppings.

If you don't have time for an extended tour of the Rockies beyond Denver, you can still get a taste of one of the higher mountains by *driving* all the way to the top! Just west of Denver, **Mount Evans** is 14,260 feet high, with a paved road to its peak. (Drive 35 miles on Interstate Highway 70 to Idaho Springs and then south on Route 103 to Route 5.)

WEST CENTRAL COLORADO

An ambitious tour of the major resorts of West Central Colorado will take you on a beautiful 360-mile circuit through the Rockies, but you may prefer to aim for just one of the big three:

Aspen is the best known resort town in the state. At 7,937 feet it provides wonderful winter sports opportunities, but it's an equal delight in summer both for its music festival and for the hiking, camping, fishing and riding in the surrounding **White River National Forest.**

In the 1880s the town made its fortune out of seven silver mines, but the market collapsed in 1893 and the town was deserted until revived as a sports and cultural centre after World War II. Some of the old Victorian buildings have been preserved with considerable charm and taste, particularly the Opera House and the lovely Hotel Jerome.

The **Aspen Music Festival** in summer presents opera, classical music and jazz of the very highest order. International stars just like to hang out here. They take advantage of the easy-going atmosphere in the downtown mall of shops and outdoor cafés or excursions into the spectacular **Maroon Bells** mountains south-west of

Negotiating the Colorado River

144

town. In winter, the skiing opportunities vary from the family slopes on Buttermilk and nearby Snowmass to the tough challenges on Aspen Highlands or the famous Ruthie's Run on Aspen Mountain.

Vail, north of the White River National Forest, is a very successful modern ski-resort with Swiss-style chalets. In summer it caters for tennis and golf enthusiasts—the only problem with the golf course is that the scenery is so spectacular it may distract you from your game. Surprisingly, there is also enough gentle landscape around to make bicycling a special pleasure. Anglers fish for some excellent trout in Gore Creek and Eagle River.

Glenwood Springs offers the ultimate luxury of a 405-foot-long swimming pool fed by a stream of natural warm water to a temperature of 85°–90° F. The waters were much prized by Indians as energizers before going on the hunt or warpath. They'll relax you before or after some exhilarating rafting down the **Colorado River.**

SALT LAKE CITY *(Utah)*

A unique phenomenon in American life, Salt Lake City is a community founded and sustained on theological doctrine—that of the Mormons, or, to give them their full name, the Church of Jesus Christ of the Latter-day Saints. It

also manages to be a highly agreeable town of friendly, outgoing people with bright shopping centres and outdoor cafés as well as impressive monuments to their historic spirit of adventure and courage.

All this is carved out of a desert of salt flats that stretch from the foot of the Wasatch Range of the Rockies around the Great Salt Lake clear across Utah to the mountains of Nevada. Their geographical isolation has motivated the people of Salt Lake City to keep up a busy cultural life of ballet, choral music and art exhibitions.

Temple Square is the all-important centre of town. This is a 10-acre compound surrounded by a 15-foot-high wall containing the nucleus of the Mormons' church buildings.

The solid granite Temple, 40 years in the building, is closed to non-believers but the celebrated **Tabernacle** is open to all. Its vast 250-foot-long and 150-foot-wide turtleback dome, originally of wood shingles but now encased in aluminium, was constructed only with wooden dowels, no nails, since iron was too scarce in Utah in the 1860s. The dome stands on 44 sandstone pillars at its periphery and provides wonderful acoustics for the great Mormon Tabernacle Choir. The 375 singers hold free rehearsals on Thursday evenings. A monumental 10,814-

145

pipe organ enhances the rather stark interior (free organ recitals every day at noon).

The **Church Office Building** (Temple Square East) contains a unique collection of genealogical records, largest in the world, possibly including yours. Go in, they'll be glad to help you track your ancestors.

Beehive House (67 E. South Temple) was built in 1854 as Brigham Young's residence and is now a museum devoted to the great man. The life of the early community is portrayed in the **Pioneer Museum** (300 N. Main Street). State Capitol, a copper-domed, Corinthian-style building of Utah granite and marble, affords a sensational **view** of the Wasatch Mountains.

The **ZCMI** (Zion Co-operative Mercantile Institution) at 15 S. Main was the country's first department store in 1868. Now its charming, ornate cast-iron façade with its slender Corinthian columns serves as the front of a bustling shopping mall with 60 attractive boutiques, art galleries and gift shops. Similarly, **Trolley Square** (5th South and 7th East streets) has converted old trolley barns into restaurants, shops and a theatre, with minstrels and mimes wandering around to entertain the shoppers. Monday night, the Mormons' Family Evening, is a popular time for locals to visit the ice-cream parlours and movie houses.

Just south of the square, **Liberty Park** makes a lovely picnic ground, with arbours, swimming pool, tennis courts and a boating lake. There are also sum-

> ### Too Many Wives
> *The Mormons' founder, New Englander Joseph Smith, began and ended his religious career with divine revelations. The first, in the 1820s, was that the American Indians were the Lost Tribes of Israel to be redeemed from paganism by Smith and his followers. Twenty years later, with 15,000 converts in Nauvoo, Illinois, he was directed by revelation to follow the path of polygamy, since the prophet Isaiah had said in the Bible that "seven women shall take hold of one man". Smith in fact took 27 wives and others followed suit until a conflict with dissidents ended in his lynching. Brigham Young succeeded as the Mormons' Prophet, inheriting 5 of Smith's widows to add to a dozen of his own wives, and led his people on an arduous 1,000-mile trek across the prairies, Great Plains and the Rocky Mountains to a new promised land. "This is the place" were his much quoted words on surveying the dry expanses of Utah's salt flats. Polygamy remained the official practice until the United States made its disavowal the condition of Utah statehood in 1896.*

mer concerts, an amusement park and an aviary.

The Salt Palace auditorium holds 28,000 people for pop concerts and sporting events. On the same grounds, the **Bicentennial Arts Center** combines theatre, ballet and the music of the Utah Symphony Orchestra with art exhibitions.

Visitors Center, Temple Square

You should not leave without visiting the **Great Salt Lake** itself, even if you prefer not to float in its hot, sticky, 25 per cent saline water. The lake is surrounded by marshland and salt flats, indeed forbidding to all but the hardiest Mormons. More refreshing is the lovely **Wasatch National Forest,** a pleasure for hiking, camping, trout fishing and autumn hunting for deer, moose and elk.

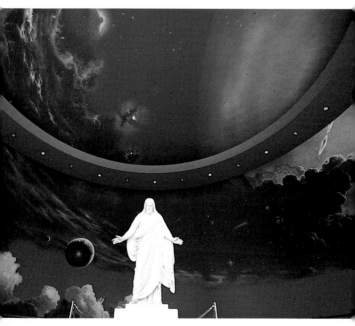

THE SOUTH-WEST

The region *par excellence* of America's wide open spaces, the South-West stretches across most of the much touted "Sun Belt". It covers the vast ranchlands and oil country of Texas, the rugged highlands of New Mexico first settled by the Indians and Spanish conquistadors, and Arizona's deserts rising to pine-forested mountains. Their culmination is the nation's most awe-inspiring sight, a phenomenon that humbles the most blasé of world travellers—the Grand Canyon.

Perhaps it's the sheer majesty of these open spaces that sustains in the people of this region that American individualism and independent spirit that have been a little tamed in the cities of the East and West coasts and the Midwest. It makes South-Westerners perhaps somewhat less accessible to the outsider at first, but if you win the confidence of the man on the next barstool or the woman selling cakes at the county fair, you'll find the most cordial, cheerful and colourful company in the country.

Don't even consider visiting Texas, New Mexico and Arizona without a car. While buses and planes will take you from town to town, the distances around the towns and between the sights are more than shoe leather or local

bus services were meant to deal with. Spring and summer bring the great dry heat of the desert or the enervating humidity and high temperatures of towns like Houston. The region was settled by doughty pioneers and you must come to it with some of the same spirit.

Texas is an acquired taste. The endless cattle ranges, the inexorable pumping of the oil derricks and the sparkling prosperity of the skyscrapers in Dallas and Houston are insistently impressive. But in the end, the name Texas evokes not only a geographical location but a special people with a special attitude to life, and this is what is hard to get hold of. The pushy arrogance and braggadocio have become legendary, to a point where Texans who might by nature—just a few of them—be shy, retiring types feel obliged to live up to the popular image. Since the 1959 admission of Alaska (2½ times its size), Texas is no longer the largest state in the U.S., but the self-image as biggest and best has remained. Houston and Dallas will show you the dynamic modern form this Texan self-confidence has taken and San Antonio will show you the historic background from which it has come.

Part of the joy of New Mexico is the predominance of a completely different architecture from that of the rest of the U.S. Adobe

(dried mud) houses with tranquil courtyards, arcaded plazas and fountains give a welcome illusion of coolness in the summer. You won't find them everywhere, but there are enough to make you forget for a while the rectangular blocks of skyscraper-land. Another special pleasure here is the desert landscape and the glowing pink and gold light which gives its aridity a jewel-like quality, an excellent ambiance for meditation. It's not surprising that the state attracted so many artists, flower-children and hippies in the 1960s. They've stayed on and grown into mellow forty-year-olds with a *mañana* view of life that fits in well with the local mores. Don't hurry around New Mexico, let it seep in slowly.

After the skyscrapers of New York City, the rugged desert and mountain landscapes of Arizona are the most likely component of the world's image of America. For history and Hollywood, this is as far as the Far West gets. The Hopi Indians settled here in what was Europe's Middle Ages and the Navaho followed. In the 19th century, the cattle and sheep ranchers fought for control of the plains and battled with Apache heroes Cochise and Geronimo. Copper, gold, silver, uranium and other ores made the state rich, and the year-round sun has since warmed the hearts of retired colonists from the cold Midwest.

150

For the visitor, Arizona offers the matchless wonder of the Grand Canyon, the awe of the deserts and the mirage-like towers of Phoenix.

DALLAS *(Texas)*

Television, movies and the national tragedy of John F. Kennedy's assassination have made this one of the best-known cities in America. The skyline looming out of the plain says it all. A forest of towers sheathed in silver or bronze mirror-glass reflect the dawn as more golden, the noon's blue sky more blue, the rosy sunset blood-red.

From Dallas-Fort Worth Airport you may pass **Texas Stadium** on Route 183. It sets the stage. This gigantic, domed arena has a large hole in the roof. It's the home of the Dallas Cowboys, the most razzmatazz American football team there is, known locally as "God's Team". The hole in the roof, say the Dallas fans, is to let God watch the game. If you happen to be there in season, try to get a ticket. Even if you don't understand the game, *especially* if you don't understand the game, the spectacle will not easily be forgotten.

Downtown, the most attractive skyscrapers are the gleaming slabs of the Hyatt Regency Hotel standing beside **Reunion Tower** topped by a huge geodesic sphere (300 Reunion Boulevard, off the Stemmons Freeway). The Tower is 570 feet high and has a revolving cocktail lounge, restaurant and observation deck for a fine **view** of the Texas infinity.

The **John Fitzgerald Kennedy Memorial** (Main and Market) is a stark and eloquent monument to the shooting of the president, on November 22, 1963, one of those dates when everyone remembers what he or she was doing when the news came. The 30-foot-high walls enclose a broken square which you approach along a gently sloping ramp, a space invit-

---

Bar Tips

If you want to make friends with Texans in a bar, don't order white wine or fancy cocktails. If you think you can manage it with a straight face and without spluttering, ask the bartender for a "long neck" (bottled beer) together with a shot of whisky. Don't say "Scotch", don't specify rye or Bourbon. Just drink the whisky, it'll be Bourbon, at one gulp. Smile politely at your neighbour. Ease your way gently into conversation, don't get bumptious or pushy. Don't talk dirty. Don't argue the merits of European and American football. Don't even try to explain the rules of soccer. Just ask how good the Dallas Cowboys are this year compared with the past. Don't talk about Houston in Dallas or about Dallas in Houston. They don't want to know.

Bathroom Cowboy

The cowboy look has come in and out of fashion a dozen times. Bankers wear pointed boots and stetson hats. The whole world wears blue jeans. But in any good Texas gentleman's outfitters, you can study and acquire the "real thing" (pronounced "thang"). Start with the hat. There are four basic cowboy hats: the Bullrider, straw for the summer, felt for the winter, with a slight crease in the high crown and the brim pulled down front and back. Normally it takes a season of rodeo bullriding to get the right shape, but you can work on it in the bathroom mirror. The R.C.A. takes its name from the Rodeo Cowboy Association and differs from the Bullrider by its side vents, wedge-shaped centre crease in the crown and narrower brim. The Rancher, as its name suggests, is for the boss and so made of beaver skin and is wide-brimmed. The Hi-Roller is for city-slickers, low crowned, curled brim, good for gambling, pulls well down over the eyes.

Jeans, as people have known for a long time, should look worn-out from the beginning. But not just worn-out anywhere, only on the inside of the leg, from riding, and the back pocket, from your chewing-tobacco tin. Again, you can simulate all this in the bathroom, with a good floor-scrubbing brush. Belts should be of hand-tooled Texas cowhide with your full name (not just initials, that's sissy) on the inside. The buckle, loop and belt-tip should of course be sterling silver (not gold, that's considered vulgar ostentation) and should have a simple, elegant floral motif, no ranch or rodeo scenes. Similarly, your boots should not be ornamented, just good plain leather. Pointed toes are not indispensable but high heels are—not for making you taller, of course, but to hold the stirrup. Soak them in the bathtub, dry them in the oven, cover with mud, scrape with harsh knife, soak and dry again, kick them front and back against the wall. O.K., you're ready to ride.

---

ing meditation. The assassination is understandably something the people of Dallas would rather forget, but visitors just won't let them. And so the municipality has provided a map on a plaque near the Memorial showing, among other landmarks, the nearby **Texas Book Depository** (now used as a courthouse) from the sixth floor of which Lee Harvey Oswald is said to have fired the fatal shots. A **John Fitzgerald Kennedy Museum** (501 Elm Street) offers an audio-visual presentation of his life and assassination, called "The Incredible Hours".

West of the JFK Memorial is the little **Log Cabin** (Market and Elm), a replica of the one pioneer John Neely Bryan built in 1841 when he came to settle in this part of Texas, the site of the future city of Dallas. The tiny cabin, which was brought here, perhaps as a cheerful antidote to the assassination monument, served both as post office and courthouse.

This resolutely forward-looking town has preserved just one area in which it has assembled the remnants of its past—**Old City Park** (Gano and St. Paul streets). Here you can picnic on the grass among restored Victorian houses, old log cabins, an 1886 railway depot, a bandstand, 1900s shops and an elegant Greek Revival mansion from 1855.

But otherwise, it's the people rather than the buildings that carry the past with them in this town. And you can see them at their best at **Farmer's Market** (1010 S. Pearl), a collection of ramshackle tin-roofed stalls where they sell Texas-sized fruit and vegetables, chew tobacco, spit, pick a mean guitar or a playful fight—good ol' boys to a man.

One of the more important local monuments is **Neiman Marcus** (Main and Ervay), a legendary department store. Nothing is too outrageous for them to sell—solid gold bathroom fittings, "His" and "Her" jet aircraft, pet lion cubs, a Monopoly game in which the board, the pieces, the money and property-cards are all made of chocolate (it doesn't specify whether the winner has to eat it all). The Christmas catalogue is a great collector's item.

The **Dallas Museum of Art** is a showcase of treasures you can't buy. But you can view the collection, particularly strong in 19th- and 20th-century art, housed in a starkly effective building designed by Edward Barnes.

In the midst of the formidable fanfare of downtown Dallas, you can retreat to a moment's tranquillity in the lovely triangle of Thanksgiving Square, a peaceful little oasis of immaculate lawns, trees, channels of water and a bridge leading to a spiral chapel inspired by the great mosque of al-Mutawakil at Samarra, Iraq.

HOUSTON *(Texas)*

Houston is oil and space. It's a hot, humid town that has burgeoned into one of the most prosperous business communities in America (though its Blacks and Mexicans are relegated to squalid slums for which Texan commercial ingenuity has not yet found a solution). To deal with the heat and humidity they have an underground network of air-conditioned concourses (fuelled by local oil) linking the downtown skyscrapers—and the highest air-conditioning bills in the nation.

Oil is proclaimed on its skyline by the striking black wedge-shaped towers of **Pennzoil Plaza,** designed by Philip Johnson. You can see how the black gold is drawn from the earth at the **Museum of Natural Science** (5800 Caroline Street at Hermann Park). The displays of drilling and refining technology include a fascinating model of an offshore oil rig. The Medical Science department lets you give yourself a check-up — listen to your own amplified heartbeat, test your lung capacity and blood pressure.

The **Museum of Fine Arts** (1001 Bissonnet) has good collections of Indian and pre-Columbian art, and the contemporary art section is a constant source of surprise as the wealthy local donors bring back new treasures from Europe. For local colour, the most exciting works on display are the vigorous studies of cowboy life by painter and sculptor Frederic Remington. His are the images that have made bucking broncos and gunfighters the icons of the Wild West.

The **Rothko Chapel** (3900 Yupon Street) is a lovely if somewhat austere non-denominational place of worship, housing the starkly contemplative, purple-and-black canvases of Mark Rothko. In the grounds is Barnet Newman's equally simple and moving rust-brown CorTen steel **Monument to Martin Luther King,**

a shattered finger-like inverted obelisk balanced on a pyramid.

Some 25 miles south-east of Houston on Interstate 45, the **Lyndon B. Johnson Space Center** is the controlling hub of the United States space programme. This is the 1,620-acre astronauts' training ground, looking like a university, and NASA's monitoring centre for manned space flights. The Visitor Orientation Center is a splendid museum of space equipment, rockets, lunar modules, space capsules and moon rock. It provides guided tours around the Mission Control Center by incredibly cheerful and knowledgeable cadets, and you can also visit by yourself the Skylab Training Room, the living and working quarters of NASA's space laboratory.

SAN ANTONIO *(Texas)*

For the outsider, San Antonio is the most accessible of Texan towns, the historic centre of the state's Spanish-Mexican beginnings and delightfully inviting to the public today with its River Walk through the heart of downtown.

The **Alamo** (Alamo Plaza), built as the Spanish Mission San Antonio de Valero in 1718, is the hallowed fortress where 187 Americans fought and succumbed to 5,000 Mexican soldiers under General Santa Ana in 1836. They'd been sent to put down

American resistance to Mexico's authoritarian rule of its Texas province. The Americans' heroic stand inspired the revolt which finally won Texas independence and subsequent admission to the U.S. as the Lone Star State. Today the Alamo is a museum of that momentous battle. Among other memorabilia it displays the fa-mous Bowie knife, the curved-bladed weapon fashioned by Colonel James Bowie, co-com-mander of the Alamo. The other commander, William Travis, was the one who issued the order: "Victory or death." But best-known of the Alamo heroes was Davy Crockett, who'd devoted his life to self-promoting acts of courage and strength in Tennessee until he was defeated in a congres-

Taos Pueblo

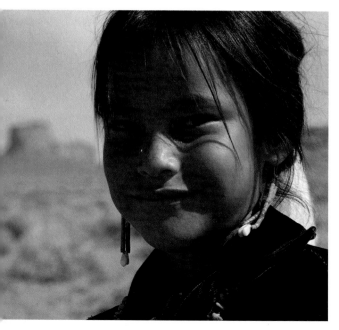

sional election and told his constituents "You can all go to hell, I'm going to Texas." And there he died.

You can see where the Spanish used to rule Texas at the **Spanish Governor's Palace,** a rather grim edifice dating back to 1749, still emblazoned with the Habsburg eagle of Spain's ruling family over the main entrance. The house is furnished with authentic pieces from the Spanish and Mexican eras.

You can also see the Mexicans' old adobe houses and stone patios in **La Villita,** the residential neighbourhood south of the river along Villita Street. For Mexican shopping, go to the old market place, El Mercado (515 W. Commerce).

The river is San Antonio's pride and joy. The **Paseo del Rio,** or River Walk, takes you nearly

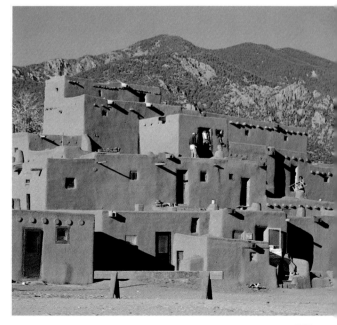

157

3 miles around a horseshoe curve through the town. Below the bustle of traffic, you can walk past banana plants and bougainvillea shading outdoor cafés and ice-cream parlours, nightclubs and craftware shops. Water-taxis and pedal-boats are available at the Market Street Bridge or take a candle-lit dinner on the pleasure barges.

The nicest museum in town is the **Hertzberg Circus Collection** (210 W. Market), part of the public library, where working models present a comprehensive history of the circus from its early days in England to the American heyday of the P. T. Barnum era. Clown costumes, Tom Thumb's dwarf carriage and a complete circus ring make a wonderfully nostalgic exhibition.

For a panoramic **view** of San Antonio and the surrounding country go out to **Hemis-Fair Plaza,** left over from the 1968 World's Fair, where there's an observatory on the 652-foot **Tower of the Americas.** The plaza is also the site of the **Institute of Texan Cultures,** devoted to the folklore of the 26 ethnic groups who have created the state of Texas—Germans, Hungarians, Poles and Irish among others, as well as the Mexicans and Indians.

Mission Road running south of town takes you out to the missions which were the basis of Spanish colonization in the 18th century, with Catholic priests converting the Indians to Christianity while a garrison of soldiers subdued the recalcitrant and searched for gold. **Mission San José** (5 miles south on U.S. Highway 281) is the best preserved of these spiritual and military installations. Founded in 1720, this "Queen of the Missions" has a Spanish Baroque entrance, once lovely, now spoiled by gunmen who have used it for target practice, and souvenir-hunters who have chipped away pieces of the sculpture. Inside, you can visit the soldiers' spartan quarters, the granary and Indians' workshops.

SANTA FE *(New Mexico)*

Founded by the Spanish in 1610, Santa Fe is the oldest capital city in the United States. The atmosphere in the historic centre of town, for all the invasion of hotels and souvenir shops, still gives a hint of that more leisurely Spanish and Indian era. The rose-coloured adobe structures with their *vigas*, log-beams holding up the ceilings and roofs, managing miraculously to be both solid and graceful in form, offer their shady arcades as a delightful shelter from the heat of the day.

The **Plaza** is the focus of old Santa Fe. On its north side is the Palace of the Governors, the oldest public building in the U.S. (1610), now housing part of the **Museum of New Mexico** devoted to the history and prehistory of the state. The arcade running along the façade of the palace is the preserve of Pueblo Indians selling handmade silver and turquoise jewellery (turquoise of good quality still coming in considerable quantities from the hills of New Mexico). Navajo and international folk art are displayed in annexes of the museum located along the old Santa Fe Trail.

Canyon Road, running along the south bank of the Santa Fe River, is the sleepy quarter where the painters, sculptors and craftsmen have their studios and galleries. Walk in and watch them work. The landscape artists tend to be the best, the ambient colour and light being such an inspiration.

The **Santa Fe Opera** is housed in a superb open-air setting, an amphitheatre carved out of the hillside (partially roofed in the unlikely event of rain) 7 miles north of town on the road to Taos.

TAOS *(New Mexico)*

Early this century, Taos was an art colony much beloved by English novelist D. H. Lawrence. It continues to attract many artists and their groupies, who live an easy hand-to-mouth existence just off the town **Plaza.** The town's colourful street life blends society's bohemian element with Taos Indians, Spanish-American

farmers and assorted sightseers. Back in the days of Spanish rule, Taos was the centre of the Pueblo Revolt (1680) which drove the Spaniards from New Mexico.

North of town, the **Taos Pueblo** is a centuries-old Indian village with 900 residents still inhabiting the sprawling five-storey apartment buildings—forerunner of modern America's condominiums. The jewellery, blankets and baskets sold here make good gifts.

At Ranchos de Taos, 4 miles south on Highway 68, the 1772 **San Francisco de Asis Mission** is the most attractive of the region's adobe churches. A sturdy, buttressed affair, it looks like a massive piece of sculpture.

PHOENIX *(Arizona)*

This may well be your starting point for the Grand Canyon. There are flights directly up to the Canyon or, if you like desert drives, rent your car here. One warning: drive within the 55 mph speed limit, the local highway patrol is very strict and the long straight roads encourage excess speeds. The most spectacular thing about Phoenix is its setting in the **Valley of the Sun,** the perfect backdrop to a Western movie, with the forbidding red Superstition Mountains to the east and towering Camelback Mountain north-east of town.

If you pass through Phoenix in summer, you may find that it's

159

just too hot to get out of your air-conditioned car. However, there are a couple of museums well worth visiting. **Heard Museum** (22 E. Monte Vista) is one of the best Indian museums in the country. It traces the history of the Indians of the South-West from the first cave-dwellers and Pueblo Indians —with a superb collection of Kachina dolls—to modern times. It is fascinating to observe in the Indian art of our era the continuity in forms and themes drawn from nature, fundamentally unchanged over the centuries.

The **Pueblo Grande Museum** (4619 E. Washington) is an on-site archaeological excavation of a Hohokam Indian settlement believed to date back some 2,000 years. The ruins, spread across a broad mound, mark out a civilization that disappeared with the Hohokam around the year 1400.

You might like to prepare yourself for the flora you'll see on your desert drive with a visit to the **Desert Botanical Gardens,** 3 miles east of Pueblo Grande. They give a good idea of the marvellous variety of species in the world's cacti.

THE GRAND CANYON

This is one place where you cannot rely on a writer or photographer to show you what it's like. No picture, no words ever matched the reality of the Grand Canyon's beauty. You have to see

it for yourself. You'll see it and still won't believe it. There's a moment when nature combines magnitude with light, colour and texture to silence and humble man into simple contemplation. That moment will come when you approach the **South Rim** of the 277-mile-long serpentine canyon. Look down to its mile-deep floor where the mighty Colorado River has eroded a passage and millions of years of earth upheavals have gouged out a theatre for the performance of grand geological drama.

Plan your trip to the Grand Canyon like a military operation. There are camping facilities and hotels on the North Rim but that's really for *habitués.* First-timers should concentrate on the South Rim. Whether you want to camp or lodge in the hotels and cabins of **Grand Canyon Village,** make reservations well in advance. The Park Headquarters at Grand Canyon Village provides information about the bus tours of the main Rim Drive, bicycling around the rim, hiking or riding mules down to the canyon floor or rubber rafting along the Colorado River. Hiking and riding mules are for the hardy who are prepared to rise at dawn, face high temperatures at noon and generally rough it. Rafting is a

The Grand Canyon

spectacular way of seeing the canyon and perfectly safe in the hands of experienced guides, with good picnic and camping facilities en route. Another spectacular view of the canyon can be had on a helicopter flight into the heart of the canyon — best at dawn.

The **Visitors Center** at Grand Canyon Village is a must for initial orientation. The rangers here and at key spots along the Rim Drive provide fascinating information on the geology, flowers, animal life and anthropological history — on Indians whose dwellings, built into the canyon cliffs, are still visible today on the North Rim.

There are some wonderful **nature trails** which the rangers will show you up on the rim through forests of juniper and piñon pine. Every now and again you emerge in a clearing on the edge of the canyon to peer down at the giant mounds or buttes rising like Egyptian pyramids or Aztec temples, and indeed bearing such names as Zoroaster Temple or Cheops Pyramid. Some of the other fanciful rock formations bear such prosaic names as The Battleship or, more ominously, Skeleton Point and the Phantom Ranch, suggesting the fate of hikers who didn't take enough drinking water.

Free buses shuttle along the 8-mile **West Rim** (closed to private cars from May 1 to September 1)

stopping off for superb views at Hopi Point, Mohave Point and Pina Point. Other buses pass frequently and will pick you up if you get out and walk a while.

If you do decide to hike, the best for beginners is the **Bright Angel Trail,** leaving from Bright Angel Lodge. Start at daybreak, count on a good three hours down, six or seven hours back uphill. It zigzags down 1½ miles to a first resthouse (with telephone), another 1½ miles to the Jacob's Ladder resthouse, still zigzagging and then straightening out to the beautiful **Indian Garden** at Garden Creek. This is a ranger station and campground where you can stay overnight. Beginners head back, stalwart hikers continue the next day along Garden Creek around the self-explanatory **Devil's Corkscrew** down Pipe Creek to the River Resthouse beside the Colorado River. A more challenging hike is the steeper **Kaibab Trail** from the Yaki Point Road east of the village. The joy of the hikes, of course, is that they do take you away from the madding crowd of the Rim Drive.

But everywhere in and around the Grand Canyon you can always walk a hundred yards further and enjoy this phenomenon alone. In a country as people-conscious as America, the Canyon is the ideal place to take time off from your fellow man.

THE WEST COAST

The West Coast is America's most varied playground, catering to the crazy, the lazy, the swinging bachelors and the easy-going families. Only those in search of the hectic are discouraged—on *this* coast nobody rushes. While Las Vegas carries the madness inland to the desert, Seattle on the north Pacific coast introduces a note of sanity in its healthy green state of Washington.

But these are the appendages to the American mecca of all dreamers, European and American alike—California. A land blessed with sun and sea and oranges and ice-cream, California is quite simply the ultimate fantasy land. It is as far west as Western man can go without starting to go east. Stand on the beach at Malibu, stare out at the Pacific or back at the Santa Monica mountains and everything seems possible: balmy winters, shining summers, snow if you want it.

It's no accident that this is the chosen home of America's cinema. California offers every imaginable landscape, for any story, any dream you can think up—Swiss Alps, Sahara Desert, English meadows, African jungle, it's all just a few miles from the freeway. And what isn't already there—a Roman forum or Egyptian pyramid—can be built in a few days with the great wealth that California has amassed in a civilized history of little more than a century.

Its prosperity is truly overwhelming, and constantly renewed—beginning with the gold of the Sierras, spreading across the great Central Valley to the gigantic combines of agribusiness (mere agriculture was just a passing phase), and on to the coast for oil and the aerospace industry. Californians are perfectly prepared to work and work hard, but they can't wait to get back to the tennis court or swimming pool, go surfing in the Pacific or hiking in Yosemite.

In constant quest of the new, in clothes, music, ideas, toys and religions, the people cling to their joyously accepted role as America's latest pioneers. Hula-hoop, skate-board, wind-surfing, roller-disco—it all starts, flourishes and fizzles out in California, while the rest of the world takes note and, more often than not, follows suit. Tough-as-iron blue jeans began life in San Francisco to withstand the wear and tear of the 1849 Gold Rush and then became the universal unisex clothing of the last half of our century. Flimsy-as-gossamer bikinis made their first appearance on the beaches of Southern California to attract as much sun and attention as possible. With a few modifications and abbreviations, their principle of merry exhibitionism has survived.

Many Californians would like to divide their state into two new separate entities, North and South California—corresponding to two distinct frames of mind represented by San Francisco and Los Angeles. But in fact there's a little bit of both—San Francisco's sophistication and Los Angeles' sunny craziness—all over the place.

Our itinerary begins in San Francisco and its nearby wine valleys and works its way down the Pacific coast to Los Angeles and San Diego before taking off for the national parks of Yosemite, Sequoia and Death Valley National Monument. You can turn this itinerary upside down, but either way, if you have the time, you should also make an excursion to California's favourite out-of-state playground—Las Vegas.

You can get to almost all these places by train or bus, and air travel is relatively cheap compared with the rest of the country, and a great bargain compared with Europe. However, California is inevitably the land of the car and it will be difficult for you to enjoy the full scope of the vast and varied landscape without driving. San Francisco is a town for walking, with buses and cable cars to help you up and down the hills, but Los Angeles is resolutely a drivers' town. Yosemite and Sequoia are splendid for hiking.

SAN FRANCISCO
(California)

San Franciscans are unashamedly in love with their town. All over the place you see the boast: "Everybody's Favorite City". The town's natural setting, nestling in the hills around the bay, make it uncommonly cosy, the zip in the air is invigorating and even the fog rolling off the ocean is romantic rather than chilling. The pervasive enthusiasm of the residents is difficult to resist. Just one tip: if you're thinking of showing your new-won familiarity with the city by calling it "Frisco", don't. It makes real San Franciscans shudder.

If you have a car, the best way to begin your visit is to take the **49 Mile Scenic Drive,** a comprehensive tour that gives you an overall picture before you start to explore in detail. Stop off at **Twin Peaks,** south of Golden Gate Park, for a panoramic view of the city and its bay.

Then put away the car and use the city's first-class public transport and a pair of good walking shoes. Start at the bridge. There are more than one, but *the* bridge is of course the **Golden Gate Bridge.** It is, in fact, not golden but a deep burnt sienna or reddish-brown, depending on the light; the masterpiece of engineer Joseph Strauss. At 4,200 feet, it's not the longest, but few would deny it's the most beautiful suspension bridge in the world. Completed in 1937, it took four years to build and now takes four years to repaint—a job that begins again as soon as it's finished. Walking across the bridge is as exciting an urban adventure as climbing the Eiffel Tower or the Empire State Building. The bridge sways beneath your feet and the lampposts rattle as the wind whistles through the swooping cables.

(While you're here, spare a thought for the far from unattractive **Oakland Bay Bridge** just visible in the distance. The silvery bridge swings across to Oakland via Yerba Buena island and at 8¼ miles is one of the world's longest. It's the bridge you'll take to Berkeley.)

South of the Golden Gate Bridge is the **Presidio,** site of the original garrison, built by the Spanish to protect their settlement in 1776. It is now the headquarters of the Sixth Army and remarkably green and pretty for a military establishment.

On your way down to the Yacht Harbor, you'll pass the **Palace of Fine Arts,** a weird rebuilt relic (the original was chicken wire and plaster) from the 1915 Panama-Pacific Exposition. The exterior, a hodge-podge of classical architecture and reinforced-concrete "Roman ruin", contrasts with the modern technological wizardry of the Exploratorium museum in-

> ### The Cable Caper
> *One delightful way of coping with San Francisco's hills is aboard the fabled cable cars. It's clearly one of the most enjoyable rides imaginable. Especially standing on the outside step—dangerous but legal—hanging on for your life as the Powell Street car clangs up and down Nob Hill, with the sights passing by in slow but bumpy motion.*
>
> *The cable cars were first installed in 1873 and one of the originals can be seen in the museum, which is also the system's fascinating working centre at Washington and Mason streets. The handmade cars are constantly being refurbished and overhauled, so don't be surprised if one or another of the cable-lines is not in service.*
>
> *By the way, you're not allowed on with an ice-cream, because the bone-shaking ride would almost certainly land it on the lap of a fellow passenger.*

side. What with holography, lasers, solar-operated musical instruments, it's great for the kids on a rainy day.

From the western Yacht Harbor make your way along Marina Boulevard, past its fine waterfront houses, to **Fisherman's Wharf.** Stroll around, look at the boats and nibble shrimp or crab from the seafood stands along the wharf. It's also a major centre for

the revival of street theatre and music that seems to have caught on all over the world. Check out the delightful shopping centres, **Ghirardelli Square,** a converted red-brick chocolate factory, and **The Cannery,** once a fruit processing plant. Both now include a variety of attractive shops and restaurants.

The Hills

There are 40 of them, and they're San Francisco's pride and challenge but you don't have to tackle them all. A tour of Nob Hill (Powell or California Street cable car), Telegraph Hill (bus) and Russian Hill (cable car) will give you a good sense of the past and present splendours of San Francisco's wealthy, many of whom have preferred to stay in the city.

The monumental Victorian houses of **Nob Hill,** where the "nobs" or nabobs lived, were wiped out in the 1906 earthquake—with one notable exception: the imposing brownstone house of James Flood, now the highly exclusive Pacific Union Club. You can't get in there, but you can loiter (with appropriate decorum) in the hill's two landmark hotels—the Fairmont and Mark Hopkins. Each has a panoramic bar and the stiff price you pay for a drink in either of them is worth it for the view.

Oakland Bay Bridge

167

The best reason for climbing **Telegraph Hill** is to see the other hills from the top of Coit Tower. Built in 1934 to honour the city's fire department, its shape is meant to resemble the nozzle of a fire hose.

Russian Hill may be less obviously opulent than the other two hills, but its gardens and immaculate little cottages make it the most appealing. The constant ups and downs of the city's streets reach a crazy climax on **Lombard Street,** between Hyde and Leavenworth. After you've negotiated the incredible serpentine plunge, weaving in and out of backyards and around seven sudden bends, you're not going to quibble about its claim to be the "crookedest street in the world".

Downtown
North Beach is not a beach at all. It's the district north of the Broadway and Columbus intersection that is both centre of the Italian community and focus of the city's artistic and intellectual life. Before the earthquake, part of it was known as the "Barbary Coast", an infamous den of iniquity where sailors came for the brothels, while their captains shanghaied drunken or otherwise unconscious civilians for their crews.

Since the 1950s when poet Lawrence Ferlinghetti gathered his fellow beatniks around his City Lights Bookshop, North Beach has been the place where California's new ideas, intellectual and other, are first tried out. The few relatively literate hippies of the '60s congregated here to escape the mindless nonsense of Haight-Ashbury. In the '70s it was the turn of the "mellows", the smiling younger brothers and sisters of the hippies, gliding around on quiet roller skates, eating frozen yoghurt and espousing low-risk ecological causes. Whatever trend emerges for the '80s, a couple of Grant Avenue coffee shops have survived to offer you ringside seats to watch it all begin.

The Italian neighbourhood, clustered around Columbus, Stockton, Vallejo and Green streets, is crammed with small grocery stores, pastry shops, espresso bars and cafés and restaurants redolent of garlic and tomato sauce. But the seedy tradition of the Barbary Coast lives on in the flourishing "topless" and "bottomless" joints on Broadway —San Francisco's gift to the Western world.

Chinatown has evolved from a ghetto imposed on the Chinese in the 19th century by the founders of the city into a proud, self-assertive community. Gone are the days of the Tong wars for control of the community's underworld and opium dens. The vicarious thrill that those adventures provided has now been replaced by a general civic pride, especially among San Franciscan gourmets. More than 80,000 Chinese live in San Francisco, making it the largest Chinese community outside Asia. The main neighbourhood is bounded by Broadway, Bush, Kearny and Stockton, with eight blocks of Grant Avenue as its colourful centre.

An ornamental arch at the Bush Street end of Grant marks the entry to Chinatown. Flanking it are two hamburger houses of Chinese design. Beyond the arch, life is more resolutely Chinese. The restaurants, grocery, porcelain and silk shops display English translations alongside the Chinese signs, but banks and travel agencies don't always make the same concession.

On a smaller scale, but with the same cultural pride, is **Japan Town**—J-Town to San Franciscans. Its Cultural and Trade Center at Geary between Laguna and Fillmore streets includes schools of cookery and Japanese flower arrangement, a Japanese theatre and a hotel with Japanese amenities—sunken baths, mattresses on *tatami* mats, kimonoed maids and indoor rock gardens.

After which you might want to remind yourself of America's dominant culture, the Anglo-Saxon variety. In the wedge formed by Market Street, the city's main thoroughfare, and Van Ness Street you will find a sprawling complex of municipal, state and federal buildings, known collectively as the **Civic Center.** It was initiated in an ambitious burst of city planning after the 1906 earthquake, and the early structures—note especially the gold-domed City Hall and the handsome Main Public Library—are in Renaissance style. Also part of the complex are the twin Veterans' Building (housing the San Francisco Museum of Modern Art) and Opera House, where the United Nations Charter was signed in 1945.

For a shopping detour, work your way down Market Street and turn off at Powell. **Union Square** is the place to go for fashionable boutiques, speciality shops, flower stands and large department stores. Continue on to Montgomery Street, the heart of San Francisco's financial district, also known as the "Wall Street of the West". Here, in the home of the Gold Rush heirs, take a look at the **Old Coin and Gold Exhibit** of the Bank of California (400 California Street). You're not likely to miss the **Transamerica Pyramid,** an 853-foot spike at the corner of Montgomery and Washington streets. It's one of those buildings that purists start off hating for its clash with the "spirit" of San Francisco and then defend in the next generation as the epitome of its age.

Golden Gate Park

Away from the skyscrapers of downtown, take the bus to get to Golden Gate Park. Originally nothing but sand dunes, it was turned into its present lush parkland quite by chance—or so the story goes—when 19th-century urban planner John McLaren accidentally dropped the oats from his horse's nosebag and they sprouted. McLaren carried on from there and today San Franciscans have a delightful landscape of small lakes and hills, an arboretum, botanical gardens, playing fields, stables and a popular open-air chess hang-out. At the eastern end of the park there's a superb children's playground and one relic of the Haight-Ashbury district's 1960s flower children, Hippy Hill (between Kezar, South and Kennedy Drive), where teenagers still loll in the sun. (Haight-Ashbury, east of the park, is depressingly not worth a visit, except for the sociologically inclined.)

The park includes three major museums clustered around the Music Concourse. The **M.H. de Young Memorial Museum** has some Old Masters in its permanent collection but is better known as host to important travelling exhibitions. The **Asian Art Museum** next door contains the rich Avery Brundage collection and the **California Academy of Sciences** houses a zoological museum, an

aquarium and a planetarium. Afterwards, you can rest in the lovely **Japanese Tea Garden.**

There's a splendid panorama of the Pacific at the imposing **Palace of the Legion of Honor,** a striking copy of the one in Paris. The exhibition of French art inside includes an excellent group of Rodin sculptures. To enjoy the ocean go down to Ocean Beach.

Alcatraz

Of the many cruises you can take on San Francisco Bay the most entertaining (from Pier 41, near Fisherman's Wharf) is out to the abandoned prison of Alcatraz. The U.S. Rangers conduct informative and witty tours of the old home of Al Capone and other convicts too hot for normal prisons to hold. Alcatraz—the name comes from the Spanish Isla de los Alcotraces (Isle of Pelicans)—is a 12-acre rock with no arable soil. All the water for the shrubs and trees growing here today had to be brought by the U.S. Army, for whom it was a "disciplinary barracks" until 1934. One and a half miles of ice-cold treacherous currents, sharks and raw sewage separate Alcatraz from the San Francisco shore. It was the ideal location for America's most notorious federal civil penitentiary, but enormously expensive in upkeep. In 1963, with each inmate costing $40,000 a year, they closed it down.

Getting Away from it All
Officially, nobody ever got away safely from Alcatraz. In all 39 tried, seven were killed in the attempt, and five have never been found but are assumed drowned.

In 1962, at the very end of Alcatraz's grim history, John Paul Scott made it unharmed to San Francisco by greasing his body to resist the cold. Some students found him exhausted at Fort Point by the Golden Gate Bridge. Good-naturedly, not knowing he was an escaped prisoner, they called the police to help the poor fellow in his moment of distress.

EXCURSIONS

The Bay Area

Immediately north of San Francisco are the two charming little harbour towns of **Sausalito** and **Tiburon,** which you can reach either by car across the Golden Gate Bridge or by ferry (from the Ferry Building for Sausalito or Pier 43½ for Tiburon). With Tiburon the quieter of the two, the towns have a colourful Mediterranean atmosphere, with a number of boutiques and pleasant bistros and cafés out on the boardwalk looking across the bay to San Francisco.

Sausalito and Tiburon are at the southern tip of the Californian phenomenon of Marin

County, home of hot tubs, Jacuzzi whirlpool baths and other sensual delights of communal living, spearhead of mellow fellowship. The perpetrators are not freaks, at least not any more, they've grown into lawyers and investment bankers.

The Wine Country

Wine-lovers will enjoy a drive through the vineyard of **Napa Valley** and across the Maacama Mountains to Sonoma. Bus tours are available and it's a good idea to contact an agency specializing in wine tours. The wineries, as they call themselves, provide tours and tastings in the cellars and organize picnics in the vineyards. Harvests begin around mid-August — Californian weather being so much more predictably sunny than in Europe.

Some of the more interesting wineries are at Sterling, where you visit the vineyard by aerial tramway across the valley, and at Mondavi, Martini, Beaulieu and Beringer in Napa, and at Souverain and Sebastiani in Sonoma. Homesick Frenchmen may want to visit the Domaine Chandon in Napa, owned by Moët et Chandon. Important tip: avoid Tuesdays because, following a tradition of the French national museums, with which some would like to be compared, most of the best restaurants of the region are closed.

California Vintage

California is proud of its wines and for good reason. Wine-growers have refined and matured their techniques and improved the honesty of their marketing. In the old days, the wineries churned out red and white wines that they indiscriminately labelled "Burgundy" and "Chablis".

Now with a nationwide interest for good wine increasing every year, as well as international appreciation, California wine-growers are taking more care.

Generally, wines are distinguished by labels specifying the varieties of European grapes from which they were grown. The reds include Cabernet Sauvignon *from the French Médoc,* Pinot Noir *from Burgundy and* Zinfandel, *whose origin puzzles the experts. (Some believe it to be Italian, but you won't find it outside California.) The most important whites are* Chardonnay *from Burgundy,* Sauvignon Blanc *from Bordeaux,* Gewürztraminer *and* Riesling *from Alsace, the German Mosel and Rhineland. The vintage displayed on the labels of these wines represents the authentic year of at least 95 per cent of the wine in the bottle.*

All these improvements have meant an inevitable increase in price, but Californian wines now hold their own with French, German and Italian ones.

PACIFIC COAST

Take Freeway 101 south from San Francisco and join Pacific Highway, Route 1, at Castroville, to get to **Monterey,** the old Spanish and Mexican capital of Alta (Upper) California. The bay was discovered in 1542 but was not settled until 1770 when Father Junipero Serra set up a mission here with the garrison protection of Gaspar de Portola's presidio. Monterey was a bleak, disease-ridden place and Portola recommended it be handed over to the Russians, who also coveted it, "as a punishment". But Father Serra accepted the hardships and led the taming of the Monterey wilderness. His statue looks down on the bay from Corporal Ewin Road.

The town is proud of its past and offers a sign-posted tour of the Old Town's historic buildings from the 19th-century Mexican administration and early American period. The architecture is a strange mixture of Spanish adobe and American colonial clapboard, two storeys with a balcony; an attractive enough hybrid to earn it the name of "Monterey style". At the Chamber of Commerce, on Alvarado Street, you can get a map showing the major houses.

Look for the **Larkin House** at Jefferson and Calle Principal, home of the first (and only) U.S. Consul in the 1840s, and the **Robert Louis Stevenson House,** 530 Houston Street, where the writer lived while he was working on *Treasure Island*. On Church Street you'll find the site of Father Serra's original baked-mud church; rebuilt in 1795, it's now the **Royal Presidio Chapel** or Cathedral of San Carlos de Borromeo. To the left of the altar is a colourful 18th-century Virgin Mary from Spanish Mexico.

Nearer the waterfront are the Pacific House, on Custom House Plaza, with a pleasant, flowery and tree-shaded arcaded courtyard, and the Custom House (1827), taken over as the first U.S. federal building on the Pacific coast. Casa del Oro, at Scott and Oliver, is said to have been a storehouse for gold.

More distinctively American is **California's First Theater** on Scott and Pacific streets, a pinewood shack built by one Jack Swan in 1847 as a saloon with a dubious boarding house upstairs. Customers were attracted—and still are—by Victorian melodramas, but the "boarding house" no longer operates.

Fisherman's Wharf, like San Francisco's, is a collection of

Big Sur, California

175

shops and restaurants out on the dock, but offering a more intimate view of the boats of the marina. The fish here are almost always fresh, but not abundant enough to keep Cannery Row going as more than a weather-beaten curiosity. The sardine fisheries closed down in the 1940s—for lack of sardines—and today the timbered canneries made famous by novelist John Steinbeck as "a poem, a stink, a grating noise" have been turned into restaurants, boutiques and art galleries.

The 17-Mile Drive takes you down to **Carmel,** a delightful resort and artists' colony, ideal for a rest, a suntan and some serious shopping and gallery hopping. Despite the golden light and the Spanish-style adobe houses, this immaculate tree-lined town with its leisurely, discreet atmosphere will remind you more of New England than of the California coast.

South-east of the town is the **Carmel Mission,** Basílica San Carlos Borromeo de Carmelo. Its restoration has been admirably carried out and its peacefulness is the perfect complement to the tranquillity of the town. Father Serra is buried here.

The **coast road** from Carmel to Big Sur is only 30 miles long, but it takes more than an hour of careful driving. And every hairpin turn of the road opens up another spectacular vista of forest, hills and sea.

Big Sur and the Pfeiffer-Big Sur State Park offer marvellous opportunities for picnics, camping, hiking and fishing in the Big Sur River. This was the home of writer Henry Miller. Other artists lived here and you'll find it a great place to escape the crowd. Back on the coast, Orson Welles built a redwood honeymoon cottage for Rita Hayworth in the days when film stars did the romantic things expected of them. Now it has been expanded into a restaurant, worth a visit for its matchless view of the ocean, if nothing else.

The rugged shoreline road continues down 65 more miles to where William Randolph Hearst, the man Orson Welles immortalized in *Citizen Kane*, built his unbelievable dream castle at **San Simeon** (guided tours organized by the State Department of Parks and Recreations).

The thing is total fantasy. Nothing real could look like a Spanish cathedral, a Roman palace and a Gothic castle at the same time. Hearst himself referred to the 123 acres of castle, guesthouse *palazzi*, terraces, gardens, Roman baths, private zoo and tennis courts as "the Ranch". Building began in 1919 and was still not completed when Hearst died in 1951.

The 275,000-acre estate lies 1,600 feet up in the hills. After parking your car in the lot, you take a tour bus which drives past zebras, barbary sheep and goats grazing on the slopes, remnants of Hearst's private zoo.

San Francisco architect Julia Morgan built "the Ranch" to Hearst's specifications as a "functional showcase" for his art collection. The incredible mixture of that collection begins to register as you pass the 100-foot swimming pool with its Greek colonnade and a copy of Donatello's Florentine statue of David standing on two authentic 17th-century Baroque Venetian fountains that Hearst had joined together. A Roman sarcophagus and 3,500-year-old Egyptian goddess are both genuine, but the "Ranch House" façade, its equestrian friezes on the balcony and Gothic canopies are made of reinforced concrete. Over the gigantic main entrance, in quiet simplicity, is a (genuine) 13th-century Madonna and Child.

Inside, the hodge-podge runs riot. A vestibule with a 60 B.C. Pompeian mosaic floor leads to a salon with 15th-century Flemish tapestries over Italian choir stalls behind sofas that have 1930s slip-covers borrowing motifs from the tapestries. The dining room has a magnificent cedarwood coffer ceiling from a Bologna monastery and is decorated with the flags from the Sienna *palio* pageant.

LOS ANGELES
(California)

Los Angeles is the quintessential 20th-century creation. Only modern technology could have turned this desert into one of the most flourishing metropolises on earth. Engineering genius brought water hundreds of miles across mountains and deserts to feed the city and its industry and nurture its lush gardens. The fabled freeway system arrived in time to link the people scattered across its vast area and create the burgeoning monster that never ceases to astonish.

People who don't know it complain that Los Angeles is nothing but a bunch of suburbs looking for a city. The cliché is not so much untrue as irrelevant. When you visit the various neighbourhoods and townships that make up greater Los Angeles—Hollywood, Westwood, Santa Monica, Malibu, and dozens more—you find that nobody's looking for a city, they know where they are. Up in the hills, down at the beach, in the valley, around the university campus, they're all integral parts of Los Angeles. It is not a city in the traditional sense of a downtown urban core interacting with surrounding neighbourhoods, outskirts and suburbs. LA is more a state of mind. And a huge state of mind at that, covering 460 square miles, bounded by sea and sand to the west, mountains to the north and east and desert to the south, all topped off by an almost permanent canopy of sun. With all these possibilities, it's not surprising that leisure and pleasure are worshipped here.

"The Beach"

The beach (Angelenos always refer to it in the singular) stretches some 40 miles from Malibu through Santa Monica, Venice,

Marina del Rey, Hermosa and Redondo to Palos Verdes before the white sands hit the pollution of Los Angeles Harbour and the Long Beach shipyards. And there's no better way to get the special feel of Los Angeles than to go straight down there. In LA, beaches are not just resorts for holidays and weekend cottages, they are year-round residential areas.

Malibu is the favoured beach home of the more relaxed members of the film community. Rather than barricade themselves behind electric fences guarded by Doberman pinschers as they do in Bel Air and Beverly Hills, film stars and hot young directors can be seen jogging along the sands or shopping for yoghurt and diet drinks in the supermarket. Malibu Lagoon's Surfrider Beach attracts champion surfers from all over the world. Sunning and swimming are a little more peaceful down at Las Tunas and Topanga. Malibu Pier is a good place to fish. The one hazard disturbing Malibu's sunny peace is the occasional "cat's paw" tide or mountain landslide that washes the handsome beach houses into the Pacific.

Santa Monica is built on more solid ground, and its beaches are more of a family affair. But it's neighbouring **Venice** that attracts all the attention. The beach and beach-park here are a non-stop open-air amateur circus of freaks, acrobats, weight-lifters, clowns and jugglers entertaining themselves quite as much as the passing crowd. In 1892, millionaire Albert Kinney had wanted to set down on the Pacific coast a replica of Italy's Venice, complete with canals, gondolas, a *palazzo* or two, hotels and amusement arcades. Then somebody discovered oil and the idea was abandoned. Four canals remain with a couple of sad attempts at a Bridge of Sighs, but the neighbourhood has revived as a bouncing bohemian community of serious artists and happy-go-lucky oddballs.

Movieland

London buries its heroes in Westminster Abbey, Paris puts great Frenchmen to rest in the Pantheon, and Los Angeles offers the hand, foot and hoof prints of its stars in the cement courtyard of **Mann's Chinese Theater** (at 6925 Hollywood Boulevard). Start your pilgrimage here. Sid Grauman had the idea in 1927 of getting the immortals' prints when they attended gala premières at his great exotic cinema. Most stars followed the example of Mary Pickford, the Marx Brothers and Rita Hayworth: they got down on their knees and made a hand print. But it was natural for Fred Astaire to leave a foot print, and cowboy Tom Mix preferred leaving the hoof print of his horse. If you go to see a film in LA—and it would seem silly not to, like not eating in Paris—go to one of the old preposterous movie palaces like the Chinese or the Egyptian across the street. The outrageous pagoda and Theban-temple décors may be better than the film.

Walk along **Hollywood Boulevard**—one of the parts of LA where walking is customary—and you'll see over 2,500 actors' names on bronze stars embedded in the pavement. The street itself is less scintillating—rundown shops and pizza parlours—but the second-hand bookstores are excellent. You'll pass Hollywood Professional School where babes hardly out of the cradle were turned into the likes of Mickey Rooney and Judy Garland. Between La Brea and Western Avenue, the boulevard has the fine, tacky splendour of the 1920s and '30s, with its low, flat stucco buildings and a droopy palm tree or two; even pre-war Packards and Buicks parked on the street.

A few blocks north of the boulevard is **Hollywood Bowl, the** splendid open-air auditorium where the Los Angeles Philharmonic Orchestra holds concerts against a background of the gigantic illuminated letters of H-O-L-L-Y-W-O-O-D, planted up in the hills.

South of Hollywood Boulevard is LA's most famous street, **Sunset Boulevard.** The Hollywood section is known simply as "The Strip". It's where people cruise up and down in convertibles looking at each other, a street of sleazy nightclubs and cheap motels side by side with hip boutiques and elegant restaurants.

One of the most enjoyable Hollywood trips is a **tour of the film and television studios.** The major TV networks (CBS, NBC, ABC) welcome you onto the sets for a look behind the scenes of some of America's most popular shows. A limited number of tickets to live shows are available on request. Universal Studios (Lankershim Boulevard, north of the Hollywood Freeway) offers an elaborate tour in open trolleys with guides who have all the hokum and show-biz flair of Hollywood itself. Participating in the special effects trickery, you'll be attacked by spaceships and the shark from *Jaws* and generally be subjected to all the avalanches, flash floods and fires you ever saw in a disaster film. You'll visit sound-stages, back-lots and dressing rooms and learn the screen techniques of back-projection, blue-screen and matting used to create film's great illusions. You'll see how Moses parted the waters of the Red Sea in *The Ten Commandments* and ride through a "town" that includes a New England fishing village, a Bavarian square, French bistros and an Italian pizzeria, all in the space of four blocks.

Beverly Hills is exclusive and assertively separate from Los Angeles. The streets are lined with Rolls Royces and Bentleys and the architecture of the mansions is an astounding mixture of Spanish, Gothic, Bauhaus and Renaissance, in every pastel shade.

The town is phenomenally clean and litter is almost a capital crime. It's policed with formidable efficiency and, except for in the great shopping streets such as Rodeo Drive, walking is viewed with suspicion, especially at night. If you do want to take a walk here, put on tennis or jogging clothes and the police will assume you're a sportsman. Only burglars, it seems, walk around Beverly Hills in normal clothes.

Downtown

Downtown Los Angeles is not a place you need to spend too much time in. But the **Music Center** (at First Street and Grand) is important for concerts and plays at the Dorothy Chandler Pavilion, the Mark Taper Forum and Ahmanson Theater. The colourful Mexican life of the city is best enjoyed at **Grand Central Market,** north of Pershing Square. (The other great food market is Farmer's Market, west of Beverly Hills at Fairfax and Third.)

Watts, besides being famous as the black neighbourhood of Los Angeles that erupted in violent anger in 1965, offers one of the city's more bizarre and somehow exhilarating monuments, the **Watts Tower** (1765 East 107th Street, off the Harbor Freeway). In 1921 a tile-setter named Simon Rodia started to erect three tapering towers of coloured pottery shards, sea shells, glass and pebbles cemented to frames of scrap steel and baling wire. When he'd raised the towers 104 feet, 33 years later, he announced that he'd achieved his ambition "to do something big" and walked away, never to be heard of again.

Disneyland

Anaheim (27 miles south-east of downtown LA on the Santa Ana Freeway) is the home of Disneyland. Since 1955, Walt Disney and his successors have been dispensing the good clean pleasures of a make-believe world inspired by the sweet uplifting fantasies of his films. Applying the techniques of the cinema and advanced electronics technology, Disney takes you around his smiling Technicoloured "theme-park" on a daylong outing that is simply stupefying in scope and impact. You buy a book of tickets, each of which entitles you to "ride" through the various "themes".

Main Street sets the tone with its sunny evocation of small-town

U.S.A. at the turn of the century. You may notice that all the houses and shops are three-quarter size. In this effort to escape from the realities of the outside world, everything is a little smaller than life. **Adventureland** is a boat ride through simulated jungle foliage on a river that passes successively through Asia, Africa and the South Pacific, complete with plastic tigers and alligators, stuffed elephants and hairy gorillas that emit tape-recorded roars and beat their chests. A miniature railroad takes you through **Frontierland,** the pioneer country of the Old West where a loudspeaker warns you to "watch out for Indians and wild animals". Just the faintest uneasiness is aroused by a settler's cabin on fire with a wax-model pioneer lying outside, killed by an Indian's arrow. But at the end of each ride are ice-cream and soft-drinks stands. One of the most exciting themes is **Tomorrowland,** constantly being renovated to keep pace with progress. The rides include a submarine, a spaceship to Mars and the most up-to-date experiments in public transport such as the monorail and People Mover whizzing around the whole exhibition.

Museums

A sensational convergence of art and architecture adorns downtown Los Angeles. The understated red-sandstone building of the **Museum of Contemporary Art** (MOCA) at California Plaza displays works by 20th-century masters like Jasper Johns, Willem de Kooning, Jackson Pollock and Frank Stella.

The **Norton Simon Museum** at Pasadena (Orange Grove and Colorado, off the Ventura Freeway) is where Simon put together in two decades a remarkable collection of European paintings, drawings and sculpture from the early Renaissance to the 20th century, along with Indian bronzes and Asian stone carvings.

The **J. Paul Getty Museum** (17985 W. Pacific Coast Highway, Malibu—call ahead 454-6541 for reserved parking in the museum garage) is somewhere between the Norton Simon collection and Hearst Castle. The Malibu museum is a painstaking replica of the Villa dei Papiri (excavated

from volcanic mud left by Mount Vesuvius in A.D. 79), complete with mosaics, geometric gardens and Corinthian colonnades (of plastered concrete).

The collection of antiquities is impressive, highlighted by "the Getty bronze", a 4th-century B.C. statue of an Olympic champion, believed by some experts to be the only existing work of Lysippus, court sculptor to Alexander the Great. The paintings include works by Raphael, Rubens, Van Dyck and Rembrandt.

SAN DIEGO *(California)*

This is where California's history began, where Juan Rodríguez Cabrillo, a Portuguese captain, first set foot on Californian soil in 1542. Sixty years later, its bay was explored for Spanish galleons to stop off at on their way to and from the South Pacific, but it wasn't until 1769 that Father Serra built his first mission. Today, San Diego is California's second largest city after Los Angeles.

The best way to appreciate San Diego's beauty is from the sea. Take a **cruise** along the bay—they start from Harbor Drive at the end of Broadway—past the man-made Harbor and Shelter islands around the tip of the peninsula to Point Loma out on the Pacific. The fishing, sailing and U.S. Navy vessels make a splendidly varied skyline along the shore.

Back on dry land, you can visit one of the 19th-century ships moored on the Embarcadero as part of the Maritime Museum Fleet, the most picturesque being the iron-hulled square rigger, *Star of India,* built in 1863. Or drop into Seaport Village, a lively complex of shops, restaurants and galleries.

San Diego's discoverer is celebrated by the **Cabrillo National Monument** on the Point Loma promontory (follow the signs south-west on Rosecrans Street). Cabrillo's statue, donated by the Portuguese government, faces the spot at which he landed.

Old Town (bounded by Juan, Twiggs, Congress and Wallace streets) is a six-block area of restored adobe buildings from the city's Mexican era, plus the brick houses of early American settlers. You'll enjoy a rest under the palms and eucalyptus trees of Plaza Vieja, originally the centre and bullring of the old pueblo. More restoration is under way in the Gaslamp Quarter, a mostly Victorian neighbourhood.

The modern town is blessed with enlightened urban planning —and the superb **Balboa Park.** Set right in the centre of town, the park offers a wealth of sports facilities and many of the city's cultural attractions. There's an Elizabethan playhouse, site of the summer Shakespeare festival, and running the gamut from space and science to natural history and fine arts.

But the star of the park is the **San Diego Zoo,** justly acclaimed as one of the world's finest. Certainly it's one of the most humane, giving the animals as large, free and natural a living space as possible in the confines of a manmade park. The collection of animals is particularly strong in Australian species. You can fly over the zoo in the Skyfari aerial tramway or take a guided tour by bus.

Another great park is at **Mission Bay,** offering first class aquatic facilities. Paddle around tiny islands and lagoons in canoes, or sail in catamarans and full-size sloops. It is also the home of **Sea World,** where you will see the famous 3-ton killer whale, performing sharks and skating penguins, not to mention dextrous dolphins and an otter circus— sheer entertainment mixing scares and laughs for everyone.

NATIONAL PARKS

The best times of the year for Yosemite and Sequoia are spring and autumn, but there isn't a bad time of year. Winter offers some good cross-country and even downhill skiing in Yosemite and lovely snowscapes in Sequoia, but you should check ahead to find out which roads are closed. Summer in both parks is high season and relatively crowded, but the peace of the high country is always within reach. Death Valley is best from late autumn to early spring. In the height of summer temperatures can rise to 100° F or more.

Yosemite *(California)*

"Base camp"—which might be a plush hotel room, modest lodge accommodation or simply a tent—is at the heart of Yosemite Valley along the Merced River. From the valley meadow, you can hike, bike (rentals at Yosemite Lodge or Curry Village), ride a horse or mule, or take the shuttle-bus to all the great sights. Soaring granite cliffs enclose the valleys—Half Dome at the north-east end (8,842 feet above sea level), Glacier Point, Sentinel and Cathedral Spires down the south wall, and El Capitan, Three Brothers and Washington Column up the north wall.

You can grade the hikes according to your capacity and endurance, but try at least one hike, in sturdy shoes, for the sheer exhilaration of making it to the end. In the Merced River Canyon, **Vernal Falls** is within the scope of any normally healthy person. You follow a well-marked path that begins at Happy Isles Nature Center, where knowledgeable U.S. Rangers will answer your questions.

If you're up to it, push on along the Mist Trail, past Emerald Pool to **Nevada Falls** and you'll begin to lose the crowd. Here you're on the John Muir Trail, named after the Scottish naturalist who explored the Sierra Nevada and made their conservation against the encroachments of civilization his life's work. The trail goes on past Merced Lake and heads for the lovely **Tuolumne Meadows** in the high country. The final destination is Mount Whitney, that's over 200 miles away—Muir did it, but perhaps it's a little more than you want to do on this trip.

Less exhausting is a drive or shuttle-bus ride past Badger Pass to **Glacier Point,** 7,214 feet above sea level. Both the altitude and the view over the whole valley and the High Sierras beyond are, yes, breathtaking. You can see Yosemite Creek drop half a mile from the opposite wall in two spectacular plunges—Upper and Lower **Yosemite Falls**—and you'll get an outstanding view of the majestic **Half Dome.** From here you may be willing to leave the bus and hike and picnic on your way back along the Panorama Trail via the Nevada and Vernal falls—8 miles downhill in all.

Another beautiful hike is out to **Mirror Lake,** especially in spring or early summer when the waters are perfectly still in the early morning or at sunset, capturing the marvellous colours from the trees and Mount Watkins behind.

Sequoia/Kings Canyon
(California)

It's a haven of peace and contemplation among the giant sequoias, many of them 3,000 years old and more. The forest offers a gorgeous array of dogwoods, sugar pines and white firs as well, and a rich flora of orange leopard lily, white corn lily, lupine, chinquapin and bracken fern. This is no place for a hurried look; walk slowly, sit quietly and listen, fall asleep under a tree. Watch for the birds — woodpecker, raven, spotted owl, but also W.C. Field's favourite, the mountain chickadee, and the yellow-bellied sapsucker.

Start at the Giant Forest Village with its motels, camping facilities and the U.S. Rangers' Visitor Center at Lodgepole. Get a map and information about the best walks in the forest and hikes in the back country. Watch the

186

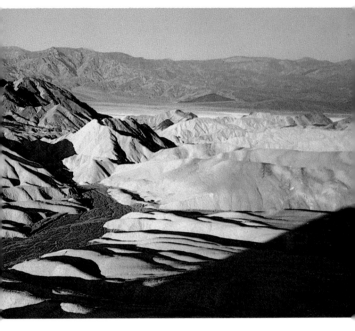

Death Valley National Monument

informative documentary film about the park.

The best introduction to the forest is the **Congress Trail.** It's an easy three-quarters of a mile walk, but worth lingering over for a couple of hours to absorb the beauty of the largest living creations. The trail begins at the **General Sherman Tree,** biggest of all, 275 feet high, 103 feet around its base and still growing. Reaching up for their light well above the rest of the forest, the branches start 130 feet above the ground. As you move among the great sequoias—the President, the Senate Group, the House Group and the General Lee—you can understand old John Muir waxing lyrical about "the first tree in the forest to feel the touch of rosy beams of morning and the last to bid the sun goodnight".

187

Another beautiful walk, by no means an exhausting hike, is out to **Crescent Meadow,** passing such venerable trees as the Bear's Bathtub, the Shattered Giant and the Chimney.

If you want to get away and explore the back country, carry on 11 miles from Crescent Meadow to **Bearpaw Meadow.** This is not too formidable a hike and has a comfortable camp to rest in. A nearby lake and streams offer good fishing for brown trout and hardhead. You'll have a fair chance of spotting some of the park's wildlife—bobcats, coyotes, golden eagles, black bear, spotted skunk, cougar and puma.

Death Valley National Monument (California)

A convenient way to see Death Valley is to combine it with an excursion to Las Vegas. Come in from the east, either on highway 95 and via Death Valley Junction on 190, or further north via Beatty, on 58.

This desert is perhaps the greatest surprise of all the wonders of California. It's not one but a dozen landscapes, not a monotonous expanse of sand dunes but an endless variety of terrains, rock formations, colours and plants. Go there in winter and you may see a flood of spring flowers blooming in the wake of the sparse rains that the Panamint Mountains deign to let into the

valley from the west. But above all, there's the light, uncannily clear, distorting distances, pink at dawn, white at mid-morning, piercing silver at noon and then shimmering into gold as the afternoon progresses.

Don't be put off by the name, Death Valley. It was bequeathed by gold-rush hopefuls who crossed from Arizona and Nevada and suffered bitter hardships here. Some never made it, but they didn't have air-conditioned cars or the excellent resort facilities at the oasis of Furnace Creek.

Get up at dawn—really, you won't regret it—and drive out south-east along highway 190 to **Zabriskie Point.** As the sun rises and the light hits Tucki Mountain and the tips of the Panamints to the west before plunging into the valley's primeval salt lake-bed below, you're likely to be set wondering about the world's creation. By mid-morning (if you visit in winter) the temperature will still be in the cool 50s on your exposed ridge, but walk down the hill to the lake-bed and you'll feel the heat rising to meet you, reaching the 80s by the time you get to the bottom.

Continue over to **Dante's View** (altitude 5,745 feet), looking down at Badwater, 282 feet below sea level. It is the lowest point in the United States. Make up your own mind whether this is paradise, purgatory or hell. On the other side of the valley you can see, from north to south, Wildrose, Bennett and Telescope peaks.

Retrace the road towards Furnace Creek and turn off left, travelling along the Death Valley floor. Follow the crumbling lakebed known as the Devil's Golf Course as far as Badwater and walk out across that expanse of baked salt. The degree of desolation is almost exhilarating. Look closer at the salt and you'll discover it's set into bizarre funnel shapes, swirls and other intricate patterns. Drive back north again and cut off at the arrow pointing to **Artist's Drive.** Here you can explore a canyon of multicoloured rocks and shrubs that culminates in Artist's Palette. The rocks have oxidized into bright mauve, vermillion, ochre, limegreen, turquoise and purple.

LAS VEGAS *(Nevada)*
If, as we claim, European and American dreamers go to California, where do Californian dreamers go? Well, they take Interstate Highway 15 from Los Angeles east across the Mojave Desert, between the Soda Mountains and the Devil's Playground, through Lava Beds and countless Dry Lakes, and over the Nevada state line until they see a town rise out of the desert, blinking its joyously evil neon signs in the twilight:

Sodom and Gomorrah with airconditioning—Las Vegas. "You can fly out here," said a dealer at one of the casino blackjack tables, "but you shouldn't be in too much of a hurry to go to hell, it's better to creep up on it, nice and slow."

Las Vegas is one of those myth-laden towns that everybody should see before they die. No amount of familiarity with all the films that have shown the meretricious marvels of this gambler's paradise can quite prepare you for the shock of the hot and cold reality. At **Casino Center** downtown, the neon signs are so overpoweringly bright that midnight can look like noon back in the Mojave. Mosaics of monster dice, poker chips, roulette wheels and playing cards are imbedded in the intersections of the main streets. Every lit-up window shows dozens of people frenetically tugging the levers of the "one-armed bandit" slot machines. One sign declares: "For every U.S. coin you got, we got the slot." Others invite you to "Cash your paycheck here" or "Exchange any foreign currency". They'll take your money any way you want to give it to them.

Primed with this first taste of things to come, head out to **The Strip** (officially Las Vegas Boulevard) between Sahara and Tropicana avenues, solid miles of hotels and casinos, each with a nightclub advertising America's top comedians and singers and a score of girlie-shows, on ice, in water, even on an ordinary stage. You'll also see wedding chapels attached to little motels, where you can get married for $15, "witnesses available $2.50 extra" and spend your honeymoon next door. If your marriage doesn't work, there are also offices along The Strip where you can get an instant divorce, at a slightly higher, unadvertised fee.

Even if you're not staying there, visit the most extravagant hotels on The Strip. These are the true monuments of Las Vegas, palaces of the Orient, Ancient Rome, Persia and many other fabled places that never existed except in the minds of hotel and casino operators. The most outrageous are **Caesars Palace,** with its fountains and colonnades, the **Sahara,** the **Sands** and **Aladdin,** all three vying for some image of the Arabian Nights.

But the décor is overwhelmed by the gambling—hundreds of slot machines spilling out from the casinos into the lobbies, plus roulette tables, baccarat, blackjack and bingo. Poker is usually played in a roped-off area at amazingly sedate tables dealt to by house-dealers too busy keeping the game going to crack a joke. The most enjoyable tables to watch are the dice or craps games, where the players get excited, whoop, yell and groan as their fortunes go up and down. You'll notice there are no clocks, no windows in the casino—the management doesn't like you to think about what time of day it is; action is available round the clock.

Even if you don't gamble, the spectacle in the casino is fascinating and the floor shows are first-rate. The best way to handle Las Vegas and survive is to arrive at sunset—for that view of the first neon lights in the desert—stay up all night, sleep late, have a good breakfast and leave immediately.

SEATTLE *(Washington)*
Bright and energetic, Seattle is blessed with one of those natural locations that render public relations superfluous. Its bay on Puget Sound is surrounded by the green, green country of Washington with the snow-capped Olympic and Cascade mountains looming in the background and 14,410-foot Mount Rainier towering over them all. The climate is fresh and moist enough to earn the town's sobriquet of the "Emerald City". In spring and summer, it positively sparkles.

Seattle's fortunes are very much tied to the prosperity of the Boeing aircraft manufacturers, though the lumber which got the town started in the 1850s is still a thriving industry. The deepwater

Pacific harbour has made it a natural gateway for trade with the Orient and the town benefits from a lively Chinatown, as well as a Japanese community. It was also the springboard for the Alaska and Klondike gold rushes of the 1880s and 1890s.

Pioneer Square (First Avenue and Yeslerway) is the only vestige of the good old days. Its Victorian red-brick has been spared the urban developers' wrecking ball, and the pleasant tree-shaded little square is surrounded by some good restaurants (both expensive and moderate) quality boutiques and excellent jazz clubs. Look out for the ornate pergola, in fact a bus shelter.

You can explore Seattle's lower depths on an **Underground Tour** (from 610 First Avenue; call 682-4646 for reservations). It leads you through the subterranean city that was burned out in 1889 and buried under today's sidewalks, streets and buildings, which were simply erected on top. You'll see old shops and façades and eerie galleries, illuminated by the guide's amusing stories of the town's beginnings.

Like any self-respecting port, Seattle is liveliest along the **waterfront.** Seafood restaurants, fish stalls and chandlers share the area along Elliott Bay with parks and the **Seattle Aquarium** (Pier 59). Stop by to feast your eyes on octopus, sharks, eels, seals and salmon, or watch a film on the watery depths in the Omnidome theatre. Afterwards, when it's time to get out on the water yourself, harbour tours (Pier 56) and a variety of ferry rides (Pier 52) will fill the bill.

Also on the waterfront, **Pike Place Market** (Pike Street and First Avenue) presents a delightful mixture of stalls with farmers, fishmongers and butchers selling their own produce.

The **International District,** bounded by Fourth and Eighth avenues and Main and Lane streets, includes Chinatown and the Japanese neighbourhood. You'll find dozens of jade and jewellery shops here, great restaurants, a Buddhist temple and the **Wing Luke Memorial Museum** (414 Eighth Street), which traces the intriguing history of Chinese immigration to the West Coast during the mining and railway construction days of the 19th century.

The great symbol of Seattle is the 607-foot **Space Needle** standing on a tripod, a proud relic of the 1962 World's Fair that gave Seattle a much-needed boost after its 1950s slump. There is a revolving restaurant and an observatory at the top from which you have a splendid **view** across the city to the Olympic mountains and the Cascade Range dominated by Mount Rainier.

Immediately below the Needle is the **Seattle Center,** which also grew out of the World's Fair. It groups the Opera House, Playhouse, Coliseum and two first-rate museums. The **Pacific Science Center** is a spectacular structure designed by Minoru Yamasaki to house exhibits on space exploration, laser technology, the rich Indian culture of America's north-west, but above all the oceanography of Puget Sound. The **Art Museum Pavilion** (a branch of the Seattle Art Museum in Volunteer Park, known for its excellent Asian collection) features contemporary American and regional artists, as well as major travelling exhibitions.

If the silhouette of Mount Rainier has proved too inviting to resist, take an excursion out to the **Mount Rainier National Park,** two hours south of town, for some exhilarating hiking on its rugged slopes.

BRIEFINGS

Alaska, largest state of the U.S.A., encompasses a vast area full of infinite variety—a popular misconception is that it is all one frozen wasteland.

The **south-eastern Panhandle,** from Ketchikan via Juneau up to Haines and Skagway, has a moderate climate, plentiful rain, a green and fertile land, with considerable forests. The **Gulf Coast,** north and west of Haines around the Gulf of Alaska, is the most densely populated, centering on Anchorage, the state's only real metropolis.

The **Western region,** including the Alaskan Peninsula and the Aleutian and Pribilof islands, is foggy, wet and windy, great for sea- and bird-life. The **Interior** south of the Brooks Range from the Canadian Yukon border towards the Bering Sea has a dry climate, a land of extremes, hot in summer, bitterly cold in winter. And the **Arctic,** extending from Kotzebue above the Seward Peninsula in the west around Barrow to the North Slope at Prudhoe Bay offers the bleak polar landscape of permanently frozen soil.

A good way to see Alaska is by boat. Cruise ships leave from Seattle and (in summer) Vancouver, San Francisco and Los Angeles.

Hawaii. This 50th state of the U.S.A. is an archipelago of seven inhabited islands, a collection of islets, reefs, sandbars and rocks strung out over 1,500 miles in the North Pacific.

The state's capital, Honolulu, is on the island of **Oahu.** The long white beaches and blue, blue ocean are perfect for swimming and sunbathing, and surfers will swear by the waves to be found on Oahu's north shore. When the sun has gone down, Waikiki offers the most vigorous nightlife.

The island of **Hawaii,** with Hilo its main city, is known locally as the Big Island because of its size and to distinguish it from the state name. There is plenty of sun and sand on the island's west coast, but the main feature remains its volcanoes, particularly the still-active Kilauea Crater.

Maui has superb beaches and plenty of sports facilities, as well as the old royal capital of Lahaina. A visit to the 10,000-foot, dormant volcano, Haleakala, is a must.

Further north, **Molokai** and **Lanai,** are ideal for those who want a quiet holiday—splendid opportunities for hiking, mule-trekking or rugged jeep-trips, while the rivers and waterfalls of **Kauai,** the Garden Island, are a delight for fishing enthusiasts.

The Berlitz HAWAII travel guide provides a comprehensive survey of all there is to see and do on the islands.

WHAT TO DO

Sports

Few countries are more sports-conscious than America. The competitive spirit runs high in every activity. With no new geographical frontiers to conquer, the urge remains to swim and run faster, jump further, climb higher and hit the ball harder than last week. The facilities are first-rate.

The Atlantic coasts of New England, New York and New Jersey, the Carolinas and Florida and the Pacific coast of California provide every imaginable **water sport**—swimming, diving, boating—and they're inventing new ones every season. For surfing, snorkelling, scuba-diving, wind-surfing and water-skiing, there are shops at the seaside resorts where you can rent the necessary equipment. Inland towns like Chicago or Detroit provide the same kind of facilities on their lakes and rivers.

(Many hotels have their own swimming pools, perfect to cool off and relax in after a long hot drive.)

Comparisons are invidious, but long-time reputations hold that southern California is best for surfing and the Florida Keys is best for scuba-diving. For surfing, the best waves are to be found at Malibu on Point Duma and Surfrider, at Santa Monica State Beach north of the pier and at La Jolla on Windansea and Boomer.

For sailing, Long Island South (New York and Connecticut), Cape Cod (Massachusetts), Newport (Rhode Island), the Chesapeake Bay (Maryland and Virginia) and Fort Lauderdale (Florida) are among the best on the East Coast, while Pacific sailors swear by San Diego (California) and Seattle (Washington).

Canoeing, a leisurely sport in the Florida Everglades, becomes an exhilarating test of endurance on the Colorado River in Arizona and Utah or in Yellowstone Park. On the national park rivers, try rafting with the whole family.

Deep-sea **fishing** provides high adventure in the Caribbean waters off Florida, but it's equally satisfying up around Cape Cod, along the Outer Banks of North Carolina or off the northern California coast.

For freshwater fishing check with local information centres for licensing regulations. **Hunting** in the Rockies for moose, elk and gamebirds is carefully regulated but by no means forbidden.

Hiking has become a major sport in these health-conscious times. There are marvellous opportunities in the national parks of the West or the hills of New England. The famous Appalachian Trail runs all the way from

Hawaiian waters are ideal for surfing

195

Maine down to Georgia. It is absolutely the best way to get away from the crowd. Be sure to have good walking shoes or boots, not just tennis shoes, for the longer hikes, and warm clothes for the sudden cool of the evening in the mountains. The rangers who run the national parks can help you with maps for the more interesting nature trails.

If you want to try **mountain climbing,** it's best to go with an experienced guide, especially over unfamiliar terrain. You can usually rent equipment in the national parks.

Jogging is still popular everywhere, healthiest of all barefoot along a sandy beach. The sports stores will try to sell you a lot of jogging "equipment" — haute-couture track-suits, Swiss timers, sweat bands, pedometers. But all you really need is a good pair of shoes and a towel. The town parks often have marked trails with exercise stations en route. In Boston, for instance, the parks, which Bostonians call their "emerald necklace" strung along both banks of the Charles River, are perfect places for jogging. If you want to get around a little faster, rent a **bicycle** or — if you don't mind grazed knees and elbows — **roller-skates.**

Tennis and **golf** are much cheaper than in Europe, and **squash** is growing in popularity. Tennis has become such an obsession that many towns provide floodlit courts for night-time games. Frequently the hotels have at least one tennis court in their grounds and can sometimes help you gain access to the local golf clubs. It helps to take your home golf-club membership card, but there are also many municipal golf courses open to the public, particularly in Florida and California.

Horse riding is good in New England and California. In the national parks, it's one of the more satisfying ways to get off the tourists' beaten track. In Yellowstone, Yosemite and Grand Canyon, **mule riding** is a more sedate alternative — and often a wiser one over the rugged terrain.

If you're taking a winter holiday, **skiing,** both cross-country and downhill, is spectacular in Colorado, Utah and California, but there are also first-class family resorts in New England. You may find the après-ski a little slow, but the slopes are fine and the people more disciplined at the ski lifts than in Europe.

Spectator Sports

Don't let ignorance of the basic rules of **American football** or **baseball** discourage you from watching these wonderfully colourful pastimes. Consider them rituals

Perfect ski conditions in Colorado

of anthropological interest. They provide fascinating insights into the mysteries of American society. An hour of the raucous humour of a baseball crowd at the New York Yankees or the Boston Red Sox, the militant religious fervour of the football fans at the Dallas Cowboys or the stoical fatalism at the Chicago Bears will teach you more about the local community than any sociological monograph. Hot-dogs taste better at baseball. Cheer-leaders at college football games are prettier but less sensual than those at the professional games. And if you feel the need for some exercise of your own, take advantage of baseball's "seventh inning stretch"—midway through the seventh of the nine innings, there is a pause while the spectators stand up and stretch.

Other sports that are better known outside America, such as **basketball** and **ice-hockey,** are played out in a particularly electric atmosphere, charged up by a lot of gambling on the "points-spread" (points difference between the two teams) in the one and by the violent body contact in the other. This is the stuff of Roman circuses. In comparison, the American version of **soccer** is rather tame.

Just what 20th-century America can do to the once sedate game of **tennis** is best witnessed at the U.S. Open Championships at New York's Flushing Meadow in September. The only thing drowning out the roar of the jumbo jets flying over from La-Guardia Airport is the clamour of the spectators. And yet the tension somehow brings the best out of the players.

The most unusual sport on show in Florida is **jai alai** (pronounced "high lie"), a local version of the high-speed Basque game, pelota. It's played in a three-walled court, trapping and hurling the ball with a scooped reed-basket known as a cesta. Night games are played at the Biscayne Fronton in Miami.

Horse racing attracts some colourful characters to Aqueduct and Belmont in New York, to Hialeah Park in Miami—in a unique setting, surrounded by a lake, landscaped gardens and a resident colony of pink flamingoes—and to Santa Anita in Los Angeles. But the great moment of the racing year is in Louisville for the Kentucky Derby (rhymes with Sir Bee) in May. If you happen to be in the country at the time, but unable to get to Louisville, you can still attend one of the countless Kentucky Derby parties held around the country, often in neighbourhood bars. Several hours are spent drinking mint juleps (Bourbon whisky, crushed ice, sugar and fresh mint), while the race itself lasts just two minutes.

Shopping

The most important advice we can give you on shopping in the U.S. is not to start on your first day or you may find you'll have to go home early. For Americans, the business of seducing the consumer has become a fine art. Advertising, promotional stunts, discounts, perpetual "sales" have been developed to a point where the only time it is safe to go out merely window-shopping is after closing time.

Best Buys on the East Coast...
The best bargain in **New York** is window-shopping. Some of Manhattan's store windows are the most imaginatively dressed in the world, an ongoing street-museum of creative salesmanship. Of course, there is also junk, crammed in piles, but at least it doesn't cost you anything.

Europeans will find the New York discount practice, widely advertised in the Sunday papers, particularly advantageous for cameras, radio and electronic calculators from Japan. In the realm of gadgets, Hammacher Schlemmer (456 E. 57th Street) reigns supreme with such extravagant oddities as electronic weighing machines that talk to you in the bathroom. The ultimate store for toys is F.A.O. Schwarz (Fifth Avenue and 58th Street). In a world of diminishing quality and synthetic fabrics, American men's all-cotton shirts are an excellent buy.

Manhattan's big department stores make up an exciting world of their own. The biggest is Macy's (34th between Sixth and Seventh avenues); the most imaginative merchandiser is Bloomingdale's (Lexington and 59th Street).

Boston's importance in the nation's history makes it an ideal place to find the best of old Americana, but it becomes increasingly difficult to get the authentic stuff at less than historic prices. In antique shops in Charles Street on Beacon Hill or around Harvard Square in Cambridge, you'll happen on some original, sturdy colonial furniture, but more often some very good (and some bad) reproductions. Look out, too, for beautifully painted, wooden decoy-ducks possibly used by Pilgrim pot-shotters. Patchwork quilts are another speciality of the colonial days, as well as decorative lacy-patterned glassware and handmade pewter (the latter at Faneuil Hall's Heritage Shop). Although whaling days are over, you can still find delicately carved scrimshaw ornaments made from whale teeth and walrus tusks (particularly in curio shops in Back Bay or around Cape Cod and, above all, on Nantucket Island). Fragrant green candles made from bayberries are a speciality of Cape Cod.

Washington being such a terrific museum town, the museums also provide the best place to buy unusual and attractive gifts. The Air and Space Museum shop has some great model aircraft and spaceships for children and their fathers. The Museum of Natural History is your best bet for jewellery of semi-precious stones and beautifully mounted pieces of rare minerals. The main Smithsonian Bookstore, located in the Museum of American History, offers a splendidly comprehensive selection of the country's arts, history and technology. Near the Mall entrance, the museum shop sells replicas of the more popular exhibits of old Americana. The National Geographic Society (17th and M streets) is worth visiting for its wonderful maps and picture-books of places near and far. For posters of the great masters, art calendars and art books, try the shops at the National Gallery of Art, both East and West, and the Hirshhorn.

Study the newspapers, especially the Sunday editions which are usually filled with advertising about the sales or "specials" currently promoted in the big stores. The major cities have discount stores, particularly good for records, cameras, electronic equipment and sporting goods. The press also gives details of local flea markets, generally held only at weekends.

...And Everywhere Else
Clothes. All the big cities are importing the fashionable clothes of French and Italian couturi-

High fashion and local crafts

ers—the trick is to find them cheaper here than back home. But we also recommend you look at California sportswear for women and at the American designers in men's clothing who seem to have the knack of combining style *and* comfort, particularly in casual attire—great shirts and well-made moccasins (for the city, not the warpath). Apart from cowboy clothing (see p. 152), styles are international.

Jewellery. If you're looking for diamonds, concentrate on Diamond Row in New York. You'll find lovely turquoise in New Mexico, silver in Texas.

Records. The selection of classical, jazz and popular records is probably the best in the world and the frequent discounts offered certainly make them the best bargains. But don't get carried away—over half a dozen and they'll really weigh down your luggage.

Gadgets and tools. In the never-ending quest for labour-saving devices, Americans will do anything to make life easier in the kitchen, the bathroom or the tool-shed. Make sure, if it's electric, that it will adapt to your home voltage and plug system.

Cosmetics and toiletries. Whereas Europeans still produce a larger range of quality perfumes and eau-de-Cologne, the Americans have a bigger selection of creams and lotions, and good

quality make-up is generally cheaper than in Europe. Try these out at the *beginning* of your trip so that you'll know which ones to stock up on at the end. There are some great-tasting toothpastes. And the giant cans of shaving foam last almost forever.

Stationery. For some reason, Americans make the best note-books, especially those long yellow legal-pads. And they're always coming up with new ideas for filing-systems, address books, folders, labels and sticking tape. Good gifts for school kids—and their parents.

One Man's Poison

A fine American institution for bargains in second-hand goods is the garage sale. Families moving away or just periodically emptying out their attics and cellars offer old clothes, furniture, books, records and ornaments displayed in the driveway of their garage. Track them down from their hand-written advertisements posted on walls, lampposts or supermarket notice boards or by just driving slowly around residential neighbourhoods on summer Saturdays—you're bound to find half a dozen. They're great places to discover the kind of old Americana—even ash-trays, car licence-plates and tobacco tins —that Americans consider junk and Europeans consider antiques.

Craftwork and curios. As a rule, the artwork you'll find in shopping centres and souvenir shops is junk, mass-produced in Taiwan, Hong Kong and South Korea (though this stuff is apparently acquiring value as Low Kitsch, the more ludicrous, the better). Your best chance of finding authentic craftwork and high quality replicas is in the gift shops of art museums. These are usually run by people who care about the aesthetic reputation of their institution and some care goes into the selection of articles for sale. Try the Museum of Modern Art and the Metropolitan in New York, the museums of the Smithsonian in Washington, and the Art Institute of Chicago. Besides posters and reproductions of paintings and sculpture, these and other museum shops sell fine jewellery of semi-precious stones set in good silver and gold, and handwoven rugs and clothes.

Entertainment

Nightlife in America is strictly a phenomenon of the big cities. In New York, Boston, Philadelphia, Washington, Chicago, San Francisco and Los Angeles, the **opera**, **ballet** and **symphony concerts** are major events of the social calendar. You have to plan well ahead to get tickets for these, but it's worth the effort (for New York, see p. 206). Your travel agency can probably help you contact city visitors information centres to make advance bookings.

The best **theatre** is still in New York, but other major towns have good repertory groups and experimental drama, particularly where there's a large university.

Discotheques continue in force, though with more varied music (even golden oldies) than the monotonous 1970s stuff. **Nightclubs** range from the spectacular extravaganzas of Las Vegas with top-flight singers and comedians, via the seedy strip-joints (male *and* female) of San Francisco to quiet supper-clubs with a dance band, or just a piano bar in the smarter hotels. Jazz is king again in New Orleans (see p. 123). New comedians try out on Sunset Strip in Los Angeles or in Greenwich Village, New York. And satirical cabaret knocks everything it can lay its hands on in Chicago. In Miami's Little Havana, they dance in the streets. In Texas, some of the nightclubs offer electronic bucking broncos and mud-wrestling. But the fashions change as fast as the light bulbs.

If you're a **cinema** buff and like to be ahead of your crowd, many of the big American movies that open in Europe in the autumn or at Christmas are released in the U.S. during the summer. These days, the major films rapidly become cult movies, and the queues of eager fans form twice around the block. Waiting to see a film,

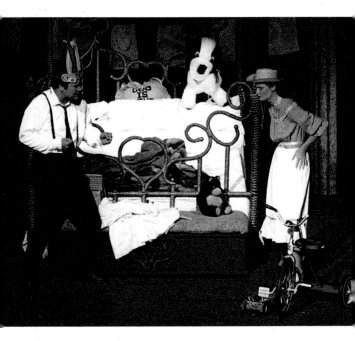

Not just on Broadway, theatre groups thrive throughout the U.S.

often for the fourth or fifth time, has become a ritual complete with musical entertainment and picnics in the street. Focal points for this delightful madness are Westwood in Los Angeles and Third Avenue, New York.

The other cultural phenomenon that fascinates many Europeans is the all-night **television**. It's a great way of whiling away your jet lag. Often the best part of the programmes is the used-car commercial. But it's also a chance to catch up on the classics—the Marx brothers cavorting in *Duck Soup* or Rogers and Astaire dancing the *Continental*.

Night Time in New York
If you could do proper justice to night-time New York, you'd never have the energy to see it by day. Some people don't.

204

Theatre is still Broadway, on sidestreets between West 44th and 50th streets for the big show and big ticket-prices. Off-Broadway and "Off-Off-Broadway" shows are smaller and cheaper, more risky for quality but more adventurous, too. Dance undeniably has its world capital in New York. The excellent resident companies—the New York City Ballet, Robert Joffrey, Merce Cunningham, Alvin Ailey, Paul Taylor, Dance Theater of Harlem and the American Ballet Theater—also attract the competition of the very best foreign companies on tour. Opera is almost equally richly endowed with the huge classical resources of the Met and the modern repertoire of the New York City Opera, both at the Lincoln Center. The New York Philharmonic is the flagship for the 30 or so classical music concerts you can choose from on any one evening—with the added summer joy of free Philharmonic and Metropolitan Opera performances in the city's parks. Going to the cinema is a highly respected pursuit in Manhattan, both for first-run fare around Times Square and up on Third Avenue above 57th Street and for old Hollywood classics and subtitled foreign films in the smaller art-houses all over town. The Film Society of Lincoln Center features programmes of retrospectives and hosts the autumn New York Film Festival.

On the nightclub scene, only really enjoyable after midnight, disco rolls on with its own fathomable momentum, with modish New Yorkers predicting its imminent death since the day it was born. But jazz is coming back strong, especially in the clubs in Greenwich Village and SoHo, the West 50s and, less funky, on the Upper East Side. For a quieter night, go dancing at the supper-clubs in the classic hotels around Rockefeller Center.

Unless you have your heart set on seeing the season's smash hit musical, you can usually pick up theatre tickets at the box office a day or two in advance (Friday and Saturday nights excepted). Do look for discount vouchers at the Visitors Bureau (2 Columbus Circle) or, if you don't mind queues, head for TKTS (47th Street and Broadway or 100 William Street in lower Manhattan) for half-price seats on the day of the performance.

But, if you like to play it safe, buy a copy of the *New Yorker* magazine before you leave home and order your tickets by mail.

Night Time in Washington

Under cellist-turned-conductor Mstislav Rostropovitch, the National Symphony has become a world-class orchestra. The visiting ballet and opera performances make grand galas — people at the Kennedy Center love dressing up. The Eisenhower Theater (political balance was necessary in choosing names though the old soldier wasn't much of a theatre-buff) stages pre- and post-Broadway productions which you may have missed in New York.

For tickets, we suggest you pick up an out-of-town copy of the *Washington Post* before you even get to Washington — best of all,

the Friday edition with the "Weekend" section — to plan and book ahead for plays, operas or concerts. Otherwise your hotel can sometimes help, or else try your luck with returned tickets at the box office an hour before curtain time.

Night Time in Boston

Those invidious categories of "highbrow" and "lowbrow" — nobody seems to like being called either — are both catered for among music-lovers by the highly respected Boston Symphony Orchestra and the jolly Boston Pops. Both perform at Symphony Hall on Huntington Avenue. The Pops moves outdoors in summer to give free concerts at the Hatch Memorial Shell on the Charles River Esplanade just west of Beacon Hill. For sheer magic, try to catch a chamber music concert in the courtyard of the Isabella Stewart Gardner Museum. The Boston Ballet is at the New Metropolitan Center and the Opera Company at the old Savoy Theater. Theatre productions bound for New York try out "on the road" at Boston's Shubert, Colonial or Wilbur theatres. Critics being notoriously unreliable and investors too impressionable, you may be lucky enough to see a good play unfairly panned here that never makes it to Broadway because the backers get cold feet.

Night Time in San Francisco

In this instance, San Francisco is much more fun than Los Angeles. Most people in LA seem to stay home in the evenings and prefer to have their fun in private. But San Franciscans go out a lot and the coffee-house and street life is booming and bouncing with vitality every night.

Bars in San Francisco are a whole way of life—downtown Irish bars on Geary, Italian coffee houses and every other ethnic variety in North Beach, and a host of late-night waterfront "joints" along Embarcadero to Fisherman's Wharf. There is no obvious distinction to be made between "tourist traps" and local hang-outs, perhaps because San Franciscans are the most enthusiastic tourists in their own town, so you'll be mixing with the locals wherever you go. Some bar-cafés around North Beach specialize in good amateur opera singing—you'll hear it as you walk by the open doors. If it sounds too much like Pavarotti or Callas, it probably is Pavarotti or Callas on the jukebox played between "sets". The San Francisco Opera is exceptionally good, but you'll be lucky to find a seat.

Broadway is also the main thoroughfare for jazz nightclubs and "topless", "bottomless" and other forms of strip-joints, most of them more innocent than they seem.

EATING OUT

The nation's Latin motto *E Pluribus Unum* (One From Many) could well apply to American eating habits. It's a country of cuisines as diversified as its ethnic groups and at the same time there's a great uniformity in the everyday meals. Texas draws on its Mexican beginnings for spicy chilli and barbecued dishes and Florida takes inspiration both from Cuban rice dishes and Jewish delicatessen. Yet in both states and all the way to Maine in the north-east corner or to the state of Washington in the north-west, you'll find the same straightforward vegetable soups, plain green salads, steak and potatoes, fruit pies and ice-cream. The great mobility of Americans has spread the original unadorned, often rather bland cooking of the Anglo-Saxons right across the country. This basic unity of taste has, for instance, guaranteed the phenomenal success of the fast-food franchises.

You'll find many areas have distinctive cuisines, notably New York on the East Coast, New England, Miami and New Orleans in the South. For the all-important wines to accompany a fine meal, the vineyards of California naturally merit particular mention in the West Coast section (see p. 173). But first there are a few basic facts worth noting.

Eating Habits

For Europeans, American eating habits may need some introduction. As soon as you sit down for breakfast, you're likely to see the waitress advancing on you armed with a pot of coffee. Serving coffee is a hospitable way of saying "good morning" and it takes firm, clear action to stop this automatic gesture if you don't want coffee immediately. The coffee is weak by European standards, but your cup will be refilled several times.

If you're having fried eggs, remember to specify "sunny side up" (cooked from below only) or "over, easy" (turned and cooked lightly on top). Toast may be white, whole wheat or rye, and English muffins (something like a crumpet) are usually available, too.

At lunch and dinner, salad is served before the main dish, which used to upset habitués of French cuisine; now, in these slimmer times of diets and health-foods, the salad makes a good appetizer. Salad dressings are often surprising concoctions not familiar to every European palate. If you want a simple dressing you can always order oil, vinegar and a little mustard and mix your own vinaigrette.

You may find that you are offered a cocktail before, during and after the meal; cocktails are not necessarily considered aperitifs. Alternatively, you can order wine immediately.

One aspect of dining out that might surprise non-Americans is the formality often demanded by the "smarter" restaurants in the evenings. That means ties and jackets for men and dresses or dressy slacks rather than jeans for women. This is enforced to maintain a certain "respectability" in the clientele. If you arrive without a tie or jacket, the establishment will usually lend you something from their own stock — most often horrendously ugly and even emblazoned with the restaurant's name in case you were thinking of walking off with it. Dresses are *not* provided for women, but customers have been known to take their jeans off and use their blouse as a mini-dress — and be allowed in!

What to Eat

Sandwiches. Served on white, rye, pumpernickel or whole-wheat bread, a roll or a bagel (doughnut-shaped rolls) or perhaps on *pita*, Arab flat bread. Classic fillings include chicken, tuna and egg salads; lox (smoked salmon) and cream cheese, a delicious Jewish speciality served on a bagel; corned beef or pastrami (a kind of cured beef), also Jewish specialities. Club sandwiches consist of three slices of toast in layers filled with turkey, lettuce, tomato, bacon and sometimes cheese.

Hoagies, heroes, submarines and grinders all refer to the same thing: a fat, mouth-stretching sandwich of French bread, stuffed with meatballs, sausages or ham-cheese-salami-onions-peppers-lettuce-tomatoes and olive oil. No need for dessert after one of these.

Soups. These days many Americans will lunch on soup rather than a hamburger, and more and more small restaurants include soups on the menu. Vichyssoise (don't let the name mislead you, it's an American dish) is a chilled concoction of leeks, potatoes and onions; chilli con carne, often served as a soup, is in fact a substantial and spicy stew of kidney beans, ground beef, onions and tomatoes.

Salads. The usual kind, served with dinner, consists of iceberg lettuce and a few slices of tomato and cucumber, but many American-style restaurants nowadays feature a self-service salad bar with an attractive assortment of greens and garnishes. Your choice of dressings may include "tomatoey" French, Thousand Islands (mayonnaise, ketchup, hard-boiled egg), Russian (mayonnaise and chilli sauce), Italian (oil, vinegar, garlic and herbs) or Roquefort.

The "chef's salad", which may contain ham, cheese and chicken, is a meal in itself; raw spinach salad with mushrooms ranks as a great American original; Caesar salad has romaine lettuce and a raw egg in the dressing; cole slaw (cabbage salad) often appears with sandwiches. Cold pasta salads often with crisp vegetables or seafood have become very popular in recent years.

Meat. Beef still takes first place — though in health-conscious America the trend is now away from red meat. It comes in enormous portions and is almost invariably tender. In steakhouses, you often pay a flat rate for a steak, a baked potato with sour cream or French fries (chips), a self-service salad bar, and in some cases a glass or two of wine, beer or *sangría*.

"Spare ribs" are pork ribs, marinated in a spicy sauce, baked or broiled and eaten with your fingers.

Fish and Seafood. Americans don't like fish as much as Europeans or the Japanese, they seem a little put off by the bones. But the fish itself is often of excellent quality, both the ocean fish of the East and West coasts and the Gulf of Mexico and the freshwater fish of the mountain rivers and lakes. Look out in particular for red snapper, blue fish, sea bass, salmon and trout.

Shellfish are perhaps best of all, particularly the clams, crab, shrimp, scallops, lobster, abalone and oysters, the latter more often cooked than they are in Europe.

You can overcome the local tendency to deep fry everything by gently stating a preference for sautéeing or broiling. Lobster is best boiled — grilling often dries it out.

Vegetables. Beans, peas, broccoli and cauliflower tend to be impeccable in appearance and colour but bland in taste. The great American vegetable is the Idaho potato, baked and served with sour cream, butter and chives. Corn on the cob is fine, off the cob it's watery. Succotash is corn mixed with lima beans.

Cheese. Swiss-, Dutch- and British-style cheeses are manufactured in Wisconsin, New York and Vermont; the sharper ones approach their European equivalents. The French cheeses, imported or locally imitated, tend to be too pasteurized to approximate their taste on the other side of the Atlantic, but the creamier versions are spiced with herbs and garlic. It's rare to find a cheese-board served except in French restaurants, though the British custom of cheese-and-wine bars is spreading.

Desserts. Ice-cream is undeniably the area in which America excels. Amazing flavours are invented every week—spearmint, peanut butter, apple pie, cinnamon—and their vanilla is terrific. Put it on the fruit pies, *à la mode,* and you're heading for blissful calorific catastrophe. Apple Brown Betty is a kind of apple crumble. Brownies are a good, simple chocolate cake usually served in small squares. In early summer when the strawberries are at their peak, strawberry shortcake—scone-like biscuit on

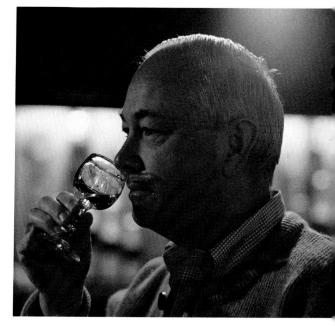

the bottom, gobs of whipped cream on top—can be sublime. Enjoy things, you're on holiday.

Regional Cuisines and Resources

New York restaurants can be very good but their chefs tend to move around as often as baseball managers. The best ones are lured away by better offers from a competitor or do well enough to open up their own places—until they discover they're better cooks than businessmen and move on again to someone else's kitchen. The best selection of restaurants is in the theatre district, the East Side or Upper West Side or down in the Village. But rather than be told where to go *this* year, just consider the variety of cuisines.

The town benefits enormously from its cosmopolitan tradition. Italian restaurants are legion. With the French, you have to choose carefully between the few authentic—and very expensive—establishments and those run by tax-dodgers with French accents. The Chinese are much more reliably competent and more varied in their regional cuisines, especially down in Chinatown itself. And then there's the whole gamut of "ethnic" restaurants—Greek, Spanish, Japanese, Jewish, Mexican, Brazilian and Indian. Increasingly, they're taking their exotica out on to the streets, vending Arab *falafel* sandwiches, spicy Indian *samosas*

or Turkish *shish-kebab* in hot competition with the local pretzels and hot-dogs.

New York's own contribution to world gastronomy begins with the hot-dog, which you can have either with sauerkraut or fried onions but not, authentically, without mustard—if only for the aesthetics of the yellow stripe down the middle of the sausage. The deli sandwich is a special Broadway institution, naming permutations of turkey, corned beef, pastrami, bacon, lettuce, tomato or whatever after some film star, pop singer or sports champion who may or may not once have ordered it. The New York strip steak is a good, thick cut of tenderloin, best eaten rare. Long Island Blue Point oysters are too good to spoil with the cocktail sauce that inevitably accompanies them. Manhattan clam chowder has tomato in it (as opposed to the creamy New England type). Although cheesecake may have come from Central Europe, it didn't taste heavenly until it reached Brooklyn and the delis on Broadway.

New York wines are mostly inferior to California's, but Napa Valley has nothing to match the Manhattan, a cocktail of four parts Bourbon whisky, one part vermouth and a dash of bitters. Here's lookin' at yuh, kid.

New Orleans prides itself on the most distinctive cooking in America. It certainly is very evocative of the city's own personality — or is it that the city derives its personality from the cuisine, rich, Latin and spicy? The Creole tradition combines a French love of intricate sauces, the Spanish penchant for mixing fish, meat and vegetables with rice, and a taste developed in the West Indies and Africa for liberal seasoning with hot peppers. Plus plain old Southern cooking.

The classic dish is jambalaya, a paella-like dish of rice and chicken, crab or shrimp with bits of sausage or ham, pepper and tomato. The poor man's version is the simple bean 'n rice, red kidney beans and rice flavoured with pork, deliciously filling. Gumbo, a West African word for okra (the green vegetable known to British India as "lady's fingers"), is the basic ingredient and generic name for thick soups of chicken or seafood, a meal in itself. Crayfish, pronounced and often spelled in Louisiana "crawfish", best served, for a change, straight boiled, is a favourite springtime shellfish to which whole festivals are devoted in April. The oysters here are plentiful and relatively cheap, encouraging New Orleans chefs to prepare them in a number of marvellous ways: fried or in gumbo; as oysters Rockefeller — rich as its name, baked with spinach and breadcrumbs; or oysters Bienville, cooked in white wine with shrimp, mushrooms and shallots; or a stupendous oysters brochette, skewered and wrapped in bacon.

The local version of the all-American submarine sandwich is the "po-boy" (long) and muffuletta (round), French bread stuffed with cold meats, oysters or other seafood, cheese and salads, often pepped up to local taste.

New Orleans claims to have invented the cocktail, or at least the word. It is, they say, a distortion of the French for egg-cup, *coquetier*, in which a Creole bartender by the name of Antoine Peychaud served his brandy and bitters in the 19th century. The dictionary, more soberly, suggests that cocktail was originally "a horse of racing qualities, but not a thoroughbred", a fair description of two New Orleans specialities: the Sazarac is rye whisky or bourbon and bitters served in a glass coated with anisette; the Ramos Gin Fizz adds sugar, lemon, lime, orange-flower water, egg-white, crushed ice and soda water to your poor, defenceless gin. If you're still conscious, try a *café brûlot*, coffee flavoured with cinnamon, cloves, orange peel and *flambé*.

In **Boston,** you should start your day with some of the "home-baked" muffins offered at breakfast time. Blueberry, cranberry, apple and date-nut are among the more interesting varieties. Or start with pancakes swimming in maple syrup. The best syrup comes from Vermont, where those in the know serve it warm.

New Englanders are proud of their culinary specialities, not the least of which is Boston baked beans. Simmered in molasses with a chunk of salt pork, this hearty dish is said to have been a decisive factor in the British abandoning their American colonies.

If that's true, the French were probably delighted to become America's first allies for a chance to sample the lobster caught off the coasts of Maine and Massachusetts, simply boiled or grilled with melted butter. The oysters, too, are good, as are the haddock, sea bass, flounder and scrod (local white fish, usually young cod). Cod turns up in fried fishcakes, a traditional Friday night supper. But clams are king hereabouts. Clam chowder is a uniquely New England soup (beware the heretical "Manhattan" version with tomatoes) of clams with potato, onions, milk and a few other seasonings that each cook keeps secret. A great summer ritual at the beach is the clambake. Over a wood fire, heat some rocks covered with seaweed. Then add potatoes, clams, lobsters and corn to steam under a second layer of saltwatery seaweed. When the potatoes are done, the feasting begins, accompanied by cold beer.

For dessert, as in the rest of America, fruit pies are legion but the cranberry is a New England innovation. Boston cream pie is actually sponge cake filled with custard and glazed with chocolate icing. For real authenticity, try Indian pudding made of cornmeal, molasses and milk. The Pilgrims loved it.

Ethnic Food

Nearly every large city has its Little Italy, Chinatown or neighbourhood Jewish delicatessens and Mexican restaurants. **Italian** food follows traditional lines, except that a favourite spaghetti dish tends to be with meat balls rather than *bolognese*. On the West Coast you will find a superb Italian version of bouillabaisse, a thick fish soup known as *cioppino*, more fish than soup, with every available shellfish spiced up or down, according to taste.

Chinese food does not have to be a full blown meal. At a dimsum parlour or tea shop you can select a smorgasbord of shrimp balls, steamed dumplings, deep-fried sweet potatoes and chopped mushrooms in wedges of rice-pastry, accompanied by pots of sauce.

Restaurants offer many variations of Chinese regional cooking—Peking, Szechuan, Shanghai, Hunan, as well as the familiar Cantonese. It's worth calling up a day in advance to order a whole Peking duck, glazed with honey and roasted slowly with spring onions. This gentle delicacy finds a sharp contrast in the spicy smoked duck you might try in a Szechuan or Hunan restaurant. But you mustn't overlook seafood. The steamed sea bass prepared with chopped green onions, black beans, garlic, ginger and sesame oil or the Szechuan shrimp, are served piping hot in both senses of the word.

Like Chinatown's dim-sum parlours, **Mexican** eating houses offer an array of snack-like food—crispy *tacos* and *tostadas* and moist *tortillas* (cornmeal pancakes) stuffed with shredded beef or chicken, grated cheese, avocado and lettuce. But the best dishes are more substantial and sophisticated—*camarones con salsa verde* (shrimp in green sauce), *carne de puerco en adobo* (pork in chilli sauce) or *mole poblano* (chicken with almonds, sesame seeds, peanuts, chilli, raisins and savoury chocolate sauce).

For the uninitiated, **Jewish** food features Eastern European borscht, cabbage soups (red or green) with sour cream, gefilte fish and minced fish balls. Blintzes, a crisper version of the Russian blini, are folded over minced meat as an appetizer or sweet cream cheese as a dessert. Corned beef and spicy, smoked, Rumanian-style pastrami make delicious sandwiches; they're served on rye bread with potato salad and pickled cucumbers. For dessert, try cheesecake.

Drinks

The cold drinks are almost invariably served iced. Iced water, iced tea, iced coffee. If you want a good serving of cola or lemonade in the coffee shops and fast-food places, specify "little ice". Beer is of course also served ice cold, but it is also much blander and more highly carbonated than European beer. You can find many foreign beers, as well.

New York State has some decent wines; those from California are better, especially the red ones. You can order domestic wine by the bottle or, in many places, in carafes as the "house wine". French and Italian wines, at quite reasonable prices, also appear on menus.

Since Americans discovered wine, hard liquor has gone somewhat out of fashion. But not the cocktail hour! Dry martinis (gin and a few drops of dry vermouth) are very potent. Bourbon, a mellow whisky distilled in Kentucky, is made of corn (maize), malt and rye; drink it straight, on the rocks or with soda. Many bars have a late-afternoon "happy hour" when they'll give you two drinks for the price of one or serve free snacks. See p. 228 for liquor (alcohol) licensing laws.

BERLITZ-INFO

CONTENTS

A ACCOMMODATION

Hotels and motels. To ensure you get the type of accommodation you want, it's wise to book in advance. You can also make reservations directly through the nationwide toll-free booking services operated by the large hotel and motel chains (listed in the Yellow Pages of the telephone directory).

American hotels and motels usually charge by the room, not by number of occupants. Rates indicated normally do not include the state and city sales taxes or daily occupancy tax. Although hotel rates are not subject to control, they are comparable within similar categories of establishment. The larger hotel chains divide into luxury, moderate and budget class. Most rooms have air conditioning, private bathroom and television. When booking your room, you normally have the choice of a single (in old hotels), twin (two beds) or double (room for two with one bed). Many motels furnish all their rooms with two double beds — very convenient for family travel. Most resort hotels offer special rates to guests who take their meals on the premises: A.P. (American Plan) includes three meals a day and M.A.P. (Modified American Plan), breakfast and lunch or dinner.

Motor hotels or motels are one of America's great bargains. Many belong to national or international chains, so you can make all the bookings for your trip at the same time.

Tourist homes (guest houses) and **Bed-and-Breakfast** establishments are found in smaller towns and holiday centres. Local tourist authorities usually have lists.

Ranches. The *Country Vacation Guide* is an excellent source of information about accommodation on ranches. There are luxury ranches, enormous complexes with all facilities from swimming pools and tennis courts to barbecues, and the simpler — but nevertheless comfortable — dude ranches, where you can take part in everyday ranch and cowboy life. For further information, contact a travel agency. Cheaper accommodation can be found on farms and family ranches.

Youth hostels offer inexpensive accommodation, usually outside towns. They are open to members of national youth hostel organizations abroad. For further details, contact your national youth hostel association or write to American Youth Hostels, Inc.:

1332 Eye St., NW, Washington, DC 20005; tel. (202) 347-3125

There are a number of centrally located residences run by the **YMCA** and **YWCA**. Rates are quite reasonable. You do not have to belong to the association to stay at the "Y", but demand is high so you should book at least two months ahead.

Students and youths can also find inexpensive accommodation at university campuses and through local student associations.

Camping. Camping in America generally involves recreational vehicles — campers, motor homes or caravans (trailers). So if you are camping the American way, follow the indispensable Rand McNally *Campground & Trailer Park Guide* or the voluminous Woodall's *Campground Directory*, both issued annually, which grade campsites according to facilities. Sites are divided into two categories: public campgrounds (found in the national parks, state parks and state forests) and private sites. Accommodation in the most popular parks must be booked directly with the individual lodge, anywhere from eight weeks to a year in advance, depending on the season. If you are sleeping rough, you must obtain a permit from the park.

AIRPORT INFORMATION FOR MAIN GATEWAY CITIES

New York. *John F. Kennedy International* (JFK), 16 miles south-east of midtown Manhattan. Hotel limousine (shared-car) and mini-bus service at frequent intervals throughout the day. Express bus (Carey Coach) to Grand Central Airlines Terminal and the Air TransCenter at Port Authority Bus Terminal (West 42nd Street) every 15–30 min.; travel time 40–65 min. (longer at peak hours). JFK Express (bus and underground/subway) every 20 min. during the day; travel time 50–60 min. Helicopter to East 34th Street every 30–40 min. during the day; travel time 20 min.

Transfer by coach from JFK to *LaGuardia* (25–40 min.), by limousine to *Newark International* (45–75 min.). Regular inter-airport helicopter service (10–15 min. depending on airport).

Miami. *Miami International* (MIA), 7 miles west of downtown Miami. Round-the-clock mini-bus (Red Top) service on request; travel time 25 min. Municipal bus (No. 20 "South" to downtown Miami, No. 34 "North" to Miami Beach) every 30–45 min. during the day.

Transfer by coach to *Fort Lauderdale Airport* (60 min.).

Los Angeles. *Los Angeles International* (LAX), 16 miles south of central business district. Airport bus service to downtown LA, Hollywood, Beverly Hills, Westwood, etc., every 10–20 min. during the day. Numerous connections to surrounding areas.

Transfer to *Van Nuys Airport* every 30 min.

Chicago. *O'Hare International* (ORD), 18 miles north-west. Airport bus service to hotels every 20 min. during the day; travel time 30 min. Express bus (No. 40) and subway (rapid transit train) service every 15–30 min. during the day, every 60 min. at night.

Boston. *Logan International* (BOS), 2 miles east of business district. Airport bus service to major hotels every 30 min. during the day; travel time 20–30 min. Shuttle bus (Massport) and subway (Blue Line) service every 15 min. during the day; travel time 15 min. Shared-cab service to surrounding towns.

C CLIMATE AND CLOTHING

The U.S. climate varies considerably from frozen north to southern sunbelt, so take your destination into account as you pack your suitcase. In summer it's warm pretty well everywhere—except northern New England, Oregon and Washington. In winter, heavy outer wear is essential, unless you're restricting your visit to the southernmost states. For New York and Chicago, rubber overshoes, or galoshes, are a good idea; some swear by "long johns"—long underwear. Even in Florida and California, temperatures can plummet to freezing point in December, January and February. Yet cold spells never last long and can be followed by a heat wave; be prepared for every eventuality. North and south, air conditioning takes the edge off summer heat and humidity, so have a jacket or light wrap handy for the chilly indoors.

With the high crime rate prevailing in cities nowadays, unobtrusive attire is the rule—no flashy clothing or jewellery. Tourists would be wise to follow suit.

Monthly average maximum and minimum daytime temperatures in degrees Fahrenheit:

		J	F	M	A	M	J	J	A	S	O	N	D
Chicago	max.	32	35	45	59	70	81	84	83	76	65	48	35
	min.	17	20	29	40	50	60	65	64	56	46	33	22
LA	max.	67	68	69	71	73	77	83	84	83	78	73	68
	min.	47	49	50	53	56	60	64	64	63	59	52	48
Miami	max.	76	77	80	83	85	88	89	90	88	85	80	77
	min.	59	59	63	67	71	74	76	76	75	71	65	60
New York	max.	39	40	48	61	71	81	85	83	77	67	54	41
	min.	26	27	34	44	53	63	68	66	60	51	41	30

And in degrees Celsius:

Chicago	max.	0	2	7	15	21	27	29	28	24	18	9	2
	min.	−8	−7	−2	5	10	16	18	18	13	8	1	−6
LA	max.	19	20	21	22	23	25	28	29	28	26	23	20
	min.	8	10	10	12	13	16	18	18	17	15	11	9
Miami	max.	24	25	27	28	29	31	32	32	31	29	27	25
	min.	15	15	17	19	22	23	24	24	23	22	18	16
New York	max.	4	5	9	16	22	27	29	28	25	19	12	5
	min.	−3	−3	1	7	12	17	20	19	16	11	5	−1

COMMUNICATIONS

Post offices. The U.S. postal service deals only with mail. Post office hours are from 8.30 or 9 a.m. to 5 or 5.30 p.m. Monday to Friday, and from 8 or 9 a.m. to 12 noon or 1 p.m. on Saturday. Some branches have longer hours; all are closed on Sunday. Stamps can also be purchased from vending machines in drugstores, air, rail or bus terminals and other public places, but you will pay a surcharge. U.S. mail boxes are blue.

Poste restante (general delivery). You can have mail marked "General Delivery" sent to you care of the main post office of any town. The letters will be held for no more than a month. American Express offices also keep post for 30 days; envelopes should be marked "Client's Mail". Take your driving licence or passport with you for identification.

Telegrams. American telegraph companies are privately run. They offer domestic and overseas services, as well as domestic telex facilities, and are listed in the Yellow Pages. You can telephone the telegraph office, dictate the message and have the charge added to your hotel bill, or dictate it from a coin-operated phone and pay on the spot. A letter telegram (night letter) costs about half the rate of a normal telegram.

Telephone. The telephone is part of the American private enterprise system. Public telephones can be found just about everywhere. Directions for use are on the instrument. Telephone rates are listed and explained in the front of the general directory or White Pages. Also included is a map showing area code numbers, information on personal (person-to-person) calls, reverse-charge (collect) calls, conference, station-to-station and credit-card calls. Evening (after 5 p.m.), night (after 11 p.m.) and weekend rates are lower.

Long-distance and many international calls may be dialled direct, even from a pay phone if you follow the posted directions and have plenty of coins on you. Dial "0" for operator assistance. If you don't know the subscriber's number, dial the area code plus 555-1212 (free of charge) and give the operator the name and address of the person you want to call. Long-distance calls cost more from a pay phone than from a private one.

All numbers with an 800 (or 1-800 depending on area) prefix are toll-free (no charge). For information on toll-free numbers, dial 800-555-1212.

CRIME AND THEFT

Petty theft and non-violent crime have become almost commonplace in many American cities and towns, and crimes of violence occur ever more frequently. But there's no need to panic. Follow a few common-sense rules and relax and enjoy yourself.

- Store valuables and any reserves of cash, traveller's cheques, etc., in your hotel safe. Carry only what you actually need from day to day. Make sure your handbag is securely fastened and keep your wallet in an inside rather than hip pocket. Never leave belongings unattended—at an airport, in a store, on the beach, or open to view in a car. It may be wise to cultivate a modest appearance: leave the glittering rings and fine gold chains at home.

- If you are in unfamiliar territory, enquire if there are any neighbourhoods which are unsafe—and keep away from them. After dark, go where the crowds are, avoiding side streets and poorly lit areas.

- If you are driving, keep car doors locked and windows up, lest some malefactor leap in when you're stopped at a traffic light. By the same token, never drive around with the windows wide open and your handbag or valuables on the seat: an invitation to some snatch-and-grab artists.

- As in most countries, be on the alert for pickpockets and bag-snatchers in any crowded atmosphere, from a packed bus to a circus tent.

CUSTOMS AND ENTRY REGULATIONS

All visitors to the United States, except Canadian nationals, must have a valid visa. Application forms may be obtained from travel agencies and airlines, or by mail or in person from any U.S. embassy or consulate. If possible, postal applications should be made at least one month before departure. Forms must be accompanied by a passport valid for at least six months longer than the intended visit, a passport-size photograph, evidence of possession of sufficient funds and proof of intent to leave the United States after the visit is over. Most visitors to the U.S. do not need a health certificate; check with your travel agent or the consulate or embassy issuing the visa.

Red and green custom's channels are in operation at major international airports like New York's JFK, Chicago, Miami and Houston, where, on the whole, customs formalities have become less time-consuming than in the past.

The following chart shows certain duty-free items you, as a non-resident, may take into the U.S. (if you are over 21 where alcohol is concerned) and, when returning home, into your own country:

Into:	Cigarettes	Cigars	Tobacco	Spirits	Wine
U.S.A.	200 or	50	or 1,350 g.	1 l. or	1 l.
Australia	200 or	250 g. or	250 g.	1 l. or	1 l.
Canada	200 and	50	and 900 g.	1.1 l. or	1.1 l.
Eire	200 or	50	or 250 g.	1 l. and	2 l.
N. Zealand	200 or	50	or 250 g.	1 l. and	4.5 l.
S. Africa	400 and	50	and 250 g.	1 l. and	2 l.
U.K.	200 or	50	or 250 g.	1 l. and	2 l.

A non-resident may claim, free of duty and taxes, articles up to $100 in value for use as gifts for other persons. The exemption is valid only if the gifts accompany you, if you stay 72 hours or more and have not claimed this exemption within the preceeding 6 months. Up to 100 cigars may be included within this gift exemption.

Plants and foodstuffs also are subject to strict control; visitors from abroad may not import fruits, vegetables or meat. The same goes for chocolates that contain liqueur.

Arriving and departing passengers must report any money or cheques, etc., exceeding a total of $10,000.

ELECTRIC CURRENT   **E**

110-volt 60-cycle A.C. is standard throughout the U.S. Plugs are the flat, two-pronged variety. Visitors from abroad will need a transformer (240-110 V) and an adaptor plug for their electric razors.

EMBASSIES

Australia. 1601 Massachusetts Ave., NW, Washington, DC 20036; tel. (202) 797-3000

Canada. 1746 Massachusetts Ave., NW, Washington, DC 20036; tel. (202) 785-1400

Eire. 2234 Massachusetts Ave., NW, Washington, DC 20008; tel. (202) 462-3939

New Zealand. 37 Observatory Circle, NW, Washington, DC 20008; tel. (202) 328-4800

South Africa. 3051 Massachusetts Ave., NW, Washington, DC 20008; tel. (202) 232-4400

United Kingdom. 3100 Massachusetts Ave., NW, Washington, DC 20008; tel. (202) 462-1340

EMERGENCIES

Many cities and towns have a special 911 number for emergencies—fire, police, ambulance and paramedics. Otherwise, dial "0" and the operator will connect you with the service you need.

G GETTING AROUND THE UNITED STATES

By Car

Rental. Cars can generally be hired at airports and in most towns. Charges vary, so be sure to shop around for the best deal. Most car-rental companies offer a flat rate that includes unlimited mileage. If you are planning to drive more than 70 miles a day, this is probably the solution for you. There are also companies specializing in older (3 or 4 years), worn but mechanically sound cars. They are much cheaper and good for local touring. You may also want to look into rent-here, leave-there deals. A major credit card is essential to avoid paying an enormous deposit; some companies even refuse to accept cash as a deposit. For tourists from non-English-speaking countries, a translation of your driving licence is highly recommended, together with the national licence itself, or failing this, an International Driving Permit.

Auto driveaway. If you'd like to cross the country cheaply, look into an auto-driveaway deal. Several companies engage people to drive someone else's car from one part of the country to a specified destination. A refundable security deposit and an International Driving Permit are required, and the driver must be at least 21 years old. You pay petrol expenses yourself, and you have to take a reasonably direct route established in advance. Consult the Yellow Pages of the telephone directory under "Automobile Transporters & Driveaway Companies".

American Automobile Association. The AAA offers information on travelling in the U.S., as well as short-term insurance for visitors. Contact AAA World Travel:

    8111 Gatehouse Rd., Falls Church, VA 22047

AAA helps members, as well as foreign visitors affiliated with recognized automobile associations, in case of breakdown or other problems along the way.

On the road. Drive on the right. Intersections are generally marked with stop or yield signs to indicate who has priority. Speed limits, almost always posted, are rather strictly enforced. An excellent interstate highway system crosses the U.S. Odd numbers designate highways running north-south, while even-numbered interstates run east-west. Interstate 80, for example, links New York with San Francisco, Interstate 5 goes from Vancouver to San Diego.

Highway terminology in the U.S. is confusing and not particularly consistent. But in general, turnpikes and thruways are high-speed, dual carriageways (divided highways) that collect tolls; parkways, which do not allow lorries (trucks), may or may not charge; freeways and expressways are usually free. Most road maps indicate which highways collect tolls. It's wise to have a stock of change on hand for the tolls—the "exact change" lanes (you drop the coins in a basket) move faster.

Speed limits are clearly signposted. Generally the limit on highways is 55 mph, but it goes up to 65 mph on rural stretches of interstate highways in many states. If you keep within the flow of traffic, you'll have no problem, but go any faster, and a patrol car will pull you over.

Expressway driving follows certain rules of the road. Rather than accelerate up the slip road (ramp) to join the traffic at its own speed, you hesitate at the top of the ramp and wait for an opening.

If you have a breakdown on an expressway, pull over onto the right-hand shoulder, tie a handkerchief to the doorhandle or radio aerial, raise the bonnet (hood) and wait in the car for assistance. At night, use the blinker.

Petrol (gas) and services. Stations are numerous and easy to locate. Many stations might be closed in the evenings and on weekends. At night, petrol stations require exact change or a credit card.

By Bus

The two largest coach companies, Greyhound Lines and Trailways U.S.A., provide transport to and from cities all over the United States. Passengers can make as many stopovers en route as they wish, provided the destination is reached before the ticket expires. Sometimes travel by bus costs about the same—or even more—than flying. So don't automatically assume the bus is cheaper. Both companies offer flat-rate rover passes for specified periods of unlimited travel. These tickets must be purchased outside the U.S.

Areas not served by Trailways or Greyhound are usually covered by regional and local bus companies.

By Train

500 major cities and towns are linked daily by Amtrak, America's National Railroad Passenger Corporation. Amtrak is currently advertising a variety of bargain fares, including excursion and family fares; the *U.S.A. Railpass*, the equivalent of the Eurailpass, can only be purchased abroad but many package tours are available in the U.S.

By Air

Air travel is by far the quickest and most convenient way of getting round the U.S. and less expensive than in Europe. Shuttle services operate on some heavily travelled routes.

The *Visit U.S.A.* fares on offer may not represent a saving for those only making one or two stops, though the rover tickets on offer outside the country usually do.

Fares change constantly, so it would be wise to consult an airline or travel agency for the latest information about discounts and special deals.

Local Transport

Municipal buses operate in most cities and towns. Some big cities have underground-railway (subway) systems. Maps of the network are usually posted at every station and in every train, and can be obtained at the ticket booth in any station. To take the subway, you need a token (purchased at the booth) which you insert in the turnstile.

Taxis are lined up at airports, railway stations and bus terminals, or you can hail a cab in the street or telephone for one (look in the Yellow Pages under "Taxicabs"). A tip of at least 15% is expected. On arrival in the U.S., if you take a taxi from the airport into town, be sure you have several small banknotes in your possession, as cab drivers will not give change for large denominations.

GETTING TO THE UNITED STATES

Because of the complexity and variability of the many fares, you should ask the advice of an informed travel agent well before your departure.

Scheduled flights. New York is the principal gateway to the U.S. from the British Isles, but major transatlantic carriers offer direct flights from Heathrow to some 20 other U.S. destinations. Direct flights are also available from Gatwick, Glasgow, Dublin and Shannon. Flying time from London to New York is 7 hours, to Los Angeles, 11 hours. Apart from the standard first-class and economy fares, main types of fares available are:

Super APEX: book 21 days prior to departure for stays of 7 days to 6 months; no stopovers.

Special Economy: book any time; offers plenty of flexibility.

Standby: bookable only on the day of travel, minimum 2 hours prior to departure.

From Sydney and Auckland, scheduled flights leave daily for Los Angeles, with connecting flights to other U.S. destinations.

Charter flights. Some are organized by scheduled airlines, others by special holiday companies. ABC (Advance Booking Charter) flights must be reserved at least 21 days in advance for a minimum stay of 7 days.

Package holidays. A wide variety are available, ranging from fully organized to flexible. Some packages include hire of a camper or camping equipment.

Baggage. You are allowed to check in, free, two suitcases of normal size on scheduled transatlantic flights. In addition, one piece of hand baggage of a size which fits easily under the aircraft seat may be carried on board. Check size and weight restrictions with your travel agent or air carrier when booking your ticket.

It is advisable to insure all luggage for the duration of your trip. Any travel agent can make the necessary arrangements.

HEALTH AND MEDICAL CARE   **H**

Free medical service is not available in the U.S., and a visit to the doctor can be expensive, hospitalization an economic disaster. Holiday medical insurance is therefore a wise precaution. You can arrange for coverage through one of the big international companies or your travel agent.

Foreign visitors may wish to ask their embassy or consulate for a list of doctors. In an emergency, local telephone operators are an excellent source of advice (dial "0").

Visitors from abroad will find that certain medicines sold over the counter at home can only be purchased with a prescription (and vice versa).

Tap water is perfectly safe to drink everywhere in the United States.

HITCH-HIKING

Except on expressways and parkways, it is legal to hitch-hike—but not really advisable. The practice does not have the best reputation—one hears too many stories of assault, robbery and worse. As a result, Americans, usually a warm-hearted lot, are wary of picking up anybody, and you may find yourself waiting hours for a ride.

L LIQUOR (ALCOHOL) REGULATIONS

Liquor laws vary a good deal from state to state and sometimes within a state. Utah is strictest, Nevada the most liberal. In certain areas you may buy alcoholic beverages in a supermarket or drugstore, in others you must go to a licensed liquor (or "package") store, even for beer. And the sale of alcohol on Sundays and holidays is frequently restricted or prohibited.

Ordering a drink in a bar or restaurant is encouraged, restricted or illegal depending on where you are. In some areas it may be necessary to join a "club"—usually a formality for nominal fee—to get a martini. Small restaurants that don't have the expensive permit to sell alcohol will generally let customers bring their own beer or wine ("brown bag" it)—but only in certain states. Only weak (3.2) beer is served in "dry" counties.

The minimum age for purchasing or drinking alcoholic beverages in a public place ranges from 18 to 21, according to the state. If you look young, you may be asked for some identification (called "I.D.") to prove you are "of age".

LOST PROPERTY

Air, rail and bus terminals and many stores have special "lost-and-found" departments. Restaurants put aside lost articles in the hope that someone will claim them. If your lost property is valuable, contact the police. If you lose your passport, get in touch with your embassy or nearest consulate immediately.

MAPS

Tourist information authorities distribute free maps and brochures. City and state maps can be purchased in bookstores and stationery stores and at many petrol stations.

The maps in this book were provided by Falk-Verlag, Hamburg, who also publish a complete road atlas to the U.S.

MONEY MATTERS

Currency. The dollar is divided into 100 cents.

Coins: 1¢ (penny), 5¢ (nickel), 10¢ (dime), 25¢ (quarter), 50¢ (half dollar) and $1.

Banknotes: $1, $2 (rare), $5, $10, $20, $50 and $100. Larger denominations ($500 and $1,000) are not in general circulation. All denominations are the same size and same green colour, so be sure to check each banknote before paying.

For currency restrictions, see CUSTOMS AND ENTRY REGULATIONS.

Currency exchange. Normal banking hours are from 9 a.m. to 3 p.m., Monday to Friday.

Only major banks in larger cities or at international airports will change foreign money or foreign-currency traveller's cheques, so it's important to carry cash or traveller's cheques in dollars. However, make sure you always have a supply of $1–$10 banknotes on hand for taxis, tipping and small purchases.

Credit cards. Credit cards play a far greater role here than in Europe. In the U.S., they are a way of life, and most Americans have several. The major cards are accepted as cash almost everywhere. When paying for goods or services, including hotel and restaurant bills, you will be asked: "Cash or charge?", meaning you have the choice of paying either in cash or in "plastic money". You'll need to show two pieces of identification when charging a purchase.

Traveller's cheques. Visitors from abroad will find traveller's cheques drawn on American banks far easier to deal with. Only cash small amounts at a time, and keep the balance of your cheques in the hotel safe if possible. At the very least, be sure to keep your receipt and a list of the serial numbers of the cheques in a separate place to facilitate a refund in case of loss or theft.

N NATIONAL PARKS

Government protected reserves are found all over the U.S. and take in everything from stretches of coastland and wayside campgrounds to wildlife reserves and wilderness areas. The 37 sites designated "National Park" or "National Monument" are areas of outstanding historical, geological and scenic importance. Almost all can be reached by car or bus and some have direct connections to major cities by rail or air. Each state also has numerous "State Parks", of lesser consequence but with pleasant scenic and recreational resources.

High season is mid-July to mid-August, when the most popular parks are likely to be crowded and advance reservations for campsites recommended. Parks often provide guided tours and usually lay on organized summer and winter activities.

Entrance fees vary. The reasonably priced *Golden Eagle Passport* (available at parks) entitles all the occupants of a private car to unlimited access to national parks.

A few of the greatest parks have been dealt with in detail in this guide. Here are a few more that you may like to visit.

Shenandoah National Park (Virginia). Nearest wilderness park to the nation's capital, this park consists of a 105-mile stretch of wooded Blue Ridge Mountain.

Petrified Forest National Park (Arizona). In the most colourful area of the Painted Desert, six forests of fallen logs, 200 million years old, have been turned into jasper and agate.

Mesa Verde National Park (Colorado). Indians abandoned this prehistoric "green tabletop" 800 years ago, leaving behind stone cities built into the cliffside.

Bryce Canyon National Park (Utah). A fantasy land of pink cliffs, dramatic rock formations and breathtaking scenery.

For further information see your travel agent or write to the National Park Service, Washington, DC. For state parks, write to the state tourist department.

P PHOTOGRAPHY

All popular brands of film and photographic equipment are available. Try to buy in discount stores where prices are much lower. Colour-print film usually takes 2 to 5 days to be developed, black-and-white film and slides up to a week.

Some airport security machines use X-rays which can affect your film. Ask that it be hand-checked, or enclose it in a lead-lined bag.

POLICE

City police are concerned with local crime and traffic violations, while Highway Patrol officers (also called State Troopers) ensure road safety, and are on the lookout for people speeding or driving under the influence of alcohol or drugs.

The American police officer is usually fair and friendly. Do not hesitate to approach any policeman and ask for assistance or information; helping you is part of their job. In case of emergency, find a phone, dial "0" and ask the operator to contact the police.

PRICES

The U.S. has a larger range of prices for any one item than you will find anywhere else, as well as a greater choice. The best prices are usually offered by huge discount houses, located just off highways and in suburban areas. Independent service stations are cheaper than those run by the large oil companies. Most prices do not include a state sales tax (normally 4 to 8%) and a city or resort tax.

To give you an idea of what to expect, here's a list of average prices in U.S. dollars. However, due to inflation as well as seasonal and regional variations, these figures must be regarded as approximate.

Camping. Entry fee $3–8 per vehicle, reservation fee $3.25, trail camps (hikers) 50¢ per night, developed campsites $6–8 per night, primitive sites $3 per night, caravan (trailer) and camper hookups $9 per night.

Car rental (international company; all prices include unlimited mileage). *Small* (e.g. Toyota Tercel) $46 per day, $170 per week. *Medium* (e.g. Ford Fairmont) $60 per day, $240 per week. *Large* (e.g. Ford LTD) $66 per day, $300 per week.

Cigarettes (20). $1.25 and up.

Entertainment. Cinema $4–6, theatre $12–45, nightclub/discotheque $6 and up for cover charge, $3–4 for drinks, jazz club $5–30.

Hairdressers. *Man's* haircut from $15. *Woman's* cut from $15, shampoo and set or blow-dry from $12, shampoo and colour rinse from $14.

Hotels (double room). Expensive $135 and up, moderate $70–135, budget or motel $35–75.

Meals and drinks. Breakfast $5–12, lunch $8–15, dinner $15 and up, carafe of wine $6–7, glass of beer $1.50–3, whisky $2.50–5, soft drink $1.50, coffee $1.

YMCA/YWCA. Double room $40, single room $22.

PUBLIC HOLIDAYS

The following public holidays are—with a few exceptions—celebrated nationwide.

New Year's Day	January 1
Martin Luther King Day	Third Monday in January
Washington's Birthday*	Third Monday in February
Memorial Day**	Last Monday in May
Independence Day	July 4
Labor Day	First Monday in September
Columbus Day***	Second Monday in October
Veterans' Day****	November 11
Thanksgiving Day	Fourth Thursday in November
Christmas Day	December 25

> * celebrated on February 22 in some states (also called President's Day or Washington-Lincoln Day)
> ** celebrated in most states
> *** celebrated in most states, on October 12 in some states (also called Pioneers' Day, Farmers' Day, Fraternal Day, Discoverer's Day)
> **** also called Armistice Day

Lincoln's Birthday (Feb. 12) is widely observed in the northern states, Robert E. Lee's Birthday (Jan. 19) and Confederate Memorial Day (late April/early May) in most southern states.

If a holiday, such as Christmas Day, falls on a Sunday, banks and most stores close on the following day. There are also long weekends (such as the one following Thanksgiving) when offices are closed for four days. Many restaurants never shut, however, not even at Christmas.

R RADIO AND TELEVISION

You'll almost certainly have radio and television in your hotel room, with a vast choice of programmes. Some television networks broadcast from 6 a.m. until 3 or 4 the next morning; others never go off the air.

American commercial television aims to appeal to the largest possible number. The non-commercial Public Broadcasting Service (PBS) screens music and drama programmes along with its own news and information broadcasts.

There are numerous AM and FM radio stations. Most broadcast pop and country-and-western music, but each large city has at least one classical-music radio station.

RESTAURANTS

In the U.S., there's something for every taste and budget. You can dine in the luxurious surroundings of a fashionable restaurant or eat on the run at an informal lunch counter.

Most restaurants charge more for dinner than for lunch. You can order as little or as much as you want, but sometimes there's a minimum charge. In simple places, you often pay the cashier on your way out, after leaving the tip on the table. See also TIPPING and PRICES.

Breakfast is served from 7 to 10 a.m., lunch between 11 a.m. and 2.30 p.m. and dinner from 5 or 6 to 10.30 p.m. or so. Brunch is featured on Sundays between 11 a.m. and 3 p.m. Reserve a table in advance if you plan to eat in a well-known restaurant.

If you feel hungry at an unusual hour, you'll be able to find a fast-food establishment, diner or coffee shop serving hot food, sandwiches or snacks at almost any time of day or night:

Coffee shops and **cafeterias** offer sandwiches, hamburgers, salads, simple hot dishes and pastries. They do not serve alcoholic drinks.

Delicatessens (deli), a cross between grocery stores and restaurants (some are just restaurants), are known for their gargantuan sandwiches. Other specialities include salads and hearty soups. Some delicatessens are kosher.

Diners. Originally a sort of coffee shop on the road built in the shape of a railway dining car, some have now become quite elaborate and serve alcohol. But they're still open long (often 24) hours.

"Ethnic" restaurants, a term covering all foreign restaurants—Greek, Italian, Japanese, Chinese, Spanish, Mexican, Indian, Middle Eastern, German, Russian, Scandinavian, and so on. There's something for every taste.

Fast-food outlets. You'll see plenty of reminders that you're in the land of McDonald's and Kentucky Fried Chicken.

French restaurants. Approach these with caution, for each excellent one there are another hundred that are mediocre and far too expensive for what they offer.

Health-food restaurants and **juice bars.** Every imaginable kind of fruit and vegetable juice is served, plus delicious salads, wholefood and vegetarian specialities. The ingredients are often organic.

Open-air or sidewalk cafés have become very popular in recent years. They serve hamburgers, *quiches*, *crêpes* and sandwiches, and will usually let you linger over your coffee.

Pizzerias serve a wide variety of pizzas, usually big enough for three people. You can also buy pizza by the slice.

Take-outs are small shops where you can order sandwiches, salads, assorted groceries and drinks to take out and consume elsewhere.

T TIME ZONES AND DATES

The 48 conterminous states of the U.S. are—from east to west—divided into four time zones: Eastern (G.M.T. –5 hours), Central (–6), Mountain (–7) and Pacific (–8). The major part of Alaska is on G.M.T. –9 hours, Hawaii on G.M.T. –10.

Under Daylight Saving Time, observed in all states but Hawaii, Arizona and parts of Indiana, clocks move ahead one hour the first Sunday in April and turn back again to Standard Time the last Sunday in October.

In the U.S., dates are written in the order month/day/year; for example, 1/6/99 is January 6, 1999.

TIPPING

In general, a service charge is not included in the bill; you are expected to tip the waiter, waitress or bartender about 15% (more in luxury establishments). Cinema or theatre ushers are not tipped, but doormen, cloakroom attendants, etc., should be remunerated for services rendered—never less than a quarter.

Some further suggestions:

Porter	50¢–$1 per bag (minimum $1)
Hotel maid (not for overnight stay)	$1 per day or $5 per week
Lavatory attendant	50¢
Taxi driver	15%
Bus tour guide	10–15%
Hairdresser/Barber	15%

TOILETS

Americans use the terms "rest room", "powder room", "bathroom" (private) and "ladies' " or "men's room" to indicate the toilet. If you encounter a pay-toilet, the usual charge is 10 cents.

TOURIST INFORMATION AGENCIES

For information prior to arrival, contact:

United States Travel Service
22 Sackville St., London W1X 2EA; tel. (01) 439 7433

or

International Visitors Information Service
801 19th St., NW, Washington, DC 20006; tel. (202) 872-8747

State tourist departments distribute general information and maps of the state, while local *convention and visitors bureaus* put out free city maps and leaflets on principal tourist attractions.

Travelers Aid Services dispenses just about everything, even — for the traveller genuinely in distress — pocket money. Offices are located in most major cities.

Convention and visitors bureaus in the principal cities:

Atlanta Convention and Visitors Bureau, 233 Peachtree St., NE, Suite 200; tel. (404) 659-4270

Baltimore Office of Promotion and Tourism, 110 West Baltimore St.; tel. (301) 752-8632

Boston. Greater Boston Convention and Tourist Bureau, Prudential Plaza, P.O. Box 490, Suite 1944; tel. (617) 536-4100

Chicago Convention and Tourism Bureau, McCormick Place on the Lake; tel. (312) 225-5000

Dallas Convention and Visitors Bureau, 1507 Pacific Ave.; tel. (214) 954-1454

Denver Metro Convention and Visitors Bureau, 225 West Colfax Ave.; tel. (303) 892-1112

Detroit. Metropolitan Detroit Convention and Visitors Bureau, 100 Renaissance Center, Suite 1950; tel. (313) 259-4333

Houston. Greater Houston Convention and Visitors Council, 3300 Main St., tel. (713) 523-5050

Las Vegas Convention and Visitors Authority, 3150 South Paradise Rd.; tel. (702) 733-2323

Los Angeles. Greater Los Angeles Visitors and Convention Bureau, 505 South Flower St., Level B; tel. (213) 239-0200

Miami/Miami Beach. Greater Miami and the Beaches Tourism Council, 555 17th St., Miami Beach; tel. (305) 673-7070

New Orleans. Greater New Orleans Tourist and Convention Commission, 334 Royal St.; tel. (504) 566-5033

New York Convention and Visitors Bureau, 2 Columbus Circle; tel. (212) 397-8200

Philadelphia Convention and Visitors Bureau, Suite 2020, 1515 Market St.; tel. (215) 636-3300

Phoenix and Valley of the Sun Convention and Visitors Bureau, 505 N. 2nd St., Suite 300; tel. (602) 254-6500

Salt Lake City Valley Convention and Visitors Bureau, 180 South West Temple; tel. (801) 521-2822

San Antonio Convention and Visitors Bureau, P.O. Box 2277; tel. (512) 270-8700

San Diego Convention and Visitors Bureau, 1200 3rd Ave., Suite 824; tel. (619) 232-3101

San Francisco Visitor Information Center, 900 Market St., Lower Level, Hallidie Plaza. Dial (415) 391-2000 for information and 391-2001 for a recorded summary of the day's events.

Santa Fe Chamber of Commerce, P.O. Box 909, tel. (505) 988-3044

Seattle King County Convention and Visitors Bureau, 1815 7th Ave.; tel. (206) 447-4240

Washington, DC Convention and Visitors Association, 1575 Eye St., NW; tel. (202) 789-7000

W WEIGHTS AND MEASURES

The United States is one of the last countries in the world to resist the metric system. As yet there is no official changeover programme. Some British and Canadian visitors will be happy to go back to the good old days of feet and inches.

Milk and fruit juice can be bought by the quart or half-gallon, but wine and spirits now come in litre bottles. Food products usually have the weight marked in ounces and pounds as well as in grammes.

There are some slight differences between British and American measures, for instance:

1 U.S. gallon = .833 British Imp. gallon = 3.8 litres
1 U.S. quart = .833 British Imp. quart = .9 litres

Conversion charts

Length

Clothing sizes
Dresses, blouses, knitwear

U.S.A.	8	10	12	14	16
Great Britain	10/32	12/34	14/36	16/38	18/40

Note: Men's suits and shirts (collar sizes) are the same in the U.S. and Great Britain.

SPEAKING A DIFFERENT LANGUAGE

Even English speakers take time to adjust to the American accent, which varies from region to region. In addition, certain words have different meanings for Americans and British. This list will help you to avoid confusion.

U.S.	British
admission	entry fee
apartment	flat
bathroom	toilet
bill	banknote
billfold	wallet
candy	sweet
check	bill (restaurant)
chips	potato crisps
collect call	reverse-charge call
comfort station	public lavatory
cookie	biscuit
cracker	biscuit
dead end	cul-de-sac
detour	diversion
diaper	nappy
divided highway	dual carriageway
eggplant	aubergine
elevator	lift
fall	autumn
faucet	tap
first floor	ground floor
flashlight	torch
French fries	potato chips
garters	suspenders
gas(oline)	petrol
general delivery	poste restante
generator	dynamo
hood	bonnet
jelly	jam
jumper	pinafore dress
kerosene	paraffin
line	queue
liquor	spirits
mail	post
muffler	silencer

U.S.	British
pants	trousers
panty hose	tights
pavement	road surface
person-to-person call	personal call
pocket book	handbag
private school	public school
purse	handbag
railroad	railway
rest room	public convenience
roundtrip ticket	return ticket
second floor	first floor
sidewalk	pavement
stand in line	queue up
straight	neat (drink)
subway	underground
sunny-side up	egg fried on one side
suspenders	braces
tail lights	rear lights
trailer	caravan
truck	lorry
trunk	boot (car)
tuna	tunny
underpass	subway
undershirt	vest
vest	waistcoat
wash up	wash oneself
windshield	windscreen
yard	garden

U.S.A.

240

0   200   400 km
0   200   400 miles

A   D   A

MINNESOTA

Isle Royale N.P.

Lake Superior

MICHIGAN

St. Paul

Minneapolis

WISCONSIN

Milwaukee

Madison

Lansing

Lake Michigan

Lake Huron

Lake Ontario

Niagara Falls

Buffalo

VERMONT

MAINE

Augusta

Montpelier

Concord

NEW HAMPSHIRE

MASSACHUSETTS

Albany

Boston

Providence

RHODE ISLAND

Detroit

Lake Erie

NEW YORK

Hartford

CONNECTICUT

NEW YORK CITY

IOWA

Chicago

ILLINOIS

Cleveland

PENNSYLVANIA

N.J.

Trenton

Philadelphia

Des Moines

Indianapolis

OHIO

Harrisburg

Baltimore

Dover

DELAWARE

Springfield

Columbus

WASHINGTON D.C.

Annapolis

MARYLAND

Kansas City

Jefferson City

INDIANA

Charleston

WEST VIRGINIA

Shenandoan N.P.

Richmond

Topeka

St. Louis

Ohio

Frankfort

Williamsburg

MISSOURI

KENTUCKY

VIRGINIA

Nashville

Great Smoky Mtns N.P.

NORTH CAROLINA

Raleigh

ARKANSAS

TENNESSEE

Mississippi

SOUTH CAROLINA

Columbia

Little Rock

Atlanta

Savannah

Charleston

LOUISIANA

Montgomery

GEORGIA

Savannah

Jackson

MISSISSIPPI

ALABAMA

Baton Rouge

Tallahassee

Houston

New Orleans

FLORIDA

Cape Canaveral

Orlando

Palm Beach

Fort Lauderdale

Miami

Everglades N.P.

Gulf of Mexico

ATLANTIC OCEAN

N

MANHATTAN

0 500 1000 m
0 500 1000 yards

N

NEW JERSEY

Hudson River

North River

Holland Tunnel

West Side Highway

Eleventh Ave.

W. 26th St.

Tenth Avenue

General Post Office

Ninth Avenue

CHELSEA

West 23rd Street

West 14th St.

Eighth Avenue

West 20th St.

GREENWICH

Cherry Lane

W. 7th Ave.

Madison Square

Seventh Avenue

Theodore Roosevelt House

Walker Park

VILLAGE

Avenue of the Americas

Fifth Avenue

Union Square Park Ave.

Gramercy Park

Washington Square

Broadway

Police Academy Museum

West Broadway

West Houston Street

Stuyvesant Square

Canal Street

Hudson Street

Grand Street

St. Mark's-in-the-Bouwerie

14th Street

Second

World Trade Center

Broadway

Church St.

Broadway

Lafayette Street

LITTLE ITALY

First Avenue

Houston

Bowery

Avenue A

Tompkins Square

Trinity Pl.

City Hall

CHINATOWN

Delancey Street

LOWER EAST SIDE

Avenue B

N.Y. Stock Exchange

Trinity Church

City Hall Park

Buddhist Temple

Canal Street

Avenue C

West Side Highway

Federal Hall National Memorial

Avenue D

Battery Park

Pearl Street

Madison

East Broadway

Seward Park

Hamilton Fish Park

Fraunces Tavern

Elevated Highway

Franklin D. Roosevelt Drive

Statue of Liberty

Brooklyn Battery Tunnel

Staten Island

South St. Seaport

Brooklyn Br.

Manhattan Br.

Elevated Highway

Grand St.

Corlears Hook Park

East River

Brooklyn-Queens Expressway

Williamsburg Bridge

038/708 RPC 17